PITT SERIES IN POLICY
AND INSTITUTIONAL STUDIES

Making Regulatory Policy

Keith Hawkins and
John M. Thomas,

EDITORS

UNIVERSITY OF PITTSBURGH PRESS

Published by the University of Pittsburgh Press, Pittsburgh, Pa., 15260
Copyright © 1989, University of Pittsburgh Press
All rights reserved
Baker & Taylor International, London

Manufactured in the United States of America

Library of Congress Cataloging-in-Publication Data

Making regulatory policy / Keith Hawkins and John M. Thomas, editors.
    p. cm. – (Pitt series in policy and institutional studies)
  Bibliography: p.
  Includes index.
  ISBN 0-8229-3615-1
  1. Administrative procedure – United States. 2. Administrative procedure –
United States – Decision making. I. Hawkins, Keith. II. Thomas, John M.
(John Michael), 1938- . III. Series.
KF5411.M35 1989
342.73′066 – dc19
[347.30266]   89-4784
                                                CIP

Chapter 8, by Daniel J. Gifford, is a revised version of an article that appeared in the
Southern California Law Review 57 (1983): 101.

Contents

Preface

THIS BOOK is concerned with policymaking in regulation, where policy is broadly defined as consisting of decisions which provide substantive direction to the legal mandates of a governmental agency and determine the way regulatory programs are to be enforced. In this context, the policy process involves issues such as how public regulatory agencies make rules, the relationship between rule making and enforcement, decisionmaking concerning the management of discretion by regulatory officials, and the use of knowledge and information in policy decisions.

The individual chapters in the book apply a variety of concepts from law, organizational analysis, and behavioral theory to the study of regulatory policymaking. These chapters provide several detailed case studies which explore aspects of policymaking in areas such as nuclear power regulation, environmental pollution control, and federal trade regulation. The essays approach these complex subjects from the perspective of a number of disciplines, primarily law, sociology, and political science.

A central theme of the book is the relationship between legal frameworks for designing and implementing regulatory policy and the bureaucratic setting in which these legal frameworks are defined and interpreted. The individual studies attempt to integrate conceptual analysis with rich descriptions of actual decisionmaking practices in several types of regulatory organizations. Examples of policymaking issues are used to propose new frameworks for understanding the way decisions are made, and, in several instances, to examine normative implications for managing the regulatory process.

In organizing this volume, we have deliberately avoided forcing our authors to take a unified conceptual approach. Rather, given the book's multidisciplinary character, we thought it wiser to define themes and issues which emerge from the individual studies. Our efforts to examine the general topic of regulatory policymaking from several disciplinary perspectives using empirically based case studies carry forward several themes that were treated in an earlier volume, *Enforcing Regulation* (Boston: Kluwer-Nijhoff, 1984). Both books presuppose a recognition of the importance of understanding the complex, interdependent relationships between policy formation, implementation, and the enforcement of legal rules. We offer this work as a preliminary step toward the development of a more inclusive, general framework for understanding the phenomenon of *how* regulators actually regulate. We hope we have identified a number of key dimensions of this complex process that may contribute to this enterprise.

The book is organized around three principal themes in regulatory policymaking: the role of information in policy decisions when information generation and transmission is fundamentally influenced by symbolic processes within the regulatory organization; the problem of formulating methods of implementing policy goals and the relationship of these procedures to the values of interest groups within the agency and external constituencies; and policymaking issues related to the delegation of discretion to officials charged with enforcement responsibilities. The introductory essay discusses the relevance of two general concepts for understanding the regulatory policymaking process, namely the notions of bounded rationality and social construction. This chapter applies these concepts to an analysis of several basic issues which define the bureaucratic context of regulation and are themes in the essays that follow: the use of information; the interaction between the regulatory agency and its external environment; the influence of professional values and ideology; and internal agency politics.

Making Regulatory Policy

1

Making Policy in Regulatory Bureaucracies

Keith Hawkins AND *John M. Thomas*

"ALL REGULATION," Breyer observes (1982:6), "is characterized by administration through bureaucracy." Several studies of the regulatory process have emphasized the important role played by the agency bureaucracy in imposing constraints upon the effective solution of regulatory problems and in setting the approach taken to the implementation of regulation. This role has been interpreted in various ways. For instance, according to Joskow and Noll, "once a regulatory organization is established it develops behavioral patterns and a dynamic of its own that are constrained by Congress but not completely" (Joskow and Noll, 1982:49). According to Kagan, agencies may respond to particular issues in predictable ways because they tend "to develop philosophies of decision-making, presumptions and norms of rule application thereby creating a 'lean' in favor of a particular balance of stringency and accommodation" (Kagan, 1978:90). In another study Wolf has argued that an important source of failure in the regulatory process is what he terms "internalities": the goals that apply within nonmarket organizations to guide, regulate, and evaluate agency performance and the performance of agency personnel (Wolf, 1979:116). And in a penetrating analysis which demonstrates the pitfalls of the simplistic assumption that regulation always serves the interests of industry, James Q. Wilson has concluded that regulatory actions take the form they do in part because of "coalitions of diverse participants who have somewhat different methods" (Wilson, 1980:373).

According to other writers, the prominence of the agency bureaucracy results from the political nature of most regulatory issues. Legislatures typically react in a highly general way to demand that something be done about problems, creating or authorizing an agency to design a program and demonstrate results but offering little or no guidance as to how ends are to be attained. They address the issue not in general policy terms, writes Mashaw, "but as a problem of institutional design. The need for a policy is redefined as a need for an institution that can focus on the policy question over time and can devise solutions in the light of this experience. The regulatory agency is, of course, such an institution" (Mashaw, 1979:45).

Regulatory policymaking operates at several levels. Perhaps most generally, it requires choices to be made among competing societal objectives which are bound up in the process of interpreting a legal mandate. One such choice, for example, would be between reduced risk and economic efficiency; another involves how far to go in the design of procedures and institutions of public participation that will lend legitimacy to substantive rule-making problems (see Stewart, 1979:78). While both of these issues require a proper allocation of legislative, executive, and judicial roles, we will seek to show in this essay that regulatory agencies inevitably enjoy considerable autonomy in the policymaking process.

A focus on agency behavior is important for several reasons. The whole regulatory process, as Breyer has noted, is essentially adversarial in character. The collision of values is particularly explicit in the implementation of regulatory policy. A variety of interest groups, as well as the entities being regulated, attempt to influence the definition of problems and the ordering of policy agendas, which in recent years has caused the legislative branch to become increasingly involved in efforts to oversee and monitor agency action. Demands upon agency policymakers to account for the economic impacts of decisions – to consider various goals and tradeoffs – also contribute to the adversarial nature of the process. As a consequence, the way the agency actors interpret external constraints within an adversarial context is profoundly important, critically influencing not only the substance of policy and its effectiveness but also the efficiency and equity of policy decisions. For example, in interpreting the motives and behavior of their significant publics, agency staff employ interpretive frameworks which incorporate assumptions about the motivations of regulated firms to act in certain ways (Kagan and Scholz,

1984). Regulatory bureaucracies are also organizations, of course, and like all organizations have a very human concern with self-preservation. Thus, as Joskow has observed, agencies "seek to minimize conflict and criticism appearing as signals from the economic and social environment in which they operate" (Joskow, 1974:296; also see Wilson, 1980).

Understanding the decisionmaking process in regulatory agencies, however, is no simple matter, partly because regulatory tasks by their nature can involve highly technical problems. Such tasks may also be clouded by high levels of uncertainty yet demand the application of value judgments about the probability of harm and the degree of acceptable risk (see generally Lowrance, 1976). Recent case studies indicate that policy decisions are frequently not made with the careful analysis of technical evidence which might be expected, as some of the essays in this book also suggest. In an important assessment of these studies, Crandall and Lave have emphasized the influence of agency discretion and policymaking under conditions of scientific uncertainty:

> Regulators do not seek scientific contributions in a way that is likely to elicit the most helpful analysis and are not able to use the material they do receive. Both problems stem partly from an inability of agency heads to understand the limitations of science and to interpret inconclusive information. . . .
>
> Regulators have learned that scientific data and analysis often cannot provide firm answers to their questions. With few scientific constraints, regulators find themselves driven by political forces, using an intuitive decision-making process. [Crandall and Lave, 1981:16–17]

Each of the essays in this book illustrates in a different way that agency policymaking reflects a persistent and complicated interconnection of political, legal, economic, technical, and bureaucratic factors. The purpose of the present chapter is to consider some of the existing theory and research on this topic in light of the essays which follow. At the outset, it is important to note that this essay does not attempt to provide an integrated conceptual framework of the regulatory policymaking process (for one such effort see Sabatier, 1977). Instead we seek to define some of the basic questions and illustrate the value of addressing the issue from different disciplinary perspectives. We conclude the book by considering some of the implications for the design of regulatory policy which emerge from the following analysis.

The Tasks of Policymaking: Two Perspectives

Policymaking in regulatory agencies may be regarded as comprising a set of distinct tasks. These tasks encompass both "external" and "internal" rules (see Diver, 1983:76). External policymaking includes rule making that governs the conduct of the regulated public and rule making that governs methods of enforcement. These policy rules set forth the ways in which noncompliance is to be sanctioned or, conversely, the ways in which compliance is to be implemented. Internal policies, in contrast, refer to agency decisions for the allocation of agency resources and the control of discretion. Internal policies are thus involved with the development of decision rules for targeting regulatory problems (that is, the development of procedures for allocating resources among competing priorities) and for limiting the discretion of agency officials. Here it is important to note that internal policies may conflict with, or may contradict, the objectives of external policies. A failure properly to analyze information about the costs and benefits of various alternatives for the regulation of conduct, for example, can result in overinclusive conduct rules – standards that are inflexible and unreasonable. But on the other hand, a failure to grant a necessary degree of discretion to enforcement officials, such as field-level inspectors, can result in the misapplication of conduct rules (see generally Bardach and Kagan, 1982). Similarly, the failure to select relevant targets results in an inefficient application of rules as well as ineffectiveness, because resources are not concentrated on actual problems. With respect to such allocation decisions, it has been observed that regulatory activity "may be motivated by a popular reaction to a recent event rather than by evidence of a problem that regulation can systematically address. Also, an agency may exacerbate concern about a trivial or nonexistent problem" (Crandall and Lave, 1981:3). The converse is also true. The adoption of simple, straightforward, substantive commands of the "thou shalt not" variety can result in an inefficient allocation of enforcement resources (see Diver, 1983:76).

The approach that agencies take to their policymaking tasks may be considered from a number of disciplinary perspectives, though we want to consider, in particular, two views from organization theory and sociology: bounded rationality and social construction (see Pfeffer, 1982). Bounded rationality assumes that policymaking is directed toward the attainment of certain goals but is subject to time and resource constraints which affect efficiency and effectiveness. The concept, then, is intended to convey the idea that policymaking involves incomplete information processing under uncertainty through bureaucratic operating procedures. The process is conceived in terms of problem solving, where the assessment and analysis of the consequences of various constraints are evaluated in comparison with alternatives. In contrast, the social constructionist perspective, which derives from interpretive sociology, emphasizes that policymaking is a social process, in which actors interpret their environments, their goals, and the constraints in the process. Shared meanings arise through interaction among officials in different units of an agency and between these officials, interest groups, and other actors involved in the regulatory process, such as the courts and the legislature. As this conception implies, the inputs to policy must be understood in terms of what they mean to key agency policymakers or, put another way, in terms of policymakers' cognitive perspectives.

The concepts of bounded rationality and social construction provide complementary perspectives on agency policymaking. Their fundamental interdependence is reflected in the idea that decisionmaking is a function of what March has termed "process rationality" – the symbolic content and meaning attached to procedures for making choices (1978:592). The framework of bounded rationality incorporates elements of the social constructionist perspective, since it can be said to be based on the assumption that "most of what we believe we know about events within organizational choice situations as well as the events themselves reflects an interpretation of events by organizational actors and observers" (March and Olson, 1976:19).

Bounded Rationality

A basic issue in the design of policy is the extent to which it is the product of an incremental decisionmaking process, as opposed to one which aspires to comprehensive rationality (see Lindblom, 1959, 1979). The concept of bounded rationality draws attention to the circumstances under which decision rules will be governed, both in design and in implementation, by either of these strategies. Comprehensive rationality describes an explicit formal attempt to specify the goals of policy, to select and evaluate alternative methods of regulatory intervention, and to weigh the costs and benefits of various programs. There is little doubt that, as Lindblom aptly observes, it represents an overidealized approach to policymaking (Lindblom, 1959). Nevertheless, the idea of comprehensive rationality incorporates methodologies of policy analysis, such as decision modeling and cost-benefit studies, which are employed in decisionmaking about regulatory policy (Diver, 1981:397).

Incrementalism, in contrast, is what Lindblom calls "disjointed" problem analysis: several competing values are considered, and decisionmaking is fragmented and decentralized (Lindblom, 1979: 517). An incremental strategy is remedial and ad hoc. Regulatory problems are viewed as too complex for the application of comprehensive policy analysis. There is a primary emphasis on developing "a strategy to cope with problems, not to solve them" (Lindblom, 1965:148). Incrementalism also defines a normative structure for the regulatory decisionmaking process. Decisionmaking authority is not automatically vested in those who command knowledge of the techniques of comprehensive rationality: conflicts of value are accommodated, and policy goals are adjusted to reflect diverse political interests. It is important, as Lindblom notes, to maintain a clear distinction between problem analysis, which is incremental, and the decision process itself. He reserves the term "partisan mutual adjustment" for the latter, a phrase which connotes decentralized, pluralistic decisionmaking.

The idea of comprehensive rationality has become associated with a particular method for designing substantive policy rules. For example, it has been observed that the so-called hybrid rule-making cases – an attempt to combine informal rule-making procedures with judicial-type hearings – reflects a belief in the use of analytic methods (see DeLong, 1979:341). Efforts to promote this approach to rule making came into prominence in the 1970s as the courts and legislature stressed the use of policy analysis methods which required agencies to clarify goals and systematically identify and evaluate the impact of a broad range of alternatives. Thus the idea of comprehensive rationality has come to characterize a general demand advocated by courts and legislators for change in the agency policymaking process. In particular, agencies felt compelled by the courts to "show that they have made a conscious choice among policy options and not simply an *ad hoc* response to the pressures of the moment" (Diver, 1981:421).

Lindblom's framework helps clarify a controversial aspect of the way substantive policy is formulated, namely the role of public participation. Advocates of comprehensive rationality frequently oppose such participation because they believe it will reinforce the undesirable elements of incrementalism. "Participatory procedures," Diver observes, "are more consistent with the incrementalist impulse to accommodate conflicting values than with the policy analyst's penchant for objectivity" (Diver, 1981:424–25). According to this view, the opportunity systematically to evaluate alternatives is unduly compromised by participation. Moreover, the ideology that rational decisionmaking is subverted by participation can become the basis for conflict not only among various professionals within an agency but between the agency and external interest groups. Interest group participation is frequently equated by advocates of comprehensive rationality as irrational problem solving which lacks objectivity. According to this view, therefore, interaction between the agency and its political environment is primarily adversarial (see Lindblom and Cohen, 1979:33).

The issue of participation has been analyzed in terms of a basic conflict between the goals of "political responsiveness" and "economic efficiency" (Reich, 1979; also see chapter 4 of this volume). The latter holds that regulatory agencies should be evaluated according to their use of the policy analysis techniques of comprehensive rationality. Advocates of "political responsiveness" argue that agencies should be primarily concerned with reconciling the value conflicts and demands of diverse interest groups (Reich, 1979:38). This latter view is expressed in institutional terms in the form of hearings where partisans present opposing viewpoints and contest the validity of policy analysis. In this sense, participation is a mode of problem solving with the basic characteristics of "disjointed incrementalism," in particular, the "intertwining of analysis of policy goals and other values with the empirical aspects of the problem" (Lindblom, 1979: 517). The experience of the Federal Trade Commission (FTC) emphasizes the difficulties of applying criteria of economic efficiency to such hearings: proceedings can become highly politicized, as those opposing policy initiatives make continued demands for more rational studies, creating delays in rulemaking. Thus, without clear specification of goals in legislation, the integration of methods of comprehensive rationality with a formal process of participation becomes highly problematic, as chapter 4 shows.

In terms of incrementalism in agency policymaking, effective bargaining has also become more problematic because of the trend toward ensuring accountability by making the regulatory process increasingly a matter for judicial intervention. It has been argued that the informal rule-making procedures of the Administrative Procedures Act, and efforts to implement "hybrid" rule making, have resulted in procedural requirements which impede useful bargaining (see Schuck, 1979). Opponents of this view, however, argue that the formation of substantive policy lends itself to a less formal process of negotiation, again a form of problem solving which incorporates the characteristics of incrementalism. According to Schuck's assessment of the nature of regulatory issues, "policy problems can be solved only by taking account of numerous interdependent and highly variable factors which oblige the decision-makers to manage a kind of cybernetic process involving tentative probe, feedback, adjustment, and reconciliation" (Schuck, 1979:29). This approach depends on the reciprocity of bargaining and is inconsistent with highly formalized agency proceedings which are judicial in character despite the fact that these requirements have been adopted in the belief that they help promote greater objectivity and dispassionate analysis in regulatory policymaking (DeLong, 1979; Majone, 1980; Pedersen, 1975). Ironically, however, such pressures may actually result in more active bargaining and negotiation because of the difficulty of integrating analytical studies into formal proceedings. In the FTC rule-making hearings, for example, such studies were frequently perceived as inconclusive and unreliable guides to policy formation (see chapter 4).

The Social Constructionist Perspective

In an earlier work, we discussed the utility of the concept of "social construction" for understanding enforcement behavior in regulation (Hawkins and Thomas, 1984). The emphasis this perspective gives to the shared meanings that people ascribe to acts and events which emerge from patterns of interaction is also relevant to developing an understanding of the dynamics of policymaking within the regulatory agency. As a theoretical framework having certain methodological implications, the social constructionist perspective is part of the broad tradition of interpretive sociology of deviance, and in many areas of the sociology of law, scholars have given much less attention to its potential for furthering our understanding of public policymaking in general and of regulatory policymaking in particular.

The essence of the interpretive perspective is a concern for the characteristically human quality of social action, that is, a belief that behavior has subjective meaning and relevance for people (this is the theme of Erving Goffman's publications; three other classic essays are those by Blumer, 1969; Cicourel, 1968; and Garfinkel, 1967). Meaning is a central and pervasive feature of everyday life and influences behavior. It is necessary, as Van Maanen has observed, "to recognize that the objects, facts, events and relationships seemingly present in the everyday world have no meaning apart from what the observer chooses to give them. . . . it is only through the continuous interaction with others that we can construct certain meanings to things in the world toward which we can then gear our behavior" (1979:18–19).

Meaning is regarded as relative – as dependent upon setting, not only in a given culture, but also in a particular time and in a particular place. Concern for the meaning of behavior draws attention to the interpretive work in which human beings are constantly engaged in their ordinary everyday conduct. People constantly interpret what they see and hear, and these interpretations are continually open to change in a dynamic process upon which social action is based. Life is thus seen as an emergent process of constant interpretation and reinterpretation by people in endless social interaction. Decisions which, within the positivist tradition of research on the policy process, are regarded as "taken for granted" objective reality become problematic within the interpretive framework, given the central focus on the socially constructed nature of events.

If we apply this view of social action to regulatory policymaking, the social constructionist perspective requires us to pay attention to the basic role of norms and values in the process and the interpretive behavior of actors involved in it. Indeed, the particular relevance of work in the interpretive tradition for study of the regulatory bureaucracy is that its naturalist focus provides a means of understanding how policies are actually formulated. This perspective draws attention to questions such as: policymakers' conceptions of the goals to be attained; the values which they seek to advance, preserve, and protect; and *how* bureaucratic constraints emphasized in the concept of bounded rationality influence the way information is actually perceived and defined. Thus a deeper understanding of policymaking requires close, empirical study of routine decisions and working procedures, a focus on the social processes in a bureaucratic setting by which policy actually takes, and changes, shape.

The interpretive perspective has an important virtue in that it is less vulnerable to some of the shortcomings of positivist or rationalist assumptions about the nature of policymaking. Some of these flaws have been well documented in the context of policymaking by Paris amd Reynolds (1983), who have called attention to the danger of assuming that individuals will always behave as if they were calculating, rational actors. "In the Vietnam war," they write,

> theoretical discussion and practical prediction that a "rational" enemy would not continue a war given certain military pressure led to literal disaster. Similarly, if the views of the potential "targets" of policy are not well understood, the reaction may undercut what seems to be an otherwise sensible policy. For example, in 1966 James Coleman and others completed a massive, data-based study of the correlates of educational achievement. Rightly or wrongly, it was taken to imply that busing for integration would be one of the few, if not the only, policy which would boost black student performance. That policy was pursued in the face of tremendous opposition in white areas. By 1975, Coleman himself had admitted that "white flight" had rendered this policy nearly useless. Had it been understood what this policy meant to many white families, it might not have been pursued or pursued in the way it was. Without taking any position on the virtue of the policy or the opposition to it, we can say that sensitivity to agents' viewpoints here was crucial to the empirical premises of policy arguments. [1983: 180–81]

It follows, then, that one of the implications of considering the analysis of policymaking from an interpretive perspective is to reveal the inadequacy of more orthodox forms of inquiry. Paris and Reynolds provide an example from Aaron Cicourel's celebrated study of the handling of juvenile offenders (published in 1968). In their analysis of that study, they argue that the empirical premises of policy arguments framed in orthodox terms involve a fundamental positivist assumption that delinquency is an unproblematic, observable phenomenon and not something socially created by ideologies and practice. As a consequence, conventional analysis will tend to overlook the fact that statistical indicators of trends or patterns in crime, or lay theorizing about criminal behavior, are socially created and maintained. The result is a double misunderstanding:

It ignores the world-view and self-conception of the target of policy efforts (the delinquent) as well as that of the public official who produces policy aimed at that target. To the extent that orthodox approaches ignore policy-relevant understanding of citizens they may produce ineffective policy (such as the Coleman report and "white flight"). To the extent that they ignore policy-makers' ideology and understandings, they may take as facts or data what is the result of social processes (e.g., juvenile justice data). An understanding of the process by which policy-makers interpret the social world may suggest discrepancies between typical explanations or expressed rationales and the actual logic of (conscious or unconscious) understandings of policy in actual practice such as the role of "broken" homes in dealing with delinquents. It may also clarify the influence of organizational rules or routines on those understandings. Information on the understandings of both policy-maker and citizen may be important to obtaining sound, relevant empirical premises for policy arguments, and this is precisely what such participant observation attempts to offer. [Paris and Reynolds, 1983: 183–84]

The application of this type of inquiry to the field of regulation is clearly no easy task. The methodologies of the social constructionist approach, which rely on ethnographic techniques, particularly participant observation, are time-consuming. Furthermore, such techniques are more suited to the study of processes involving continuous activity (such as policing). It is difficult to adapt these methods to the study of policymaking, which is often introspective and secretive. More important, this empirical work requires reflection on a complicated and fragmented process over a substantial period and the capacity to unravel subtle and shifting events.

Though the essays in this book are concerned with regulation in very different settings, they illustrate themes which pervade the making of policy by regulatory bureaucracies. Of particular relevance for an increased understanding of policymaking are the role of knowledge and information processing, the relationship between the agency and its environment, the influence of professional values and beliefs, and internal agency politics.

Processing Knowledge and Information

The concepts of bounded rationality and social construction are particularly relevant in considering the problem of information processing, an issue addressed in several chapters of this volume as a problem of defining, communicating, and interpreting data in areas of regulation where risk is frequently defined by the low probability of a catastrophic harm. Policymaking, for example, systematically relies upon regulated firms for assessments of health and safety problems but rarely considers information about the potential victims' perceptions and attitudes toward risk (see Perrow, 1984:314–15). Moreover, it has been observed that certain agencies gather huge amounts of particular kinds of data which infrequently enter into crucial policymaking decisions. The Environmental Protection Agency (EPA), for example, regularly assesses the relationships between industry costs and the amount of risk that a given investment of resources might eliminate but fails to use this analysis as a basis for targeting enforcement resources (Ackerman and Stewart, 1985: 1363).

Information and research are crucial to the creation of informed regulatory policy, particularly the task of designing rules and determining standards, the highly visible basic elements of an agency policy. However, these are not necessarily straightforward matters. "The central problem of the standard-setting process," Breyer writes (1982:109), "and the most pressing task facing many agencies, is gathering the information needed to write a sensible standard." Of course, in some potential arenas of regulatory control, uncertainty about whether to adopt a regulatory policy, as well as which policy to adopt, is compounded by a lack of adequate scientific theory or by emotional controversies over the interpretation of data. Areas of protective social regulation are often characterized, ironically, by a high level of information coupled with a high degree of uncertainty. This dilemma is familiar in many of the areas in the EPA's policymaking where problems may often be marked not simply by scientific uncertainty but even by outright conflict, such as the precise nature and extent of the depletion of the ozone layer by chlorofluorocarbons (CFCs) produced in manufacturing. As Rabin illustrates in chapter 5, when the EPA tried to regulate CFC emissions, there was substantial doubt about the sheer credibility of ozone depletion theory. As a result, the problem has been all the more acute for policymakers, for if the theory is correct, or even partly correct, the absence of regulatory control could have drastic consequences.

The making of regulatory policy inevitably incorporates elements of predictive decisionmaking, which is at best an extremely difficult matter. The difficulties, however, are compounded when efforts are made to formulate policy for potentially catastrophic events, as might occur in the nuclear power industry, where judgments and the assessment of risk assume correspondingly greater importance. Essentially the problem involves making policy not only for events which have not yet occurred but also for events which, although extremely unlikely to occur, may be of enormous gravity if they do. Yet the understandable anxiety to regulate for the catastrophe may come to preoccupy regulatory policymakers because of their public position, their public image, and their need to dramatize the activity and effectiveness of their agency to a public consumed by a sense of dread. The problem of policymaking is the more acute in the absence of actual data drawn from past experience. Furthermore, to the extent that regulatory agencies depend upon the results of research and are concerned with indexes of impact or effectiveness, they often operate in a world of vague indicators or unclear impacts, so that research has results which are either confusing or have little of significance to display. Policymakers need imagination to envision the possible and to design policy which precludes it. Indeed, unlike most regulatory policymaking, nuclear regulation is ostensibly concerned not with how many accidents to allow but with how not to allow any accidents at all.

But knowledge derived from scientific inquiry is, in itself, insufficient for policy purposes, as Manning argues. Indeed, at the outset, Manning rejects the positivist paradigm by arguing that interpreted meaning, not information, is the basis for regulation. Information must be available and must then be interpreted correctly. Some questions of regulatory policy are particularly complicated and intractable because they are essentially concerned with values which sometimes conflict with the interests of technical or economic efficiency. Thus it is helpful to regard policymaking in regulation as a form of information handling involving a social process which connects a sender and receiver of knowledge. Policymaking is presumably only as good as the information collected by, or made available to, regulatory agencies, which is then interpreted and understood as to its implications by those in key policymaking positions. Furthermore, Manning argues, matters central to protective social regulation, such as safety and health, are to be regarded as broad and symbolic in character, so that difficulties arise in their definition, measurement, and assessment and they become less obviously a part of routine operational data gathering (see chapter 3).

Agency and Environment

Precisely how matters come to be interpreted, of course, has to do with the nature of the environment in which the regulatory agency and its officials operate. Moreover, interpretations of the agency's environment determine the way in which knowledge and information are used in policymaking. According to Joskow and Noll:

> In addition to the fact that the organizations possess decision rules for processing information, their perception of the structure of the world (or that of its constituent parts) determines what information is observed and processed. For all intents and purposes, the organization's perceptions constitute the reality in which it operates. The structure of the environment that the organization perceives may be quite different from the objective reality; however, this structure or model of the economic and political environment works from the viewpoint of the organization, in that it consistently explains the behavior with which the organization is concerned. [Joskow and Noll, 1982:50–51]

From these perspectives, an agency's various constituencies will all have an interest in ensuring that the agency sees its world in a particular way. Thus values and views are expressed to regulatory officials in the course of their direct relationships with regulated groups and firms. Sometimes the agency may be well aware of pressure groups and firms. Sometimes the agency may be well aware of pressure groups and campaigning individuals who want to see more control and greater activism. Other aspects of the regulatory environment, however, may be more diffused and less obvious though nonetheless real. Changes in political administration, for example, may have profound consequences for the budget of regulatory agencies or for the appointment of new staff in key positions. Sometimes such changes may serve as a concrete expression of a shift of public opinion about the degree of social regulation required, or even about regulation's role as a function of government.

Put like this, the issues seem straightforward. The actual regulatory process, however, may be much less clear, as Rock suggests. He argues that research directed to policymaking is conducted within a framework of expectations about probable policymaking and political action. The "problem" about which policy is to be formulated usually has a prehistory which can be described as "proposals, projects, programs, and talks" (see chapter 2). Prehistory is shaped by competing publics with their own agendas and interests. Furthermore, regulatory organizations are not simply passive receivers of comment and complaint from the interested publics who compose their significant environment, as Manning notes. The environment of the regulatory agency is characterized by competing values, and this environment yields data to be interpreted or acted upon by the agency, so that it becomes, in Weick's terms, the "enacted environment" (see Weick, 1979).

The nature of the relationship between regulator and the regulated environment has long preoccupied political scientists and economists, who have argued that the impetus for control is dissipated as agencies become captured by regulatory firms (for example, see Bernstein, 1955). In the case of nuclear power generation, for example, regulatory policymaking appears to be conducted in an environment best characterized, in Manning's words, as one of "abiding warmth." In the relationship between the Nuclear Regulatory Commission and the nuclear power industry, Manning argues, power companies are able to exert an excessive degree of influence in the formulation of regulatory policy. They are able to do so because of the mutual trust between the two groups and because the relationship involves two large bodies which are very familiar with one another. Furthermore, it can be postulated that the more complex and advanced the technology subject to regulation, the more the regulators will have to rely on trust as the basis for their relationship with the regulated (see Reiss, 1984).

The relationship between the regulatory agency and its environment is also a prominent theme in Boyer's analysis of FTC rule making. The FTC had originally been strongly criticized by Ralph Nader and his colleagues. Boyer argues that changes in the agency in the mid-1970s partly responded to Nader's attacks and to changes in agency personnel. The consequence was much greater activism on the part of the agency. Yet within another five years, this activism had been dissipated. Boyer emphasizes the quality of the personal relationships between regulators and the regulated and its implications for the framing of policy. Many staff members at the FTC were new to the job and had no opportunity to develop close contacts with their regulated constituencies, so that direct feedback from them was not possible. Furthermore, when they did actually seek to cultivate such relationships, they did so unsystematically or aggressively, so that they created resentment or formed a distorted picture of the regulated public (see chapter 4).

In fact the FTC had relatively little feedback from its interested publics that would indicate their reaction to its policymaking and correct its view of reality, and the result may have been less caution than is inherent in agency policymaking. In Boyer's view, one reason for the inadequacy of the feedback was structural, relating to the agency's shift from case-by-case adjudication to industrywide rule making; the implication is that the formal or structural aspect of policymaking is significant. While critics may complain of the ad hoc and particularistic nature of case-by-case adjudication, one of its advantages is that it allows an agency to adapt incrementally to unfolding experience. Boyer concludes that to remain healthy, or even to survive, agencies do indeed need to adapt to changes in their political environment. In the case of the consumer movement, the momentum toward greater regulation was dissipating and losing its influence in the mid-1970s, and business groups were mounting a sustained period of opposition. In these circumstances, an agency might find bargaining and compromise valuable. However, if agency policymaking is characterized by missionary zeal, then a dysfunctional adversarial culture may develop. Effective adaptation thus depends upon the development of incentives that emphasize the use of rational analysis in a context of bargaining between the agency and its diverse constituencies. For policymakers, it is essential to understand that such incentives are socially constructed; they both reflect and mold a "culture" of agency bureaucracy.

The Influence of Professional Values and Beliefs

Several of the essays in this volume also emphasize the theme that policymaking is to be seen as a product of the people actually engaged in the enterprise, with their own concerns, drive, and initiative. The extent to which this is possible may well depend, however, upon the way the law is structured. For example, from his study of the FTC, Boyer proposes that the broader the discretion afforded to administrative agencies by law, the greater the part to be played in the making of policy by the personal beliefs and ideologies of the policymaking staff. These beliefs, in turn, are clearly formed by the staff's socialization and recruitment. In the case of the FTC, the staff were lawyers whose training and instincts did not encourage them to undertake systematic empirical analysis and whose personal beliefs were often at odds with the values of the regulated industries.

The effects of socialization and recruitment may also be compounded by the incentives and constraints to which staff in a regulatory agency are subject. A further impediment to careful but time-consuming empirical analysis of the issues in the FTC existed in the form of the staff's career incentives, which prompted a commitment on their part to work leading to a quick payoff. Because of the high degree of staff turnover in this agency, many individuals did not expect to see the implementation of a policy to which they had contributed. In short, they became concerned more with creating policy than with the implications of policies created.

Rabin, like Boyer, supports the view that internal organizational structure has clear implications for the manner and substance of policymaking. Boyer shows that in the FTC the allocation of staff with different kinds of expertise was crucial. In the EPA, however, Rabin's evidence (which is drawn from firsthand participation in the work of the agency) clearly indicates the importance of different operational philosophies among staff in different organizational departments.

Meidinger's essay on the "market mechanism" paradigm in air pollution policy also develops this theme. Meidinger suggests that the recent emergence of market, incentive-based strategies for the design of enforcement policy is related to the professional values which define a particular regulatory "culture." A significant dimension of that culture involves perceptions about the way conflicts in the social and political environment should be worked out. This system of beliefs, developed through interaction among professionals, essentially expresses an incrementalist perspective on policymaking which holds, for example, that scientific data cannot provide definite answers to regulatory problems despite the sophistication of methods of formal analysis and modeling. This culture of policymaking suggests that decisions should be made within a stable framework capable of including all significant values, one based on broad participation and bargaining with affected private interests.

These human processes are all extremely subtle. As Rock argues, it helps if we regard policy as emerging from the activities of individuals in organizations. People move about organizations and in doing so must reconstruct a sense of organizational history and purpose. The motives and rationales for policy are, in Rock's view, constantly revised and altered as policy unfolds. He draws attention to the developing outcomes of organizing processes which shape and are shaped by their own attendant webs of social relations (a point also well illustrated by Rabin's essay). This suggests a fortuitous element in the process, a view endorsed by one official engaged in the formulation of penal policy in England. He regards it as essential "to stress the diverse, and one might say almost haphazard, character of the process. Some of the pictures presented of policy-making suggests a simple input-output model. The reality is a good deal more confused than that. Given the breadth of the field, the variety of pressures, the many uncontrollable elements, it probably has to be so" (Moriarty, 1977:134).

Internal Agency Politics

Agency politics may be a prominent feature of the policymaking process, given the ill-defined nature of regulatory problems that value conflicts frequently entail and given the diverse motives of regulatory officials. In recognition of the influence of such motives, Wilson has argued that there are essentially three types of regulatory official: "careerists" who identify with a particular agency and do not expect to move; "politicians" who are interested in other appointive or elective offices; and "professionals" who identify with the status-reward system of an occupation and the norms of technical competence of that occupation (Wilson, 1980:374). Coalitions of officials with similar motives form around specific policy issues and the need to preserve autonomy. The existence of such coalitions, however, can adversely affect what Wilson terms the organizational maintenance goal of the agency (see Wilson, 1980:377).

The recognition that internal agency politics may be a significant force in regulatory policymaking suggests that the particular public stance adopted by agencies may be a product of bargaining among individuals and coalitions within the agency bureaucracy. In a number of studies, lawyers have been shown to be a professional group with a significant role in agency politics. Indeed Noll (1976) has discussed the evidence for "a lawyer domination" model of agency behavior where regulatory goals are displaced by the interest of the legal profession. According to this theory, such professional norms can deflect the agency from its ostensible concern with efficiency and serving the public interest. Lawyers, it is argued, may divert the agency from its primary objectives by giving undue emphasis to procedural values such as due process. Recent studies of the FTC and the antitrust division of the Department of Justice, for example, have demonstrated that the professional orientation of lawyers does indeed exert a powerful – even dominant – influence on the kinds of cases that are dealt with (Katzman, 1981; Weaver, 1977). Similarly, the influence of the beliefs and motives of legal professionals upon the agency is evident from Boyer's study of rule making in the FTC, where the activist, proconsumer motives of younger lawyers in the agency inhibited their capacity to negotiate policies which could accommodate the multiple conflicting values encountered in rule making.

The dominance of lawyers in bureaucratic politics sometimes gives rise to conflict with other professional groups. One example occurred in the early formative stage of the EPA. EPA economists were highly critical of the lack of analysis and objective evidence in orders issued by the lawyers (see Wilson, 1980:381). Another example is to be found in the FTC antitrust division, where agency infighting has frequently involved lawyers and economists (see Katzman, 1981) and has led to serious disputes over policy. The existence of such a conflict is not surprising. Lawyers tend not to think in terms of comprehensive rationality when interpreting industrial information but favor strategies which are reactive, concrete, and particularistic; they take on business conduct cases which come from complainants. Economists, on the other hand, tend to be more concerned with large, structural cases which affect the consumer economy, and in general they prefer a more abstract, proactive approach involving comprehensive planning and policy analysis.

Agency politics may become particularly significant when, as part of policy development, the agency seeks to change its own mandate through the reform of existing legislation. In this situation the task is to propose a new set of goals and procedures for the agency which may require extensive lobbying by regulatory officials. The different perspectives of lawyers and policy analyst economists may give rise to serious difficulties, as was shown when Connecticut's Department of Environment Protection (DEP) created a new enforcement policy for pollution control. Professional conflict emerged, in part, because of different functions. The economic analysis group "focused on the managerial and economic aspects of enforcement . . . , how could a system be designed that would give DEP effective leverage on polluters' behavior?" (Lynn, 1980:416). The lawyers, on the other hand, were concerned primarily with drafting policy which could resist legal challenges. More important, however, was that professional value conflict seemingly led to negative images of each other's contributions. As the leader of the economic analysis group assessed it: "the lawyers were unable to suspend the usual lawyerly thought processes to understand his economic/managerial analysis of the problems within the enforcement process" (Lynn, 1980:416). In contrast, the head of the legal team perceived the analysis group as "thinking" in "relatively conceptual terms, at a rather theoretical level, whereas . . . the need was to be extremely concrete very quickly" (Lynn, 1980:416). Such differences lead to a policy formation process which is not unified and which can jeopardize the shared objective of desirable change in the law.

Agency politics is a function not only of professional values but also of attitudes and viewpoints that develop through identification with a particular unit or role with the organization. Rabin's essay, for example, shows how two departments or offices within the EPA competed for the prize of formulating CFC emission controls to protect the ozone layer. One of these offices was able to intrude into the policymaking process by commissioning outside research (see also chapter 2) and instructing researchers to concentrate on a specific enforcement method, in this case a market incentive strategy, thereby introducing its own policy preferences as serious matters for debate within the agency. The other interested branch in the EPA had thus to share its authority and cooperate with its counterpart in order to make some contribution to the research and to have access to the data. This unit, however, was wedded to a traditional command-and-control style of regulatory enforcement, which led to a conflict of philosophy over enforcement policy. Jealousy within the organization arose when one branch realized that the other was committed to regulation by economic incentives rather than by command and control. It had reservations about a policy based on incentives and also feared that if it endorsed this approach it would lose its dominant role in policymaking. Indeed, Rabin goes on to suggest that the choice of regulatory technique in this particular case may actually have hinged on which of the EPA's internal offices achieved control of the policymaking process within the agency—on who, in effect, won the turf war.

Rabin's study of the EPA also draws attention to the role of hierarchical authority in agency politics. The conflict over enforcement policy between the two groups was dampened by the preoccupation of the EPA administration with the policy issue of whether the government should intervene at all. This larger question superseded political infighting over the particular issue of enforcement policy. This case reveals how agency politics unfolds in response to different levels of problems (such as identifying the purpose of governmental action and determining what institutions and laws should be mobilized or how specific programs should be designed); the process can be viewed as a game with rules and influence patterns (see Lynn, 1982). In the case of the CFC regulation, a consensus of senior management within the EPA ultimately allowed the coalition favoring market incentives to prevail.

Conclusion

The regulatory process illustrates the general problem of program implementation by government bureaucracies. As such it involves all the dimensions of what Clune has defined as the politics of implementation through law, "the design of government policy, the choice of policy instruments for social purposes, and the management of government policy in a complex and politicized environment" (Clune, 1984:49). While the regulatory process, broadly conceived, begins with legislative action (agenda setting and lawmaking about a perceived problem) and proceeds to implementation (formal prosecution and informal bargaining over compliance), agency policymaking falls between, and intersects, these functions. Thus defined, policymaking encompasses two fundamental problems: the promulgation of rules which reflect the agency's conception of its mission and the design of a method of enforcement. Both are based on interpretations of statutory authority and technical information about a particular problem.

References

Ackerman, Bruce A., and Richard Stewart. 1985. "Reforming Environmental Law." 37 *Stanford Law Review*: 1333–65.

Bardach, Eugene, and Robert Kagan. 1982. *Going by the Book: The Problem of Regulatory Unreasonableness*. Philadelphia: Temple University Press.

Bernstein, Marver. 1955. *Regulating Business by Independent Commission*. Princeton, N.J.: Princeton University Press.

Blumer, Herbert. 1969. *Symbolic Interaction: Perspective and Method.* Englewood Cliffs, N.J.: Prentice-Hall.

Breyer, Stephen. 1982. *Regulation and Its Reform.* Cambridge, Mass.: Harvard University Press.

Cicourel, Aaron V. 1968. *The Social Organization of Juvenile Justice.* New York: Wiley.

Clune, William A., III. 1984. "A Political Model of Implementation and Implications of the Model for Public Policy, Research, and the Changing Roles of Law and Lawyers." 69 *Iowa Law Review:* 47–125.

Crandall, Robert W., and Lester B. Lave, eds. 1981. *The Scientific Basis of Health and Safety and Regulation.* Washington, D.C.: Brookings Institution.

DeLong, James V. 1979. "Informal Rulemaking and the Integration of Law and Policy." 65 *Virginia Law Review:* 257–356.

Diver, Colin. 1981. "A Policy-making Paradigm in Administrative Law." 95 *Harvard Law Review:* 393–434.

————. 1983. "The Optimal Precision of Administrative Rules." 93 *Yale Law Journal:* 65–109.

Garfinkel, Harold. 1967. *Studies in Ethnomethodology.* Englewood Cliffs, N.J.: Prentice-Hall.

Hawkins, Keith, and John M. Thomas. 1984. *Enforcing Regulation.* Boston: Kluwer-Nijhoff.

Joskow, Paul L. 1974. "Inflation and Environmental Concern: Structural Change in the Process of Public Price Regulation." 17 *Journal of Law and Economics:* 291–328.

Joskow, Paul L., and Roger C. Noll. 1982. "Regulation in Theory and Practice: An Overview." In *Studies in Public Regulation,* ed. Garry Fromm. Cambridge, Mass.: MIT Press.

Kagan, R. A. 1978. *Regulatory Justice.* New York: Russell Sage.

Kagan, R. A., and John Scholz. 1984. "The Criminology of the Corporation." In *Enforcing Regulation,* ed. Hawkins and Thomas.

Katzmann, Robert A. 1981. *Regulatory Bureaucracy: The Federal Trade Commission and Antitrust Policy.* Cambridge, Mass.: MIT Press.

Lindblom, Charles E. 1959. "The Science of Muddling Through." 19 *Public Administration Review:* 79–88.

————. 1979. "Still Muddling, Not Yet Through." 39 *Public Administration Review:* 517–26.

————. 1965. *The Intelligence of Democracy.* New York: Free Press.

Lindblom, Charles E., and David K. Cohen. 1979. *Usable Knowledge: Social Science and Social Problem Solving.* New Haven, Conn.: Yale University Press.

Lowrance, W. W. 1976. *Of Acceptable Risk.* Los Altos, Calif.: Kaufmann.

Lynn, Lawrence E., Jr. 1982. "Government Executives as Gamesmen: A

Metaphor for Analyzing Managerial Behavior." 1 *Journal of Policy Analysis and Management:* 482–95.

———. 1980. *Designing Public Policy: A Casebook on the Role of Policy Analysis.* Santa Monica, Calif.: Goodyear.

Majone, Giandomenico. 1980. "Process and Outcome in Regulatory Decision-making." In *Making Bureaucracies Work,* ed. Carol H. Weiss and Allen H. Barton. Beverly Hills, Calif.: Sage.

March, James. 1978. "Bounded Rationality, Ambiguity, and the Engineering of Choice." 9 *Bell Journal of Economics:* 587–608.

March, James, and Johan P. Olsen. 1976. *Ambiguity and Choice in Organizations.* Bergen, Norway: Universitetsforlatet.

Mashaw, Jerry L. 1979. "Regulation, Logic, and Ideology." 3 *Regulation* (November/December): 44.

Moriarty, Michael. 1977. "Policymaking Process: How It Is Seen from the Home Office." In *Penal Policymaking in England,* ed. Nigel Walker. Cambridge: Institute of Criminology.

Noll, Robert G. 1976. *Government Administrative Behavior and Private Sector Response: A Multidisciplinary Survey.* Social Science Working Paper 62. Pasadena: California Institute of Technology.

Paris, David C., and James Reynolds. 1983. *The Logic of Policy Inquiry.* New York: Longmans.

Pedersen, William F., Jr. 1975. "Formal Records and Informal Rulemaking." 85 *Yale Law Journal:* 38–82.

Perrow, Charles. 1984. *Normal Accidents.* New York: Basic Books.

Pfeffer, Jeffrey. 1982. *Organizations and Organization Theory.* Boston: Pitman.

Reich, Robert B. 1979. "Warring Critiques of Regulation." 3 *Regulation* (January/February): 37–42.

Reiss, Albert. 1984. "Selecting Strategies of Social Control Over Organizational Life." In *Enforcing Regulation,* ed. Hawkins and Thomas.

Sabatier, Paul A. 1977. "Regulatory Policy-making: Toward a Framework of Analysis." 17 *Natural Resources Journal:* 415–60.

Schuck, Peter H. 1979. "Litigation, Bargaining, and Regulation." 3 *Regulation* (July/August): 26–34.

Stewart, Richard B. 1979. "Judging the Imponderables of Environmental Policy: Judicial Review Under the Clean Air Act." In *Approaches to Controlling Air Pollution,* ed. Ann F. Friedlander, pp. 68–137. Cambridge, Mass.: MIT Press.

Van Maanen, John. 1979. "On the Understanding of Interpersonal Relations." In *Essays in Interpersonal Relations,* ed. Warren Bennis, John Van Maanen, and Edgar H. Schein. Homewood, Ill.: Dorsey Press.

Weaver, Suzanne. 1977. *Decision to Prosecute.* Cambridge, Mass.: MIT Press.

Weick, Karl. 1979. *The Social Psychology of Organizing.* Reading, Mass.: Addison-Wesley.

Wilson, James Q. 1980. *The Politics of Regulation.* New York: Basic Books.

Wolf, Charles. 1979. "A Theory of Nonmarket Failure: Framework for Implementation Analysis." 22 *Journal of Law and Economics:* 107–39.

I

The Use of Information and Knowledge
in Regulatory Policy

A central issue in policymaking is the use of information by the regulatory bureaucracy. Often the assumption is made in formal methods of decisionmaking that information is unproblematic, objectively defined, and subject to little interpretation. Part I, in which two essays analyze the role of information in decisionmaking from the perspective of social construction, suggests otherwise. Both studies reveal how the use of information is strongly influenced by shared meanings and symbols which reflect social processes in bureaucracies.

The first essay, by Paul Rock, is based on an extensive study of the use of knowledge and information by a government department. (See Rock, A Voice from the Shadows [Oxford: Oxford University Press, 1987].) Rock demonstrates the complexity of policymaking processes and the difficulties that may be encountered in disentangling lines of influence and causation and even chronologies of events. He shows that what is often presented and made public in very simple and clear terms is often enormously elaborate. His analysis indicates that policies actually crystallize from broad, constantly changing ideas and influences.

Similarly, Peter Manning's essay draws attention to the decision behavior of policymakers as organizational actors. Manning explores the relevance of conceptions of risk, hazard, or catastrophe to emergent policy, using the occasion of the nearly disastrous incident at Three Mile Island in Pennsylvania in 1979 for illustrative purposes. Law is increasingly being called upon to regulate areas of human enterprise involving potentially catastrophic matters, and nuclear regulation dramatically embodies some of the most crucial problems and dilemmas posed for regulatory officials. Manning suggests that in such a setting policymaking may be regarded as a dramatic enterprise in which symbols have considerable influence on the meaning of events and serve to define new and specific concerns of government.

29

2

Criminology, Research, and the Making of Policy in a Canadian Setting

Paul Rock

S INCE J ULY 1981, I have been concentrating on a description of the work done by the Ministry of the Solicitor General of Canada in its construction of the "Justice for Victims of Crime Initiative." My examination of the interplay between ideas, research, and policy development in this chapter stems directly from that larger description, being grounded in a specific history, and I am not certain how wide its scope and relevance will prove to be. Further, my knowledge of institutions is refracted by the structure of a particular project, just as my knowledge of policymaking is refracted by the organization of the ministry. In effect, an episode of policymaking revealed facets of an institution, and the institution illuminated policymaking, the one constituting the other as analysis and events proceeded. I shall not offer anything like a detailed substantive history of the initiative. That has been prepared separately.[1] Rather, in this chapter I intend to provide a few general observations about the process of policy development as it was revealed in this one instance, the initiative serving as a loose framework and as a source of raw material for argument.

The institutional relations between criminological research and policy were nicely mirrored in the formal division of labor adopted by the Secretariat of the Ministry of the Solicitor General. Prominent in the wings of the Secretariat were the Programs Branch, focusing on research and program development, and the Policy Branch, whose function it is to shape and advance ministry policy. The Policy Branch is responsible for gaining intelligence about the political environment of the criminal justice system, for tendering advice to the solicitor general and the deputy solicitor general, and for "developing the strategic policy framework for the Secretariat" (*Annual Report*, 1981:3). Most important, it superintends the passage of proposals as they are navigated through the labyrinthine committee system of Ottawa.

The Justice for Victims of Crime Initiative itself was largely the child of the Programs Branch, and had been the subject of proposals, projects, programs, and talk since the mid-1970s. It enjoined groups of federal and provincial officials to examine the needs and problems of crime victims, assess and stimulate the services that might alleviate their distress, and make recommendations. It was the result of considerable bureaucratic preparation, condensing copious activity that had taken place in Ottawa and beyond. During the late 1960s and the 1970s, victims had become salient in a number of American and Canadian centers. They had been given form and bulk in the work done by women's organizations on raped and battered women; in a politics of decarceration which had sought to reconcile released or free offenders with their victims (*Correctional Options*, 1981; Dittenhoffer and Ericson, 1983); in crime prevention programs; and in the problems of law enforcement encountered by police officers. The centers had all been shaped by their own little histories and they had attached very different meanings to victimization. The initiative, which was to become their culmination and synthesis, may actually be likened to a master argument about the natural history of a Canadian social problem that brought together various materials and sought to reconcile them.

The matter of victims was transferred to the Policy Branch between 1980 and 1981. It remained under that branch's central direction after that time. In that transition, and in the business of caring for victims and helping them, may be observed a quite practical expression of what are often presented as somewhat metaphysical connections and happenings. I will be concerned with this process, although I cannot phrase my argument in detail or at length.

Before I proceed, I should note that research and policymaking are frequently harmonious. They often establish a stage for one another and merge into one another as a continuous activity. Indeed, as I shall argue, the distinction between the two is really rather opaque. By focusing chiefly on issues of difference in style and ownership, I shall give a necessarily exaggerated emphasis to certain problems. Like the space probe *Voyager*, I have produced an imagery which has been enhanced to describe the otherwise murky topography of relations in a setting. Before that enhancement takes place, the everyday life of the office tends to be amicable enough. In that sense, my analysis betrays its origin in a special problem. As Heisenberg remarked, "What we observe is not nature itself, but nature exposed to our method of questioning" (Heisenberg, 1958:58).

The Forms and Relations of Research and Policy

Most policymaking turns on the preparation of documents and argument. Before it is ever presented to public view, it has been pored over, analyzed, shaped, and arranged in copious committees and discussion papers. Each phase of that protracted work is carefully and artfully considered, designed to achieve very precise ends. Work done is done thoughtfully. It is a reflexive activity, mediated by written and spoken words, borrowing some of the structure and logic of rhetoric. It is simultaneously itself, its own framework and its own object, producing the conditions for its own reproduction. It is capable of furnishing a propitious environment and history for itself, setting in place those arguments, links and processes that give it form, causality and necessity. In Weick's phrase (1979), it enacts its own environment. Research can and will become part of that environment, acquiring significance as policymaking evolves. The consequences of research are therefore unstable and emergent, being fused with the changing policies which they engender. They will become progressively absorbed by argument over time, forming a feature of its organization and following its path of development. They will become objectified, ordered, and altered by the grammar and demands of political rhetoric. They will come to exemplify morals and lessons in the storytelling of the policy document and the verbal presentation of a case and will lose themselves in a superior history. Research thus tends to become an artifact of rhetoric.

It is not only the tendency of policy arguments to engulf research that makes it difficult to prise them apart. Research is not innocent of meaning in government settings. The funding of programs and the initiation of demonstration projects are themselves highly reflexive activities, undertaken in the knowledge that they may be read as signs of government interests and intentions. They may indeed be employed to foster those very interests. The Ministry of the Solicitor General itself took to advertising its concerns, announcing its developing priorities and inviting research applications that might bear upon them.

Moreover, the applied disciplines which touch on social problems have always been freighted with political and moral significance. Sometimes that meaning is imposed by outsiders who draw attention to the alleged bearings and provenance of a piece of work. Radical criminologists are especially bent on imposing an ideological context on every nuance of criminology. They peruse work for its politics, acting as the censors and judges of scholarship. They put criminology to the question. Thus it will be recalled that Platt believed it important to inquire: "What was and is the political practice of theorists like Sutherland, Cressey, Lemert, Turk and others in terms of their support of struggles against oppression? This is not simply a rhetorical or 'practical question.' Rather it goes to the root of explaining how ruling-class ideologies are formed and sustained and why it is important to undermine the hegemony of liberal theory" (Platt, 1973:598).

Others are also quite prepared to discredit ideas and arguments they find disagreeable. Parliamentarians sometimes give research a political reading, discounting that which upsets their case and attending to that which strengthens it. For example, in a House of Commons debate on capital punishment, some members sought to undermine the hegemony of research and appeal to public opinion. One declared "how can this government trot out data and conclusions which is [sic] done through the auspices of a pet professor of the government by the name of Fattah?"[2] And another announced of research at large:

> What is important is not what a sociologist believes or thinks, but what the majority of Canadians think and what they desire and ask. . . . There is an old maxim, Mr. Speaker: Tell me who pays you and I'll tell you who you are. The Solicitor General is the milk cow that feeds those criminologists who do not know what to do with their ten fingers. Do you think guys like that would take the chance of making the Solicitor General of Canada angry? In my view, Mr. Speaker, those criminologists are not stupid. He is the one who feeds them, who enables them to live and consequently they prepare the reports he wants.[3]

Sometimes research is accomplished for manifest political ends. After all, criminology, penology, and victimology have been marked by an appreciable evangelism devised to change the world. At the Third International Symposium on Victimology, one rapporteur defined victimology as a "movement" whose "original and continuing aim was and is to reduce as much as possible the suffering of victims" (Dussich and Kirchoff, 1981). And criminology and penology have been described in like manner. Of course, much scholarship is disinterested, but the bestowing and courting of political ambitions have tended to tinge all work at its margins.

In that milieu, the relations between criminological research and policy must inevitably be contingent and shifting, each being knowingly developed in the presence of the other and each exposed to a regress of expectation and adaptation. It is evident that politically influential research must be assembled in a manner that lends itself to use as a rhetorical resource. And it is also evident that the purposes of research may be shaped by rhetoric. Indeed, all ends must be metaphysical and rhetorical at last. In such a setting, argument may be understood as a form of the significant gesture, planned to answer the anticipated responses of others and becoming a working synthesis of research and policy in its own right. As events advance, so research and policy tend to blur into one another. It becomes increasingly difficult and unprofitable to decide whether thoughts about research really preceded those about policy. The two cannot be neatly separated and the question cannot be answered. Instead, the activity of amalgamation and anticipation seems to have engendered a more general discourse that permeates particular conferences, meetings, and papers, a discourse that does not lay itself out into areas of talk obviously constituted by research and areas obviously built on policy. To add complexity, those conferences and their accompanying speech tend to be international and cosmopolitan, allowing influences to seep from state to state and from academy to academy. Officials may act as conduits and filters for the flow of argument between universities, just as research staff and criminologists can mediate the relations of states. For these reasons, the internal structure of any one government cannot explain all the ways in which policy and research interlace: Canadian work may be grafted onto American research that was inspired by an English idea. Indeed, there is even greater complexity, because Canadians are not obliged to adopt American research. Theirs will be an act of choice, a creature of argument, which can pursue a most complicated development of its own.

Criminology must take on a special personality within the sphere dominated by government. Constituted by the talk of a special train of conferences, it can become a little remote from the preoccupations and teachings of the more abstract university course. If it is to be consequential, it must be formed into that peculiar compound and extension of policy-relevant research and research-relevant policy. In turn, its significant exponent and practitioner is likely to be one with an acknowledged presence in those conferences and in the social circles which they knit together. He or she will probably be an able and willing speaker in the dialect of the conference. After all, busy officials have little time to read and study the lengthy effusions of those they have not met and do not know. It is better to trust those who are recommended or encountered at first hand in the meetings of such bodies as the Council of Europe, Cropwood Conferences, the United Nations, and government-sponsored conventions. Typically, then, the social structure of conferences, practicality, and government activity gives prominence to particular people and problems. It creates a parochial world like any other, a world with its own central characters, gossip, and reputations. Politically, those qualities mediate criminology. Criminology ceases to be the substance of the academic course but a specially adapted and workable version that bears the imprint of its origins, uses, and audience. When I speak of criminology, I will refer to that local form.

Research, too, acquires its own situated character. It is not the free-floating activity of the university. On the contrary, it is conducted within an implicit and explicit framework of expectations about probable policymaking and political action. And being so conducted, it plays a major part in reproducing and sustaining that framework. It is addressed retrospectively and prospectively to a conception of what is topical, important, and immanent. Researchers try to establish what is about to happen and what is a fitting subject for their efforts. As Rawsthorne observes (1978:5), "It is perhaps not a particularly difficult task to formulate the objectives of policy oriented research. They might be stated as being to assist and contribute to the formulation and development of policy and to evaluate the effects of its implementation."

To be sure, the relationship between research and its framework is itself contingent, tenuous, and complicated. Policy-oriented research requires ultimate justification in politics, but its practitioners undertake it for very diverse reasons. They may be intrigued by some analytic or descriptive puzzle. They may wish to advance policies that touch rather obliquely on approved mandates for action. They may seek to promote their own and others' careers. Most work can, after all, become autonomous, fascinating, and absorbing in its own right. Moreover, as I shall argue, work has within it the capacity to transport staff through chains of experience, confronting them with novel problems, methods, and situations. In this process of transformation, research can wander quite far from its original context and style of presentation. It can develop its own dialectic and course of direction. Of course, it cannot become too obviously detached from themes made legitimate by policy. Neither should it upset the ends of the minister. It is always reflexively disciplined, so modified that it may be described in fitting and seemly ways.

Even more complex, the occasionally tenuous links between research and policy can be made, forgotten, changed, and remade as staff grow old, move about the ministry, leave their positions, and are replaced. As they migrate, so people learn and unlearn accounts, not knowing the full history of their predecessors' doings or why things are as they are. Indeed, people must learn and relearn the motives of their own actions. They tend to reconstitute their own past progressively, not quite remembering their purposes and interpretations except as retrospective accounts that shift as the fleeting present itself evolves. Research staff confessed to me that they could not always disentangle the first reasons that had prompted their actions from the later plausible arguments they had employed to describe their activity to others. Indeed, they had persuaded themselves, rebuilding their own motivation and biography as they did so. In this fashion, the connections between research and policy are forged and broken, sometimes to become altogether indeterminate, clarified only in subsequent discussion. Just as policy transforms research into an extrusion of itself, so research has its own rhetoric which folds back and alters it.

Policies themselves must be regarded as shifting. They are the developing outcomes of processes of organizing which shape and are shaped by their own attendant webs of social relations. When a particular initiative is on the move, it will tend to become the subject of a special division of labor. People will concentrate on its production. It will become an object of interest to outsiders, drawing them in and preparing a geography of relations and activities. As it unwinds, so it will resolve itself into a succession of tasks, each task leading to a possible revisiting of the initiative, to its reformulation, and to the redeployment of the people who work on it. Every stage will then repopulate the social circles that animate it. Moreover, as it unwinds, involved officials will discover themselves being propelled through new experiences which transform their knowledge of policy and their reasons for working on it. Most important, those experiences can change selves. They are embedded careers, and careers have been described by Van Maanen (1977:1) as "lives in progress." In this sense, policies place people, build social worlds, and generate pools of knowledge and motives that return to alter the direction and significance of research. They will produce coordinated changes of context, structure, and actor, a series of wave functions that ripple through ministries and affect their environment.

Policies do not form in isolation. Every stage of an initiative can coincide with some development elsewhere. When timetables and campaigns collide, events are brought together and patterns of causality are introduced to one another. An initiative may then be open to new causes and may acquire a new past. The research that once moved it along will be replaced, supplemented, or compounded with other research with a very different destination. It will be at the play of influences that were not only alien and unplanned but quite unforeseen. It will be transplanted into a kind of communal property, the shared concern of an extended range of people and organizations. Others will come to grasp it as their own, treating it as a convenient vehicle for the promotion of their ends. Moreover, an initiative, often slow and leisurely in its growth, may be expected to pass through a number of political and bureaucratic regimes in the course of its history. It will move from policy environment to policy environment. In its association with diverse contexts and priorities, it can achieve a surprising variety of meanings. A new juxtaposition can always give it sudden salience or utter insignificance.

In the case of the Justice for Victims of Crime Initiative, there were at least two principal arenas in which the connection between criminology and policy was enacted. One was the very practical environment of interaction between the staff of the two secretariat branches. The other lay in a recess of the symbolic landscape that framed that interaction.

The entire Secretariat of the ministry is small, numbering some 200, and the membership of each component branch is modest in proportion. At the beginning of 1981, the Programs Branch, excluding the Communication Division, was allotted seventy staff years and the Policy Branch fifteen staff years. The two branches occupy adjoining floors of the department's building in Laurier Avenue West, and there is much trafficking back and forth. Theirs is an intimate social world, revolving around face-to-face relations, mediated by friendships, gossip, and mutual surveillance. Staff may be promoted or transferred from one branch to another, carrying with them stocks of knowledge and a trail of acquaintances. Any existing structure is draped around the flow and turbulence of a miniature society with countless doings and no anonymity. It is refracted and made in the abundant talk of a group of people who are unusually articulate and devoted to the production of words. It is continually produced, changed, and reproduced as purposes, perspectives, and inclinations alter. Thus one official, Linda MacLeod, has written of "the dynamic creation of overlapping realities through personalities and ongoing redefinition of events."[4] Structure is given added focus and plasticity by the workings of a division of labor that brings people together to dwell on special tasks. Over time, the landscape of relations becomes distorted by the effects of cooperation: people will know particular others in particular ways as a project advances. They will withdraw from others as they become involved. Contours will appear, uniting staff across the boundaries of branches and separating those within. To make matters even more complex, staff members drag those contour lines with them as they move about. Landscapes need not reflect immediate and current preoccupations.

It will be recalled that the Programs Branch was the prime author of the initiative, having developed a series of projects, consultations and workshops that centered on the problem of criminal victimization. Most recently, the Policy Branch adopted and shaped the initiative for political acceptance.

In this sense, the division of labor had directed a few people to work for differing lengths of time on various facets of the initiative. As the initiative entered their careers, so it was modulated by their experience, aspirations, social relations, and special duties. Parts of that initiative were incorporated into the biographies of officials in an uneven manner. For some, the initiative was to be of fleeting interest. For others, it was a matter of passionate engagement and lasting involvement. Indeed, some had gathered about the initiative in order to pursue policies of grave concern to them. Outsiders began to associate the initiative with the lives and doings of named individuals, giving the policy a personality that merged with that of its authors. It became a form of bureaucratic property, the recognized attachment of particular people, bearing their mark and becoming an extension of their selves. It became a little difficult to differentiate between attitudes toward the initiative and attitudes toward its progenitors. A policy decision could then be interpreted as an assertion about a person.

Significantly, research can be read as that which is done and possessed by specific individuals; the relations between research and policy then become but an exemplification of issues of ownership, selfhood, and social control. A form of sympathetic magic may then come into play. Research will no longer be impersonal activity but an alienated aspect of the self. Lafferty (1932:206) once argued that "facts are bits of biography," and the destiny of the facts of research can be quite personal. They document and reveal a self. Thus it followed that when it was determined that research on the victims of crime had transformed them into a suitable subject for policy work, there were consequences for the fates of people, their creations, the acknowledgment of their authority, the recognition of their authorship, and the protection of their self-esteem. The passage from research to policy was eventful, accompanied by some anxiety about a loss of property and independence. Conversely, of course, biographies are bits of fact: the fate of an initiative is often tied up with the fate of people. The movements of individuals can become indexes of shifts in the direction and form of policy. Thus the promotion of a member of staff may be taken to signify that an initiative has been applauded and that it will receive more powerful sponsorship. But it may also remove the person in question from the region in which effective work is done, enfeebling an initiative.

Every stage of the research and policy development process can become the foundation of a little odyssey and can offer administrators perspectives and experiences which are removed from the normal stream of official life. There is an inevitable strain towards the compartmentalisation of knowledge, events being immediate to some individuals and not to others, and that strain can transform the stages and components of policy-making into the objects of special sentiment. From the standpoint of any one official, a policy can present itself as topography of different regions, some well known and the subject of emotion, others distant and devoid of interest. Such mapping tends to have repercussions on how control is negotiated, assumed, maintained, and relinquished. A research or policy proposal may be easily discarded. It may be the intimate property of an official.

The passage from research to policy was structured by the social relations of a small group of staff, the relations themselves having grown out of practical activity and the drift of policy. At this level, philosophical and methodological problems about research and policy may be reduced to very concrete questions about how people got on with one another. Some, in fact, claimed that the talk and action in the transitional phase were little more than the current form assumed by the competition between an able, aspiring official of the Programs Branch and an able, aspiring official of the Policy Branch. One described them as "bucks at play." Any action taken was held to reflect on their bids for fame. This may have been a gloss on more complicated structures of negotiation, but what was real to officials was real enough in its consequences.

On another level, however, explanations about the proper conduct of relations tended to hinge on an invocation of Platonic ideal forms and connections. Metaphysics became a real resource, presence, and constraint with practical urgency. Not only were the secretariat staff highly educated and thoughtful, having been trained and sometimes having taught in institutions of higher learning. They were daily preoccupied with the complicated business of taking an attitude toward problems of research design, the mediations of politics and research, and the problematics of the Canadian criminal justice system. Their actions received continuous public scrutiny, and it was imperative to describe them with care. When pressed, staff members might well have had to give an accounting which was solidly grounded in metaphysics. After all, the ministry was dedicated to the pursuit of very lofty ends: justice, order, law, and peace. Those ends became quite routine considerations in official work. The thinking of staff could not therefore avoid a metaphysical and reifying cast. The theoretical and the ideal were intensely practical, interwoven with their everyday pursuits and forming their running context. In this manner, embedded actions and Platonic forms tended to interact with one another, framing each other as particular problems progressed. Mundane activity would alternate with analytic pronouncement: both were open to objectification and transcription into academic articles and policy papers, and both were susceptible to the coaxing and the spurring that such papers and articles could accomplish. Thus research was reported in publications that articulated further research. In a typical dialectical sequence, life took on an independence which then confronted and changed it. The sacred and the secular became intertwined.

Research and policy staff have been apportioned between distinct sectors of activity. Their experience and production of time were correspondingly discrete. Very often the bureaucratic sensibility defined research as relatively slow, continuous, and incremental. It translated its work materials into a gradually expanding and diffusely interconnected program of action. Segments of that activity might have paraded under different official names as the legitimizing mantle of policy changed, but research staff regarded it as one coherent and largely uninterrupted enterprise. Since the ministry was first established in 1966, it had concentrated on crime prevention, diversion, policy-community relations, assistance to victims, and a host of other measures. Activity was really all one to the Research Division of the Programs Branch.

By extension, proprietorship was itself diffuse and incremental. No abrupt fissures or faults announced the abandoning or supersession of the Research Division's concerns. Projects and programs did not begin and end suddenly. Instead, they blurred into one another. They also tended to be slowly paced by the local standards of bureaucratic time, consisting of activities that might last three years in isolation but might stretch over much longer periods when yoked together. The life of a piece of research could then be quite lengthy, undertaken by staff or contracted to outsiders, planned, discussed, organized, piloted, executed, assessed, and reported. It might take years before an answer of any moment appeared.

Such a timetable exhibits the seeds of a disparity between the half lives of different ventures. On the one hand, policy development is frequently the fruit of sustained, intense activity that responds rapidly to opportunity. Its life may be short and busy, a kind of bureaucratic mayfly. By contrast, research is often protracted and cumbersome, a comparatively elephantine process. What complicates their relations is the tendency for research to emerge from an environment that has been constituted in some measure by policy. Approval for any appreciable research enterprise reflects upon departmental and government policy, major sums being expended only when they serve approved purposes. And, in this environment, research itself can assume a special guise: its very existence and nurture may spur and give a presence to policy. It may indeed give form to what had once been rather inchoate and may offer a glimpse of possible emerging commitments. After all, it is the beginning that is auspicious: what has been done can always be preserved, strengthened, or enlarged. Slow-paced research can then accelerate the velocity of policy work, and it runs the risk of becoming stranded in an incomplete state when that work nears completion.

Policy work is characteristically designed to grasp the propitious moment. It is dominated by a sense of the "timeliness" of things, an apprehension that political opportunities will appear and disappear. It is assumed that an occasion lost can condemn a policy, and this may lead policy officials to seize their chances even when research staff would protest that they are not ready. There is rarely a perfect coincidence of research and policy timetables because the opportune moment is often independent of official planning. A project could become timely when a government or a minister or an economy changes, and policy officials respond. To be sure, the Policy Branch can modulate its environment and create openings for itself. It can also reconstruct events and projects so that they complement one another. But there is always the problem of the adventitious happening – the colliding timetable or the sudden accessibility of funds. When the moment occurs, other timetables must be distorted or aborted. Although research work may not be in a state of readiness, what has been done will have to be used. Typically, all that can be said is that there is evidence of activity and commitment. A flag has been planted and a history has been started. At such a juncture, it cannot often be claimed that there is incontrovertible proof of the wisdom of a course of action. In this manner, research can fall prey to a kind of temporal untidiness, ideas being exploited as best they can.

The Justice for Victims of Crime Initiative had its birth in the Programs Branch of the Ministry, but it could not become part of Canadian government policy until it had been adopted by the minister and the Policy Branch, groomed, rebuilt, and then shepherded through the maze of committees and meetings that punctuate the process of ratification in Ottawa. The Policy Branch imparts political propriety and persuasiveness to proposals. Arguments must be standardized and adapted to conform to the approved formulas and sensitivities of others. They must be offered to the correct sequence of committees and at the right time. They must be so constructed that they appeal to the logic used by those committees. They must win the endorsement of their members.

In large measure, the work of structuring revolves around securing the approval of those who are influential enough to affect the future course and prospects of an initiative. Policy proposals tend to disturb the work and interests of powerful organizations in the criminal justice system. Those bodies act as the gatekeepers, censors, and juries of work, and their favor must be earned. Perspectives animated by the policy process center on power, territory, deference, and recognition, and policy proposals must themselves be presented as a kind of genuflection, deliberately left incomplete so that those who inspect them may leave their mark. The visible, conspicuous act of imposing a brand is significant; it acknowledges power. This act allows an organization to mollify its own constituencies by demonstrating its capacity to protect them and to sway decisions. What is imprinted may actually be of secondary consequence.

In this fashion, people and corporations are invited to become ostentatiously proprietorial toward a fledgling initiative, adopting others' proposals as if they were their own, assuming responsibilities, and taking a defensive role. The language of that process is not and cannot be draped around research. It is an extension of politics. Indeed, it *is* politics. It is the artful pleasing of strategic audiences. If women are politically powerful in their organized representation, women will be awarded prominence. If war veterans are mobilized politically, they will also loom large. And so it goes on. In the instance of victims, those groups that received extraordinary attention in Canada were the politically sponsored, not always those most vulnerable to crime. Indeed, young, working-class urban males have no particular champion. Neither does the victimized homosexual.

The preparation of policy thereby imparts its own grammar and forms to criminal justice. It turns proposals into neat, distinct packages long enough to be well argued and solid but not too long to tax a minister and his senior officials. There is but one minister, and he must superintend the work of thousands. Anything that reaches him must be condensed. A proposal should anticipate the more urgent of the current arguments about government priorities, budgetary criteria, and planning procedures. It is those arguments that will be enforced when proposals pass from stage to stage, and a failure to satisfy them will identify a proposal as inept and undeserving. A

policy must attract those ministers, ministries, agencies, and organizations that serve as the collective monitor of suggestions, being
tailored to advance what is thought to be their aspirations and those
of their clients. The policy must be recognizably consonant with precedent. It must dispatch the political problems that are likely to arise
when a new entity appears in the criminal justice system. In short,
it must acquire a premeditated scheme of justification and expectations that embody reactions to possible responses. It must be sufficiently clear to seem competent but sufficiently vague to allow modi-
fication. It must accommodate the sometimes discrepant claims of
different groups. It must be negotiable.

Further – and as an immediate aspect of that anticipatory work –
a political proposal will become endowed with a causality and a tele-
ology of its own. Constituted by bureaucratic imperatives and procedures, it must pass through a necessary and ordained evolution.
It must acquire a special history and future, formed of those processes which significant others would approve. It will come to have
a beginning, a middle, and an end compounded out of rhetoric and
the bureaucratic timetable. It will have a life and logic of development. Van Maanen has argued (1977:35) that "themes . . . have their
occasions. To varying degrees, they are made explicit by locating
thematic particulars over a series of chronologically-given discrete
events." I would argue that occasions have their themes, generating
significance. In all this, proposals become refurbished as carefully
built bundles of words directed at quite specific audiences, audiences
that are rarely part of the scientific community and are unimpressed
by scientific discourse. Those audiences become new causal agents
and authors in the life of an initiative, moving it toward their own
ends and doing so in a manner that satisfies them.

A special and useful phrase was employed to describe the chief
difference between policy and research in a ministry setting. In the
main, policy staff claimed that they gave emphasis to the forms rather
than to the content of argument. Forms are the winning, approved,
correct outward appearances of a proposal, arranged to comply with
all the political demands that would be placed upon it. They were
a manifestation of the general etiquette of political life. They contained all the right components, patterns, and code words to survive scrutiny. They were standardized, designed to become the outer
shell of any substantive argument. It was not necessary to know
much about substance to be a competent manipulator of form. Con-

tent, however, was the preserve of a research staff whose expertise resided in knowledge of the recondite and the particular. It was the raw material of policy, often unfinished and sometimes unfashioned, offering a stuff which could be shaped and transformed. It was a little subordinate in policymaking.

When research was entrusted to the policy staff, there was something of the distress felt by parents who dispatch their children to boarding school for the very first time. Schooling is a necessary part of growing up, and people would not prosper without it, but there are hazards when someone else acquires custody of one's children. Officials newly entrusted with ideas may lack an instant sense of parenthood. Motives and attitudes tend to be emergent and slowly gained, and raw research will be unfamiliar, the result of another's authorship. It takes time before sympathies are fully grown. In this, there can be the germ of an upsetting spectacle for some officials. To be sure, policy officials may also be most kindly to the themes and implications of research. But their sympathies usually well up out of separate and somewhat unrelated experience. There are problems of dissonance.

In transition, meticulously constructed components may be dismembered, old arguments neglected and connections severed. There can be an anonymization and generalization of phenomena, a forgetting of their authorship and the special qualities of their environment and history. After all, the little struggles, successes, and adventures that marked the research phase of an initiative are unlikely to concern political organizations or the wider public. They will be tidied away. The political argument will salvage only a portion of research. Indeed, research might be the essential prerequisite of certain policies, but political filtering leaves only a residue behind. For example, it may transpire that research will be assessed not by its methods and performance but by the names of the politically significant populations that demanded it, the groups that became embroiled in it, the processes of consultation that accompanied it, and the reports that were publicly made of it. The very fact that a project was successfully started in a particular area of the country or in a portion of the criminal justice system can form the lasting political achievement. Ultimately, to be sure, it may be reassuring to know that there is a research warrant for a particular course of action or recommendation. But that warrant is rarely invoked expressly. It is not customary to marshal arguments about research in policy documents. They are taken on trust. And in the criminal justice system, research findings tend to be fairly equivocal anyway.

Now that we are nearing the end of the current history of the initiative, and now that cabinet approval has been secured, research has again come into its own as demonstration projects and surveys are beginning to map the possibilities of assistance to victims. This work is framed by the policy developments that preceded it. In great measure, it is designed to publicize, organize, and disseminate the beginnings of a policy shift in Canadian criminal justice. Research is now guiding policy. But it is also guided by policy, becoming the first stages of a new orientation in the administration and execution of justice. The process is still evolving, and I have not yet fully interpreted it. In time, and in a separate analysis, I will describe it at length.

Conclusion

The principal thrust of my argument has been to stress that the institutional relations between criminology and public policy must be understood as the developing interaction of specifiable people in the settings which they shape and which shape them in return. Many seemingly recalcitrant and elevated problems tend to evaporate when they are anchored in the actual doings of individuals. The links between research and action are plainly mediated by processes that build selves, provide motives, and supply social worlds. What is also apparent is that research is often the precondition of policy, giving it a content and an inspiration, acting as its first tentative essay. Research can legitimate policy and can be part of a necessary display of rationality, planning, and consultation. It clears a path, disclosing opportunities. It dispenses with the manifestly absurd and fallible argument. But it will become sublated in time. It is not research that is enacted but the reconstituted proposals that research made politically possible.

Notes

My larger study flows out of the time I spent as a Visiting Scholar at the Programs Branch of the Ministry of the Solicitor General. See *A View from the Shadow: The Ministry of the Solicitor General of Canada and the Jus-*

tice for Victims of Crime Initiative (Oxford: Clarendon Press, 1986). I am deeply grateful to the members of the ministry's staff for their enormous kindness and patience. I especially thank Linda MacLeod and Sheila Arthurs for their helpful comments on this chapter.

1. See Rock, *A View from the Shadows.*
2. Mr. Munro, Member of Parliament for Equismalt-Sananich, *House of Commons Debates,* 25 May 1976.
3. Mr. Cacouette, Member of Parliament for Villeneuve, *House of Commons Debates,* 14 May 1976.
4. Personal communication, 4 March 1983.

References

Annual Report 1979–1980: Solicitor General Canada. 1981. Ministry of Supply and Services Canada, Ottawa.

Daniels, A. 1981. "Future for Alternatives." 1 *Correctional Options.*

Dittenhoffer, T., and R. Ericson. 1983. "The Victim/Offender Reconciliation Program." 33 *University of Toronto Law Journal.*

Dussich, J., and G. Kirchhoff. 1981. "A Summary of the Rapporteurs Report from the Third International Symposium on Victimology." 1 *World Society of Victimology Newsletter:* 20.

Heisenberg., W. 1958. *Physics and Philosophy.* New York: Harper.

Lafferty, T. 1932. "Some Metaphysical Implications of the Pragmatic Theory of Knowledge." 29 *Journal of Philosophy:* 206.

Platt, A. 1973. "Feature Review Symposium." 14 *Sociological Quarterly:* 598.

Rawsthorne, T. 1978. "The Objectives and Content of Policy-Oriented Research." 6 *Home Office Research Unit Bulletin:* 12–13.

Van Maanen, J. 1977. *Organizational Careers: Some New Perspectives.* London: John Wiley.

Weick, K. 1979. *The Social Psychology of Organizing.* Reading, Mass.: Addison-Wesley.

3

The Limits of Knowledge: The Role of Information in Regulation

Peter K. Manning

R EGULATION CAN BE defined as attempts to govern markets in order to make market participants observe specified standards. It logically combines the concerns of law and economics because legal standards are normally employed in formal processes of regulation. The heritage of classical economics shapes the study of regulation: "'Regulation' . . . is concerned with the rationale and effects of government intervention in the economy. This definition rules out private forms of regulation, such as professional self-regulation and judicial intervention" (Veljanovski, 1982:89). Veljanovski, trained in both law and economics, distinguishes between economic regulation, which concerns "attempts to regulate the economic variables affecting business through such devices as competitive policy, taxes, subsidies, quotas, tariffs, entry restrictions, price and rate of return controls," and social regulation, which is concerned with "the regulation of quality and the protection of consumers. It embraces environmental health and safety regulations, protective labour legislation and consumer protection law" (Veljanovski, 1982:90).

In both types of regulation, the core notions are that markets are self-organizing (or organized) and that "intervention" is a political and value-laden choice. Regulation, with whatever aim, instruments, and intended scope, is consequential in shaping exchange channels, costs, and "externalities"; it restricts entry to the market and sets the norm for the flow of knowledge among market participants. A government may seek by regulatory intervention either to decrease the "unintended external costs" of markets or to increase "external benefits."[1]

The paradigm of a market's stylistic unity (repeated patterning of exchange by forces intrinsic to that market domain), described by input and output curves, may be extended to model social regulation. All markets, whether exchanging goods and services, swine and slaves, or wives and wishes, are assumed to be a function of and to be described by techniques which produce models of social worlds that are closed, logical, mathematically described and set off from other markets by the ceteris paribus assumption.

Models of social regulation presume, with the qualifications noted above, that *information is exchanged* and that it guides market participants and regulators in making decisions. It is not clear how useful the analytic distinction between "participants" and "regulators" is in actual practice, since regulators shape both production and externalities. It is implicit in these formulations of social regulation that the units exchanged are in a comparable metric (that is, money) and that market exchange is information driven such that observers within and/or external to a market can discern the relevant processes, can monitor, collect, and measure information about them, and can anticipate them and act accordingly. Social regulation uses a "limited or imperfect information model" which assumes that what is not known can be known or at least estimated and measured. Economics and relevant cognitive sciences, such as information theory, artificial intelligence, and cognitive psychology (as combined, for example in the work of Herbert Simon), share an "information bias" in depicting exchange and what is viewed as a subspecies of it, namely the regulation of markets.[2] Thomas (personal communication) neatly captures the differential importance of information in both types of regulation: generally, one would say that the role of regulation in social regulation is to *correct* for negative externalities and/or lack of information in the market model; in contrast, the focus of economic regulation – antitrust and so forth – is to increase the benefits of the market model, that is, competition, or to prevent the formation of cartels, as in price-fixing cases. In this sense, the problem of information flow and the neglect of interpreted meaning could be applied to both areas of government regulation.

This outline of the assumptions of an information-driven model of regulation would appear also to guide the formation of regulatory policy. A substantial portion of the literature on policy creation, its implementation, and its consequences presupposes relatively un-obstructed channels of information flow within and across organizations in the regulatory matrix (the agency, the regulated entities, and the publics). It presupposes also information exchange based upon principles of self-interest and systematic representation and misrepresentation of positions (for example, a union's wage demands of x percent may be viewed as being set strategically higher than the union might actually be prepared to accept). It assumes that the consequences of regulation can be known, anticipated, and planned for (or against). The same "rationalistic biases" are found in policy analyses.[3]

The view implied by the metaphor, it will be argued, is misleading when applied to "social regulation," especially health and safety regulation. As I will show below, social regulation is qualitatively different from economic regulation. *The market context cannot be seen apart from social values and interpretations,* and therefore it is meaningless to assign costs and benefits to "internal" and "external" loci. *Interpreted meaning, not information, is the basis for regulation.* Policymaking requires models which encompass interpretation and the variegated meanings of regulation and policy itself.

Features of the production of nuclear power, a collective good requiring social regulation, present some anomalies. It is a dramatic example of some key problems of social regulation. In fact, it would appear that the social regulation model outlined above provides an inappropriate guide for analyzing the distribution of this sort of public good. Let us now examine the regulation of nuclear power and the problems of regulation and policy.

Nuclear Power and Social Regulation

Nuclear power generation fits uneasily within the social regulation model. Cross-cultural comparisons are helpful here. Vogel (1986) argues in this connection that concern for the quality of the environment and related political, legal, and economic changes emerged in Britain and America at roughly the same time and that many parallel social conditions underlie the environmental movement in both nations.[4]

There are some similarities in the pattern of development of nuclear power. America's quest for commercially available, inexpensive nuclear power began in the mid-1950s. The Three Mile Island incident in March 1979 and the related increased public questioning of nuclear power, nuclear armaments, and the proliferation of nuclear weapons in Europe have now halted the construction of nuclear power plants in America.[5] The Carter administration both encouraged the growth of nuclear power (Carter had been trained as a nuclear engineer and had served on atomic submarines in the U.S. Navy) and passed a nuclear nonproliferation law intended to reduce the spread of fissionable nuclear materials throughout the developing world.[6]

In contrast, the development of nuclear power in Britain has followed a jagged course which saw the approval and construction of several plants in the 1960s and 1970s, followed by a hiatus until the early 1980s, when Britain again considered building additional nuclear power plants. In early 1983, the government began holding hearings labeled the "Sizewell Inquiry" (after the proposed site of another reactor). These hearings focused on the merits of a pressurized water-cooled reactor (PWR) not unlike the plant at Three Mile Island produced by the American firm of Babcock and Wilcox. In early 1986, it was decided to build this reactor.

While the social and historical context of nuclear *regulation* in the two countries differs, eleven other features of nuclear power generation are strikingly similar.

1. Nuclear power generation, like defense, education, the quality of the air and water, and policing, is a collective good to which everyone is required to contribute and from which all draw in some sense equally. (But see point 10 below.)

This point requires elaboration. The accepted definition of collective goods derives from the economist Samuelson, who (1954:387) identifies two sorts of "consumption goods." The first, private consumption goods, can be formulaically represented as goods which can be individually parceled out in distinguishable units or amounts, which can be attached to particular persons exclusively, and which can be aggregated by summation. The second sort, collective consumption goods, are those "which all enjoy in common, in the sense that each individual's consumption of a good leads to no subtraction from any other individual's consumption of such a good" (Feeley, 1970:509). In fact, the benefit is simultaneously derived by each and every individual and by the collectivity. Consumption results from the condition of equality rather than from the summation of variable individual differences. Collective consumption goods have a number of other characteristics. The supply of such goods is joint, or indivisible; once they have been produced, they can readily be made available to all without loss of the good to some. It is unfeasible to exclude some from the receipt of the good. Feeley (1970:509) argues that for these kinds of goods there is a "divorce of scarcity from effective ownership . . . the satisfaction derived from such public goods by an individual is independent of his own contribution, because there is no feasible (or efficient) means of 'exchanging' the product on a *quid pro quo* basis as there is with private goods on the market. The benefits of public goods accrue to all, and are independent of any individual's particular contribution."

The state, or any organized group, produces collective goods such that, if any person in the group consumes these goods, they cannot readily be withheld from the others in that group (Olson, 1970:14). Olson continues, "A state is first of all an organization that provides public goods for its members, the citizens" (1970:15). Although the state can be said to dispense collective goods, it does so in *aggregate* terms, not in individual terms. The "service" or good cannot be measured in unit amounts, nor can it be disaggregated.

2. It is unclear whether nuclear power generators can be said to produce a single precisely identifiable *product* traded in the market at a particular rate.

3. Construction of nuclear power reactors is a private corporate activity heavily subsidized by government. The development and establishment of nuclear reactors was not a function of power-generation needs and remains tied exclusively to the defense capacity of the society (Dawson, 1976; Hilgartner, Bell, and O'Conner, 1983). As a result they are anomalous with respect to several matters of regulation. There are questions of the standards to be used for the determination of the costs of the products and of production; performance and production levels of the generators; and the relevant base for comparison of measures of efficiency and effectiveness.

4. The government, as in the case of other environmental matters, is the source, implementer, and enforcer of such standards, and the body which takes decisions about further action, for example, whether to take criminal or civil action in place of, or in addition to, applying penalties that the agency itself is empowered to use (cf. Hawkins's argument on water standards, 1984).

5. Regulation of nuclear power generation is intended to *facilitate production*, protect the market monopoly of the power genera-

tors, enhance the reputation and credibility of the producers, and promote, protect, and enlarge the market rather than, or in addition to, controlling competition (or protecting the consumer). (See Ford, 1981b:46.)

6. The "externalities" associated with the creation of the "product" include both benefits (for example, enhanced air quality because coal smoke is absent, improved recreation areas around the generator, and jobs produced) and *costs* (for example, risk of accidents and actual accidents, waste disposal, pollution, and reduced health of workers exposed to radiation). In an important sense, these costs and benefits are, because of the special sort of safety requirements involved in nuclear power, quite difficult to identify and measure. Economic models do not incorporate psychological costs such as stress or the differential political and moral tolerance of groups to some sorts of "products" and "costs."

7. Errors or accidents, unlike those occurring to the individual, are in many cases not likely to be detected by the consumer. The reason is not simply ignorance, technical incompetence, or an inability to judge but rather the concealed, pernicious, and invisible nature of the consequences of most accidents and indeed the invisible process involved in the generation of power by atomic means. Perhaps, too, the consumer could not judge these risks even if information were freely available.

8. Consumers, strictly speaking, cannot judge the quality of the collective good generally distributed. One cannot choose among producers and products or "exit" (Hirschman, 1970). One must either maintain an enforced loyalty or raise a voice of protest.[7]

9. Given the singular nature of the consumer's connection to the production of power, namely the lighting or heating of a home or business, the focus upon variation in utility rates set by the companies (with state approval) blinds consumers to the quite disparate nature of other costs and risks entailed. (See Lowrance, 1976.)

10. It could be argued that nuclear regulation is directed to reducing negative externalities associated with a "semicollective good" (Thomas, personal communication, January 1984), which is not, in this sense, directly comparable with defense, education, sewage, rubbish disposal, and so on. It is not something which all enjoy in common; there are clear inequities with regard to those who benefit and those who pay. It could, ironically, be a public good with respect to costs to society and not with respect to benefits. A catastrophe af-

fects many more individuals than do the benefits of nuclear power.

11. Interests in safeguarding the quality of life in society at large, and more broadly, perhaps, in perpetuating that society, are nowhere specifically protected in consumer regulation. These concerns are ignored or are treated as endemically present unless they are raised politically by antinuclear demonstrators and by interest or pressure groups (see Schell, 1982).

These features present problems in policy and in social regulation based upon an information-driven economic model. Policy, or a general symbolic perspective for enacting and punctuating a market-defined set of exchanges, is, as Burke once wrote about a poem, the dance of an attitude (1968). It lays out a world with a dramatically marked center and options and can vary, like communication generally, in its aim, its reference, and its specificity. Among other things economistic assumptions about the nature of collective goods (or semicollective goods) underride the policy orientations suggested, but the problems of standards, governmental role, and investment in power, the interpretable nature of "externalities," especially negative externalities, and existential character of consumers' risks cannot be so easily accommodated in a symbolic conception of policy. The implications of the symbolic conception of policy will be discussed in connection with the analysis in a later section of this chapter.

The analyses and inferences in the chapter should be viewed as tentative and as an exploratory agenda for future research. The analysis draws on comparisons between nuclear and other sorts of social regulation and between nations' approaches to regulation. Although a case is made for similarity, much additional work remains to be done.

In the following discussion of nuclear regulation, an identified set of limits on the informational bases of regulation is illustrated with reference to the Three Mile Island accident in Pennsylvania. I draw upon a lucid analysis of the accident in the *New Yorker* magazine (1981a,b) by Daniel Ford, a physicist and a member of the Union of Concerned Scientists who has engaged in research on safety in nuclear plants for over ten years. In describing the chain of events that triggered the Three Mile Island accident, I paraphrase Ford (1981a: 50, 53).

Early in the morning on Wednesday, 28 March 1979, two technicians were carrying out routine maintenance on part of the main feedwater system, which provided the reactor with one of two supplies of cooling water. They were trying to clear a clogged pipe that ran between the polishers (tanks that clean the water for the reactor) and a receiving tank. Work had been under way for seven hours when a worker accidentally closed the flow of water in the main system to Unit 2's reactor, causing it to shut down. Automatically, emergency procedures were initiated. Three emergency feedwater systems were thrown into action by an electronic alert system that monitored plant performance and responded to malfunctions. Two other events produced a crisis rather than a routine maintenance-caused accident: a relief valve meant to release the heat and steam from the overheating reactor did so and then became stuck in the open position and allowed 220 gallons of water a minute to flow out. In addition, someone had earlier closed two valves in the system that piped water from the emergency feedwater pumps into parts of the cooling system, rendering ineffective the three pumps that would have supplied cooling water. A testing procedure had created a common-mode failure – a multiple safety system failure – of the sort that, because it was supposedly very unlikely to occur, had been officially regarded as an "incredible event."

The following analysis is concerned with a number of themes found in this description: the central importance of interpretation in complex technology, the central importance of information and safety systems, and the interconnection of errors and happenstance.[8] These matters should be viewed in the context of the problem of producing policy regarding the safety of nuclear power–generating systems.

It should be noted that my critique presupposes that the influence of other factors upon the exchange of information is *constant*. I do not claim that failure to communicate (because of individual incompetence or ignorance) is any more or less a feature of behavior displayed in any model of regulation or that nuclear regulation based on a game model is misleading because insufficient resources are being allocated to regulation. Attempts to balance safety and costs characterize corporate behavior and regulatory actions. A concern with concealing and revealing information for political, economic, and dramatic reasons is assumed to be an accepted part of the process. No claim is made that "normal errors" due to personal fatigue, miscalculations, drugs, cognitive misperceptions, or human limits on memory or task complexity are more or less common in nuclear power generation than in any other complex production system. (For an alternative view, see Perrow, 1984.) Such errors are assumed to be present and to play their role. That some of the other factors discussed below increase the likelihood of certain kinds of errors does not make this a deviant case. It is true, however, that, while pushing the wrong button in the kitchen may only cause us to burn fish, doing so at a reactor control panel may irradiate human beings.

The concluding section of the chapter explores some of the policy-relevant implications of my position. Policymaking analyses might include instrumental and information-based postulates as well as encompassing the interpretive dimension of conduct and noninformationally based features of regulation.[9]

Some Limits upon Information

It is currently fashionable to cast the discussion of various modes and consequences of regulation in the language of economics, using an extension of Von Neuman's and Morgenstern's ideas about game theory (Schelling, 1963). The problem is commonly cast, especially in economic regulation, as a two-person game theory puzzle, for example, the prisoner's dilemma. The choice of metaphor is itself important, because once "inside" the game framework, one is constrained by posited limits, rules, choices, and goals. This metaphor is often misleading. Once one moves outside the framework and scrutinizes its assumptions with a critical eye, one can suggest how certain questions are obviated.

Consider the model of "man" and assumptions about the workings of such a "person" (whether a firm, a lawyer, or a federal agency). A rational actor holds positions in this scheme, a *Homo economicus* who sets goals and objectives of a clear, discrete, measurable sort, identifies a set of options, or means by which the goals may be pursued, with associated consequences, and makes a choice.[10]

The primary problem in regulatory games is the extent to which a move or series of moves is understood by both parties, regardless of the behavior that follows. The classic formulation of what Goffman (1969) terms "tight games," or games in which mutual orientation is nonproblematic among players, treats exchanges between a sender and a receiver as signals by which information is conveyed across a space (Cherry, 1978). Information and meaning are central.

One must first ask whether the assumptions of two-person game theory make it appropriate as a framework for regulatory analysis. Then we must inquire into the consequences of such a view and

specify the difficulties that arise when applying such a framework
to the analysis of nuclear regulation.

Goffman (1969:100–01) succinctly characterizes the view of economists and some political scientists of interaction (see Kagan, 1984)
as "strategic":

> Two or more parties must find themselves in a well-structured situation of
> mutual impingement where each party must make a move and where every
> possible move carries fateful implications for all the parties. In this situa-
> tion, each player must influence his own decision by his knowing that the
> other players are likely to try to dope out his decision in advance, and may
> even appreciate that he knows this is likely. Courses of action or moves will
> then be made in the light of one's thoughts about the others' thoughts about
> oneself. An exchange of moves made on the basis of this kind of orientation
> to self and others can be called strategic interaction. One part of strategic
> interaction consists of concrete courses of action taken in the real world that
> constrains the parties; the other part, which has no more intrinsic relations
> to communication than the first, consists of a special kind of decision-
> making – decisions made by directly orienting oneself to the other parties
> and giving weight to their situation as they would seem to see it, including
> their giving weight to one's own.

The appropriateness of game metaphors to life situations has
been questioned by several writers, including Goffman (1969, 1974),
Garfinkel (1967), and Louch (1969). Nonetheless, criticisms are not
seen as reasons for abandoning the metaphor. A perhaps more substantial criticism focuses upon assumptions made about the dynamics
of the process once the game is in play. As Goffman argued (1969),
regulation is a socially mediated game in which persons are delegated authority to make judgments about compliance with the rules
and to levy rewards and punishments. Once social mediation has
been admitted, socially induced alterations in game dynamics result.
(1) The character of a move may be in doubt; players may not know
what a move is intended to accomplish or what it "signals." (2) There
are opportunities for cheating – bending the rules in one's favor or
overlooking certain features of a move. (3) Alterations in the pattern
of moves can be made by collusion and compliance that does not
reflect interests posited to govern action. (4) The *option* of playing
the game is a choice that "players" can exercise. Goffman (1969:119)
summarized some of the implications of introducing social mediation to game notions:

Games which rely on a social enforcement system become exposed to many issues which tight games are free of. . . . Persons often don't know what game they are in or whom they are playing for until they have already played. Even when they know about their own position, they may be unclear as to whom, if anybody, they are playing against, and, if anyone, what his game is, let alone his framework of possible moves. Knowing their own possible moves, they may be quite unable to make any estimate of the likelihood of the various outcomes or the value to be placed on each of them. And bad moves often lead, not to clear-cut penalties conceptualized as such, but rather diffuse and straggling undesired consequences – consequences which result when persons do something that throws them out of gear with the social system.

Goffman isolates limits upon information: it is collected, used, retrieved, defined, classified, and interpreted or granted social reality by organizationally located actors who use it to serve personal, organizational, political, moral, and other ends. Much research on information exchange and on organizational action assumes the character of information and proceeds to construct models of its flow (see Feldman and March, 1981). There is little research on how it is actually used in organizations (but see Cicourel, 1968; Manning, 1980; Hawkins, 1984). Still, insights into the bureaucratic use of information can be gained from such studies and can fruitfully be applied to the analysis of problems of regulation.

Information and meaning, it is argued, are critically interrelated in each area discussed in the remaining sections of the chapter. I sequentially address (1) the nature of information and its exchange, (2) the technology of nuclear power plants as an environment from which information is "generated," (3) the ways in which information is embedded in trust, (4) the complementarity of motives of the regulated and the regulators, and (5) the assessment of risks associated with nuclear reactors. I then consider the relevance of these points for policy analysis and policymaking.

A DEFINITION OF INFORMATION

Information for the purposes of this analysis is not located in individual heads, or lodged behind people's eyes, but takes on social reality only when exchanged or, more accurately, *transacted*. Dewey and Bentley (1949:67ff.) argue that interactional analysis considers relations between posited objects and things, while transactional analysis views matters considered to be "irreconcilable separates" (such as persons, norms, values, and behavior) as extensionally and durationally one. When the conventional division between the observer or entity and the object is shattered, the unity of seeing and believing is dramatized and located in language. Information needs to be seen not as a thing but as a process connecting a sender and a receiver who are only analytically distinct.

The social reality of information is determined by factors which limit its exchange. These derive from several sources.[11] A number of useful ethnographic studies suggest that: information is seen differently within different segments of the organization (Burns and Stalker, 1961; Manning, 1977); that it is unequally distributed, often residing among the lower participants rather more than with "policymakers" (Wilson, 1968, 1978); that it is often informally assembled and applied, even by those with decisionmaking responsibility (Allison, 1971; Kanter, 1977), and that it is often strategically gathered, withheld, or produced for symbolic reasons or as a sign of rationality (Feldman and March, 1981). Information is often simply accumulated in raw and unanalyzed form and may be stored for set periods of time and then discarded, filed in computer databanks, or forgotten once it has been obtained; such is likely to be its fate in many large information-gathering bureaucracies, such as schools, police departments, and regulatory agencies.[12] Agencies tend to gather relevant data seriatim, or in numerical or chronologic files, unless crisis conditions demand alternative ways of gathering paper. Data at Three Mile Island were reported to the Nuclear Regulatory Commission (NRC) in this fashion, but trends in types of accidents or maintenance failures, for example, were not analyzed. According to Ford (1981b:51): "N.R.C., before the accident, had no coordinated method for identifying patterns in the safety-system deficiencies reported to it."

Information, of course, may not be complete, and a parameter may have to be extrapolated from known data.[13] Information may not be "fully appreciated" (Turner, 1977). Moreover, many questions can be answered only after identification of the problems in connection with which the information is needed. Rarely are such questions known and well articulated in advance by agency members. Information, it is argued here, is not always located in centralized files and available to those who need it at a given time (Weick, 1980). More globally, organizations develop images of what is needed and required for purposes of transacting information. Furthermore, these images omit certain categories of problems. Turner (1977:17) has accurately written:

> Organizations achieve concerted action by establishing and maintaining [a tacit] agreement amongst their members that certain possibilities, issues and contingencies may be ignored without incurring official disapproval. In this way, the rationality of the organization is bounded and in this way the possibility arises that some of those possibilities which have been ignored or set on one side may be much more hazardous than had been anticipated.

Information may be gathered for purposes unrelated to its exchange. It may be gathered or merely aggregated to show that something is being done about a problem; to simulate scientific monitoring of a situation; and to suggest that the organization is rational, or to suggest monitoring of internal transactions, rather than actually to implement close observation, reporting, or supervision (see Feldman and March, 1981).

Operational personnel may regard regulatory requirements for reporting as being of secondary importance. Data gathered and seen as relevant to regulation may be abandoned as in the case at Three Mile Island Reactor 2, "because of a shortage of storage space" (Ford, 1981a:109). Conversely, data with regulatory relevance, such as environmental impact or perhaps social-psychological impact (cf. Erikson, 1976), are not required to meet the plant's operational needs and are not monitored except when monitoring is legally required. The rather broad and symbolic character of such matters as "safety" and "health" are difficult both to define or label precisely and to measure and assess. They are therefore less likely to be a part of routine operational data gathering (Hale and Perusse, 1977). As in policing, certain sorts of work that are in fact quite relevant to procedural fairness and evaluation, such as arrest reports, property records, and statements, are viewed as "paperwork" or "red tape" and are avoided, demeaned, or discounted (Manning, 1980:220–24).

Even when information *is* available, use patterns predict *how* it will be used (Feldman and March, 1981:174):

> (1) Much of the information that is gathered and communicated by individuals and organizations has little decision relevance (2) Much of the information that is used to justify a decision is collected and interpreted after the decision has been made or substantially made. (3) Much of the information gathered in response to requests for information is not consid-

ered in the making of decisions for which it was requested. (4) Regardless of the information available at the time a decision is first considered, more information is requested. (5) Complaints that an organization does not have enough information to make a decision occur while available information is ignored. (6) The relevance of the information provided in the decision-making process to the decision being made is less conspicuous than is the insistence on information. In short, most organizations and individuals often collect more information than they use or can reasonably expect to use in the making of decisions. At the same time, they appear to be constantly needing or requesting more information, or complaining about inadequacies in information.

Apart from constraints upon the transaction of information, information must be interpreted once it has been transmitted. Interpretation requires not only the receipt of signals but a shared code, or set of principles that can be used to encode and decode signals. Codes vary. Some systems of signs are governed by logic and rationality, others by loosely articulated rules guiding interpretation (Guiraud, 1975:9). Logical systems, such as mathematics, chemistry, and music, have a closed and abstract character and incorporate formal principles that govern relationships between the units. Systems of signs, such as law, chivalry, and fashion, are hermeneutic and patterned by human feelings, values, social change, and the context within which the signifier and the signified are connected.

Engineering sciences and physics predominate in the educational background of the administrators of nuclear plants and of the NRC; most of the line personnel have technical backgrounds. The formal system of interpretation used in engineering, like that in mathematics, is closed, formal, and abstract. Such systems tend to have a single correct or favored way of accomplishing an outcome, an approved set of conventions about how one best achieves a given outcome, and a concern with efficient operations. Within this sort of logic, one can indeed identify "better" or "worse" ways of accomplishing an end and more or less efficient (or more or less costly) means. A logic of costs and benefits is suitable. To the extent that regulators and regulated share this language, communication is enhanced.

On the other hand, when policy or value questions arise, another language or code is employed. This is the language of "satisfycing," of taking a "least-worst" option; alternatively, the language of social amelioration, the language of reform, or the wooden bureaucratic-administrative language of deadlines and guidelines can be employed.

These languages include vocabularies of motive, by which people account for their actions (see Lyman and Scott, 1970; Mills, 1940). The two vocabularies may be used at cross-purposes, one with the aim of promoting efficient administration, the other with the aim of minimizing an error or simply of making it possible to "muddle through."

COMPLEXITY AND TECHNOLOGY

In his deservedly famous parable about the ant and the sand, Herbert Simon (1969:24–25) illustrates two basic principles of cognitive organization that describe the relationship between an organism or organization and the environment.

> 1. An ant, viewed as a behaving system, is quite simple. The apparent complexity of its behavior over time is largely a reflection of the complexity of the environment in which it finds itself.
> 2. A man, viewed as a behaving system, is quite simple. The apparent complexity of his behavior over time is largely a reflection of the complexity of the environment in which he finds himself.

The central notion is that the complexity of the behavior of reacting systems (ants, human beings, and organizations) directly results (or to what does "reflection of" refer?) from the complexity of the environment in which they are located. Extending this rather tenuous notion along biological lines, Terreberry (1968) and Aldrich have argued that organizations also evolve in the direction of increasing complexity of rules. There is little evidence that this phenomenon, when it occurs, is a function of or a reflection of an environment (Aldrich and Pfeffer, 1976). The hypothesis of consistency in the relationship between the complexity of an institution or market and the number and types of rules evolved to regulate it is untested.

In the case of nuclear regulation, obvious differences between the United Kingdom and the United States make any such generalization untenable. Consider such matters as the tendency of the lawmakers in the United States toward legalism and toward creating a large number of legal rules as a means of controlling a problem; the adversarial nature of much American regulation, which publicly tends to sanction rather than to seek compliance; and the pattern of lawmaking. The British tend to write rather brief and broad statutes, leaving much to administrative discretion and formulation of enforcement policies, while Americans seek specificity in statute law as well as in regulatory rules (see Vogel, 1986).[14]

In any case, the complexity of nuclear power-generating systems is daunting in the extreme. Ford (1981a:68, 70) writes almost casually:

> To generate power and comply with the safety guidelines, a nuclear power station typically requires some fifty miles of piping, held together by twenty-five thousand welds, eight hundred and fifty miles of electrical cables; eleven thousand five hundred tons of structural steel; and a hundred and seventy thousand cubic yards of concrete. Countless electric motors, conduits, batteries, relays, switches, switchboards, condensers, transformers, and fuses are needed. Plumbing requirements in the various cooling systems call for innumerable valves, seals, drains and vents, gauges, fittings, pipe hangers, hydraulic snubbers, nuts, and bolts. Structural supports, radiation shields, ductwork, fire walls, equipment hatches, cable penetrations, emergency diesel generators, bulkheads, walls, and floors must be installed. Instruments must be provided to monitor temperatures, pressures, chain-reaction power levels, radiation levels, flow rates, cooling-water chemistry, equipment vibration, and the performance of all key plant components. Written procedures must be provided to cover normal operations, equipment installation, periodic maintenance, component and system testing, plant security, and appropriate operator actions during reactor startup, reactor shutdowns, and all anticipated emergencies.
>
> All nuclear-power-plant systems, structures, components, procedures, and personnel are potential sources of failures and malfunctions.

It could be that this complexity is associated with the use of broad and simple regulations and the passing on of much of the detailed monitoring, surveillance, reporting, and sanctioning to regulatory agencies by legislators and to private industry by the agencies. (See Ford, 1981a,b; Perrow, 1984.)

Relationships between a regulated organization and a regulatory system reflect a form of coupling. Organizational analysis suggests that the couplings are, as often as not, loose, uncertain in their content and appearance, determined by several variables interacting with each other to produce several effects, and predicated on trust. Weick (1979), who called such couplings "loose," has argued that they are relevant to the analysis of organization and environment connections (see also Meyer and Scott, 1983).

"Organization," according to Simon (1969:4–7ff.), is an artful artificial creation, an extension of human rationality. Humans envision, foresee, and shape an environment. An "environment" is in this fashion mediated by human intentions, interpretations, and actions and is enstructured within the organization (Manning, 1982b). Data from the environment are interpreted or acted upon to create what Weick terms an enacted environment (1979:131ff.). Data flow from preestablished modes or channels, such as reporting systems, auditing and accounting procedures, and, in the case of industrial production, gauges, dials, meters, and computer printouts. These are in turn read by actors who fulfill organizational roles and by machines linked together by computers. The complexity of the internal linkages between segments of the organization, each of which creates a microenacted environment which is semiautonomous, and between the environment and the organization's boundaries, is a source of information and error fed into the organization's communicational flow.

The nature of error in such systems requires explication, for the identification, anticipation, control, and reduction of errors is one of the central concerns of health and safety regulation. Errors are "unplanned events," but this way of conceptualizing them omits consideration of the consequences of errors. It is necessary, however, to see how errors are embedded in sociotechnical systems to imagine what their consequences might be as well as to reduce the likelihood that they will appear. The social reality of error is that it is multiple in origin and that it can be either reduced or amplified by the social organization in which it is located. An error is indicated by a sign, or something that stands for something else in a particular context. Smoke, an indicator light, a word spoken, and a change in a gauge are all signs. Actions which are not planned are signified to those involved and are seen against a set of expectations. These expectations link the signifier with the referent, or the signified. These two constitute the sign. Errors are seen as signs (the link of signifier and signified) within a context of expectations. Some of these expectations may be fairly well formalized, or known, while others are tacit, unclear, and almost intutitive in character. The science of signs, or semiotics, is useful in identifying both signs and their context, or the codes to which they are routinely referred (see Eco, 1976, 1983; Guiraud, 1975). The links between signifier and signified are variable, not determinant. In identifying types of errors it is useful to examine carefully the character of the semantic links between signifier and signified. Two concepts are helpful in this context, namely that of a signal, or a mechanical link seen between two expressions (turning on a switch and the illumination of a light), and that of an index, or an interpreted link between two expressions (smoke indicates fire;

the footprints of a man on sand indicate the presence of a person). Unlike mechanical systems of signs, which produce signals with an on-off, binary quality, interpreted systems of signs produce indexes which contain a problematic based on the connection drawn between a signified, such as a warning light, and a signifier, such as the level of water in a pressurizer (Leach, 1976). In actuality, observers are constantly reading off expressions without an awareness of the quite different codes to which these expressions may be being referred (Culler, 1975). In nuclear power generators, observers (both machines and people) must take signs and place them in context (a code which associates signifier and signified), and they are then confronted with data which can be seen within either of the two systems of signs. Errors can arise from both mechanical and interpreted systems.

Consider the following types of error, bearing in mind that the discussion is restricted to errors which are present and identified by a person, a machine, or both, either in concert or in sequence.

1. *System function error* is a mechanical failure, such as overheating, leakage, or computer malfunction, which is read from a dial, a gauge, a nonworking switch, or a computer printout.

2. *Human error* is a failure to read or a misreading of a gauge, dial, or printout and/or acting incorrectly (turning off a switch that should be on, or the opposite).

2a. *Clerical error* is a subcategory of human error in which the error is restricted to failure to record, report, or otherwise document a reading or to record a reading correctly or accurately.

3. *Interpretive error* can arise from reading either a signal as an index or an index as a signal. A signal can be taken as an index, for example when a computer correctly shut off the nuclear generator automatically at Three Mile Island Reactor 2. Workers, assuming that this shutoff reflected a machine error to be interpreted, manually overrode the computer and switched the already overheating generator back into operation (Ford, 1981a:100). When an index that can be interpreted, extrapolated, or put in context is read as a signal, or a nonproblematic sign, another form of error arises. The water level in the reactor itself was not directly measured or shown on a dial. The technicians were instructed to *interpret* the water level in the pressurizer, a machine that cleans water before it flows into the reactor, as equivalent to the water level in the reactor itself. At Three Mile Island Reactor 2, when the valve connecting the pressurizer with the reactor was not reopened after maintenance, the water level in

the pressurizer was read as a signal. Workers continued to believe that water was present in the reactor when in fact because of the reduced water level the core of the reactor was beginning to overheat.

4. *A common-mode failure* is a global, ramifying failure involving several system function errors in conjunction and interaction. Ford writes that it is a "cardinal rule" of reactor safety that at least one alternative, or "backup," system must be available to carry out functions if the primary system fails. This kind of failure can be obviated when several errors create multiple malfunctions affecting *both* primary and secondary safety systems (Ford, 1981a:49).

5. *Machine-machine error* can be of type 1, an unread dial or misreading of it, or type 2, in which, for example, a computer acts incorrectly when it is given a signal. Ford, in a chilling example of an occurrence at the Rancho Seco power station in 1978, reports that a workman dropped a tiny quarter-inch lightbulb into a control panel. As a result, short circuits cut off the power supply to instruments monitoring the feedwater system. The feedwater system malfunctioned. Instrument failure meant that operators did not have the information to determine which emergency steps were appropriate. "Automated equipment was available . . . , but the correct automated actions were not carried out, either, because this equipment failed to receive the appropriate signals from the malfunctioning instruments" (Ford, 1981b:53). Then the instruments began to send erroneous signals to the plant's integrated control system, and plant operators had extreme difficulty in determining the true status of the plant because of the erroneous information in the control room (Ford, summarizing a memo from the Babcock and Wilcox report on the Rancho Seco accident, 1981b:53).

6. Error types 1–5 can be *redefined* as merely inexplicable events, caused by "gremlins," or as resulting from random error, concealed, lied about, or ignored. (The closed logical system of engineering, like medicine, tends to plug "gaps" in explanation with semantic fictions such as the "idiopathic headache," used in medicine, or, in engineering, the "gremlin-caused" error: see Kidder, 1982). These "labeling errors" are second-level errors, or amplification errors. (The Ranch Seco instrument failure is an example.) They serve to send forward "error messages" as truth and thereby have additional consequences (Ford, 1981b:52–53).

Errors also result from a combination or sequence of errors. These are sequential errors in that they arise from coupled errors. A clerk reading a printout who fails to act to correct an initial type 1 error produces a sequential error. Type 2 errors can feed back to produce type 1 errors. The errors may combine to produce an amplification loop that recycles errors as true messages. The link may result from human action or may be mechanical in origin. A sequence of errors can in turn be redefined to produce metaerrors, or amplification errors. In any given event it is possible to identify first-level errors, sequence errors, and amplification errors.[15]

Error and complexity are related in a profound fashion, and the interaction is amplified by the ways in which technology, a process by which work is accomplished, is reified and is thus converted into an object or *thing*. When technology is reified, it takes on properties or fixed attributes and is frozen symbolically into a single domain of thought. This reification has had serious consequences of the following character in the regulatory field.

When we assert that there are *classes of accidents*, certain kinds become "unthinkable" or so unlikely that little or no preparation is needed for them. The most unthinkable accidents, of course, are a full-scale nuclear war, a nuclear disaster such as the explosion of a reactor caused by the boildown of the inner core, a terrorist attack, and/or an uncontrolled chain reaction (see Schell, 1982). The Three Mile Island Reactor 2 accident was labeled a "class 9 accident," one viewed as nearly impossible. Crews in nuclear plants are only now beginning to prepare for such eventualities with simulated accidents of this kind and, as a result, to imagine their nature and consequences. Conversely, other types of accidents, some of which can be quite productive of radioactive waste, are viewed as "routine." Ford, for example, argues that the Three Mile Island incident was not an "accident" at all but the consequence of routine operations and maintenance. Such "accidents" were found to have happened in other plants so frequently as to suggest that they were not rare events in statistical terms (Ford, 1981b:99–101).

A parallel sort of reificational thinking applies to equipment assessment. Whereas it seems obvious that a generator is an integral system in which malfunctioning will have general consequences, nuclear engineers prior to the Three Mile Island incident labeled some equipment in a generator "safety-relevant" and other equipment "non-safety-relevant." This division into categories has practical consequences, for it means that "safety-relevant equipment" is defined as most in need of inspection, while other equipment may be checked

less frequently (if at all). The distinction disregards the holistic nature of the system and the systemwide potential consequences of
errors. The various sociotechnical systems (of social roles) which grow
up around technology are made invisible (see Emery and Trist, 1960).

When the entire enterprise – generator, cooler, and human staff –
is described as clean and "inherently safe," in the words of one NRC
official (Ford, 1981b:107), the imagery of the machinery and its omi-
nous potential is shrouded in semantic garbage.[16]

The American government and the nuclear industry have argued
that nuclear power since its development is essentially clean, cheap,
and safe. Nuclear power has been viewed as less risky than most sorts
of complex technology and as nonproblematic. Even disposal of the
toxic wastes associated with the production of power by nuclear
means has been considered only a rather minor external cost or nui-
sance factor. Perhaps this attitude, displayed in government propa-
ganda, has shaped the public's view of the safety of nuclear weapons,
nuclear power, and nuclear war. It has certainly been instrumental
in forming public opinion on the risk of accidents and breakdowns
and about safety in general with respect to radioactive materials.

THE ROLE OF TRUST

Trust is inversely related to bureaucratically organized rules and
procedures. When trust becomes a visible issue and requires resto-
ration or enhancing, it has already ceased to exist in a viable form.
Trust is an invisible basis for the articulation of parts of organizations through exchange. Interpreted relationships, or loosely coupled
ones, tend to elevate the role of trust (see Meyer and Rowan, 1977;
Weick, 1979). Thus the more an organization is trusted, the less
information is required by the public concerning its day-to-day
operations.[17]

As previously noted, the pattern of NRC–nuclear power industry relationships has been one of abiding warmth (see *New York
Times,* October 16, 1983, p. 1). At the planning level, manufacturers
are not required to submit detailed plans for approved plants to the
NRC; designs are *assumed* to be safe and are assumed to resemble
previous labyrinthine designs (Ford, 1981a:79). The formulation of
detailed rules and regulations concerning safeguards and penalties
for violations is delegated by the NRC to the power companies. The
power companies thus write their own ticket. Plans for the assessment of production quality are not required by the NRC and may

or may not be developed by supervised companies (Ford, 1981a: 103). At the operational level, trust abounds as well. "Grandfather clauses" are included in regulations so that operating plants do not have to be modified when new regulations are introduced – they are, in effect, automatically exempted from new controls (Ford, 1981a: 88). Quality control is presumably based on the notion that plants are safe, that power plant builders and operators will attend to safety checks, and that the procedures and rules as written are uniformly adequate. Surveillance and inspection would appear to be almost overwhelming jobs, given the size of the plants and the sort of equipment used.

Yet a very small percentage of the equipment is checked annually by inspectors. According to Ford, a federal inspector estimated that only 1 or 2 percent of the "safety-related" activities at plants are closely monitored yearly (1981a:101). An honor system based on mutual trust is used to articulate company expectations and regulatory actions (see Ford, 1981a:119; 1981b:57, 88ff.).

Trust is basic to this sort of regulation for several reasons, including the technical incompetence of the inspectors and the members of the Nuclear Regulatory Commission; the rapid change in nuclear technology that is known to only a few people (mostly young engineers employed by power companies and a few university-based physicists); and the assumption of mutual trust among similarly trained scientists. Perhaps it is also sustained by a recognition of the vast amount of information, personnel, and money that would be required to assemble and evaluate information in areas now left to mutual trust.[18]

THE COMPLEMENTARITY OF MOTIVES

Nuclear regulation in America has, from the outset, been mandated to encourage the growth of nuclear power (Ford, 1981b:63).[19] Regulation and production are guided and managed by experts in the same fields.[20] It seems to be assumed by those in the regulatory matrix, apart from the several publics involved, that in order to be efficient (and the installations are indeed extremely expensive, with costs running into billions of dollars and increasing daily), installations must operate virtually continuously. As a result, there are pressures for plants to operate *during* routine safety and maintenance checks and for "on-line" checks to be performed. Routine maintenance, in turn, according to Ford (1981a, b), is the primary cause of accidents. Accidents known to the scientific community (one assumes that many accidents are not reported, given the honor system for reporting events to the NRC) are overwhelmingly, in Ford's felicitous term, "maintenance-caused" (1981a:95ff.).

It has always been assumed that the net cost of nuclear power will be inversely related to the number of reactors in operation. It follows that, if economies of scale are to be enjoyed, many operational reactors should be present. There were early claims that nuclear power would be so cheap as to make its costs minimal or irrelevant.[21] To achieve such savings has been an aim of the NRC. These are dubious assumptions, however.

It is clear, furthermore, that there is little consensus among experts concerning safety standards with respect to the operation of generators (Ford, 1981a). The complementarity of motives means that information is not deemed critical; knowledge is often assumed to be shared as a result of professional background and training. No semiprivate collusion is formed between two units in the regulatory matrix, the agency and the regulated, against the public; rather, an implicit or tacit *consensus* exists. Much relevant information is either never gathered or never requested or not regarded as actionable if it is available, was requested, and was obtained (see Ford, 1981b:92 *et passim*).

RISKS AND RISK CALCULATION

The notion that "externalities" are associated with the production of goods leads economists to seek to measure social costs that "unintentionally" issue from market processes. For example, one might calculate the costs of socially acceptable risks (it is not indicated to whom they are acceptable) by

> an empirical assessment of three considerations (1) the size of the expected accident costs . . . , (2) the distribution of accident costs which depend on compensation programs, insurance protection, and liability arrangements and (3) the anticipated costs of preventing accidents. . . . Exposure risks are inextricably tied to each other principal "good," and the analysts must impute an implicit price for the risk component which he can derive from the market price for the package consisting of a principal "good" plus its associated injury risk. These implicit prices (which indicate the market's implied valuations for expected accident costs) are incorporated into risk premiums for more hazardous jobs, and price discounts for more unreliable ladders. [Oi, 1977:59]

As this passage implies, however, this formulaic approach works best when cost can be inferred from specified risk and true risk can be balanced against a social good. Nuclear power generation, however, presents a number of quite complex and interrelated problems, each of which has an elusive value. (The problem is not simply that "costs" can be more easily assessed than "benefits" but also that both costs and benefits partake of the emotional and affective aspects of human valuation.)

The production of nuclear power in the normal course of events pollutes the air, heats surrounding water, and damages the ecological system by changing land use patterns. Radioactivity moves through air and water into plants and animals and hence, through the transfer of strontium 90 to plants eaten by cows and deposited in milk, directly to human beings. It also produces disease and genetic damage, the most fearful and virulent being forms of cancer. It is also becoming more obvious that nuclear power generation has psychic costs to those exposed to radioactivity. These costs include fears that the body and future generations will be contaminated through genetic damage, fears regarding potential accidents as they threaten the continuity of the self in social relations, and uncertainty about the extent, mode of arrival, intensity, and locus of potential damage (see Erikson, 1976; Lifton, 1969). Nuclear power represents, in the extreme (as in the case of a large-scale disaster), a threat to essential community ties and relations (Erikson, 1976: pt. 3). The psychic costs are the greater because, with nuclear power generation, unlike smoke, asbestos dust in the air, or the black dust produced by coalmining, the risks are much more subtle. Nuclear generators produce invisible risks and invisible harm which may not appear for another generation (or two) in the form of damage to children.

The complexity of risk assessment is indicated by the range of risks – that is, the diversity of the parameters, location, the channel through which risks are communicated (air, social relations, and water), the scope of the damage, and the degree of existential dread associated with nuclear power generation. Like nuclear war nuclear accidents, especially massive, ongoing, interdigitated ones, because they are so dreadful, have been called unimaginable or "unthinkable." The difficulty of imagining the range of risks and problems and their potential seems to provide the basis for the many illusions surrounding nuclear power development: the illusion that we are safe from accidents, that nuclear installations are inherently safe, and that the risks are so low as to be irrelevant when additional construction is being considered (Lifton, 1983).

As Broadbent (1984) and other psychologists have noted, people attach subjective probabilities to events on the basis of their own personal experience, the representativeness of an anticipated phenomenon (how common or "typical" they consider the event), and their exposure to descriptions of threats and risks by the media. Broadbent suggests that perhaps single horrendous events, such as a major air or bus crash, an explosion, or a fire, tend to be more worrying than the slow creep of everyday risks to which one is exposed—bicycle accidents, heart attacks, strokes, and so forth. The dread of a single event, however, may produce a megaspill of emotion, leading to a kind of repression, denial, and setting aside of some events as literally unthinkable. Thus while it is perfectly true that people underestimate the probability of very catastrophic events and overestimate the likelihood of less damaging ones, they tend to view the most extreme of events, the destruction of the world or an explosion of a nuclear power station, as beyond rational cognition. Engineers working with objective probabilities based on cumulative risk trees, on the other hand, reach the same conclusion: the probability of a nuclear core meltdown or shutdown is highly unlikely. Neither subjective risk assessment nor objective risk assessment operates in the existential world in which fundamental questions about being and the groundedness of life processes are asked. Perhaps it is not possible to describe human risk in probability terms or to make a subjective probability assessment when the risk to be calculated is not an individual person's safety but an axial change in the quality of human life for large numbers of people.

The very complexity of the problem of risk assessment has meant that it has been collapsed by economists and operations researchers. The probability of the occurrence of certain events, or a sequence of events, such as an accident in a nuclear installation, has been studied using *trees*. "This means listing all the pathways to failure of the system, then all the pathways to those pathways, and so on. You then assign a probability of occurrence to each of the component pathways and combine them to produce an overall likelihood of that accident occurring" (Tysoe, 1983). Another approach has been to develop *hypothetical scenarios* in order to capture the consequences of various sorts of malfunctions or errors. Since the vast majority of such scenarios describe events that have never occurred, they are substitutes for experience, feelings, and empirical data.

Both risk or fault trees and scenarios are abstract logical models for which parameters (for example, how probable it is that an event will occur) must be estimated and inserted.[22] The number of kinds of errors listed above compound the estimates but must nevertheless be included, since so many "rare" or improbable events – such as the dropping of a lightbulb into a panel, computer malfunctions that send spurious electronic signals or mistake "out of order" for "no signal," or the failure to return valves to their previous positions after maintenance – have been found to combine to produce quite a number of small accidents.

There is a concern in the regulatory literature with the distribution of such risks and their costs in terms of lost production, repair expense, and salaries and wages or the likelihood of a given outcome (a core's boiling down, a processor's corroding, a valve's malfunctioning and refusal to close, and so forth). This sort of calculation is forced into a single metric (money), is composed of events that are seen as being of equal value and social significance (attached by derived weights or monetary costs), and reflects the assumption that *internal costs* are of primary importance. Such calculations assume the value of the production and identify and weigh the costs of the externalities, regardless of the social meanings attached to the events. The cost of an accidental loss of an arm, an eye, or a life can be calculated from insurance tables but not from a table of emotional values.

This means of calculating risks based on formal metrics presuming the rational weighting of events by neutral and objective criteria may be inappropriate for understanding the public's interest in the safety of nuclear power installations. This model of risk is taken from events in which, unlike nuclear accidents, the existential component is absent. People may value their health in absolute or binary terms: it is seen as either present or absent. Lowrance (1976) has suggested that the concept of risk should be contrasted with the concept of safety, which can tap the holistic concern that people have for the quality of their existence. The various kinds of costs which the public bears are not fully captured in risk trees or scenarios. These events are not of equal importance to those at risk; the fear associated with living near Three Mile Island may cost residents more than a number of small accidents involving valves, scrubbers, electrical circuitry, and computers.

People may place any risk within the context of accustomed risk, those risks and fears with which they normally cope. For example, living in the midwestern part of the United States, one learns to accept that at least one tornado will strike in the local area a year; on the Gulf coast of Texas, one expects floods; and in Michigan, one anticipates at least one blizzard every year or two. However, the occurrence of several tornadoes, or blizzards, or constant flooding tests this assumption, as does a single axial and catastrophic event such as the Three Mile Island accident, the Buffalo Creek Disaster (Erickson, 1976), or the bombings of Hiroshima and Nagasaki (Lifton, 1969). The importance of a single paradigmatic event in setting and altering this accustomed tolerance cannot be overemphasized.

Risk trees and the like are based on the notion of individual choice in the buying of the goods or being at risk as a result of industrial production. One's sense of risk, research has shown (Hale and Perusse, 1977:75), is mediated by the degree to which one feels in control of individual exposure. The various costs associated with nuclear power production are at times unknown and invisible. Furthermore, they are costs that are collective and do not involve choice. Those who "choose" to ride a motorcycle are taking an individual decision to ride, but the vast majority of residents do not choose to live near a nuclear power station. In the latter situation, one finds a communal risk: people feel they are jointly at risk. They see the risk in terms of interdependence: an injury to a neighbor, in some sense, is an injury to oneself. This notion is very close to what Durkheim called the collective conscience, or the sense in which the community is more than the sum of its parts or individual risks; it involves mutual complementarity, a joint fate, and identification and lodging of self in social relations (see Oi, 1977:60–62). Oi, an economist, argues that the level of tolerance for collective risks is lower than for individual or voluntary risks (1977:60). That is, if one is involuntarily in a situation with others with whom one identifies, and in which one is perceived to be at risk, this risk will be shared and will be seen as greater than any single individual risk.

The ratio between individual or private costs and the public good of power production varies for different social groups. This raises the question of horizontal equity among groups in the nature of the risk to which they are exposed. Regulation is a means of increasing the "benefit externalities" of production or reducing the costs. The regulatory problem of risk assessment does seem rather more complex when these externalities are existential and include symbolic costs derived from fear for one's way of life, psychic coherence, bodily integrity, or the future of one's children.

Policy Contexts and Nuclear Regulation

The economic-information-based model that involves attributing costs and benefits offers a false and misleading basis for the construction of a regulatory policy in the nuclear power regulation area. Given identified limits on information, the complexity of the technology, the role of trust and complementarity of motives and the inadequate modes of risk calculation used in conjunction with this model, new modes of policy formation are required.

It has been argued that the regulation of nuclear power production is different for a number of historical, economic, and organizational reasons. The character of the risks associated with such an enterprise are quite different. The economic model of regulation, based on information and calculative rationality, is well suited to the study of economic controls but less suited to the study of social regulation. Information has been misleadingly used as a basis for modeling the relationships between the regulated and the regulators.

What policy issues arise, given this position? Such conceptualization blinds policymaking not only to the symbolic nature of much policy but also to the interpreted nature of the relationships that are intended to be regulated. One must consider, I submit, the *intentions* of policy, the role of *symbolic reassurance,* and the *contexts* within which policy is made.

Policy has quite different *intentions,* it would appear, when it seeks to deal with events unfolding in the social world which are well understood as a result of their repeated appearance and well-rehearsed past social responses, as opposed to the occasions when it seeks to deal with events which have not yet occurred. Consider, for example, the relatively routine nature of public and agency response to disasters such as fires, floods, earthquakes, or even oil spills (Barton, 1969). Compare, on the other hand, the ad hoc, emergent, and rather confused approach to the first publicly known nuclear power generation disaster at Three Mile Island.[23]

If one extends this reasoning, of course, imaginative work is clearly required for the social construction and anticipation of certain kinds of events or accidents. Nuclear disasters and other unthinkable events (such as nuclear war or the destruction of the earth by a change in the climatic conditions or as a result of a meteor shower), having never occurred, must be imagined. Analogical or lateral thinking of a kind must be employed. The setting of policy, or the use of a logic for setting aims and the means by which they are expected to be attained under these conditions, is apparently a different sort of operation from the setting of policies for coping with events that are known to occur and that have previously been experienced.

The regulation of nuclear installations, like other social regulation, involves emotionally loaded questions, for example, the transfer of carcinogens through the air, the movement of heavy metals and chemicals pollutants into lakes and streams, the neurological damage caused by toxic sprays and chemical agents, and value questions that link it politically with other questions. Nuclear regulation is intimately connected to long-range energy supplies, national defense, and the waging of tactical and strategic war. Single events with a low probability of occurrence according to engineering logic may have vast unanticipated indirect and direct consequences for a large number of people.

Facts alone are not at issue, because when facts are known there may be debates about their relevance; or facts may be seen differently; or because an event has never before occurred, facts may be unavailable. In other words, analogical thinking is employed when the risks are assessed. Is the risk of being exposed to toxic waste at the seashore at Windscale on the northeastern coast of Britain (an operator in a nuclear power station cynically dumped waste into the sea twice in late 1983), or to carcinogens in the air near a nuclear power station, like the risk of being hit by a car while crossing the street or having a child born with diabetes? The occurrence of an event with a low probability of happening, like the Three Mile Island incident — and it is still not clear precisely what caused the incident or what damage has been done to the reactor, which remains buried under tons of waste — calls sharply into question the claims for absolute safety made by power companies and reactor manufacturers. The question that analogical policymaking must address is: what sorts of imagined events does one want to compare with the kinds of accidents one wants to avoid or to manage better? What class of events is involved, and how are they like and different from other events with which one has experience?

Analogical thinking may prompt people to consider the relevance of disordered situations, chaos, ignorance, lack of knowledge, and mistaken knowledge (based on misinterpretation) rather than trying to fit pseudorationality around events people do not understand well. What do we know about confusion, indecision, ambiguity, and behavior in stressful but unclear situations such as war, planning for the future use of a roadway, political election campaigns, and the like? Perhaps these are the sources of analogy rather than the tidy, often binary, decisions made by chess players, computers, and cryptographers.

Anticipatory policymaking involves constructing and putting in place hypothetical entities that are likely while at the same time designing public policy which denies the likelihood that such entities will appear. This is the paradox of policy directed toward controlling or lessening the consequences of anticipated events. Policy for imagined futures must encompass nonroutine thinking. In the extreme, in events such as Hiroshima and Nagasaki, the consequences are patently "nonroutine" (Lifton, 1969). The risks are existential and rather more fundamental than they are statistical and limited in character. They threaten totally, and their features are likely to freeze action and make thought painful. People may seek to avoid thought and to edge toward denial or *psychic numbing* (Lifton, 1969:31). Furthermore, nuclear disasters have the potential to destroy systems that characterize and support civilized life (see Schell, 1982). Policy for *anticipated* or future events requires not only building scenarios, or sequences, of possible events and associated risks of a subjective and objective kind but also taking into account the need to reassure publics.

Policy bearing on imagined events is concerned primarily with reassurance and with producing the appearance of control, containment, and risk reduction. The rhetoric of policy directed to the public has the symbolic character of indicating and marking the extent, nature, and implication of governmental interest (see Gusfield, 1975, 1981). In many respects, anticipated events call for drama, or the selective display of symbols to achieve an anticipated definition of the situation and to reduce the likelihood of alternative interpretations. Policymaking in this context is a dramatic device.

One can reverse this reasoning to ask: what sort of data, empirical results, safety checks, or regulatory machinery in and of itself could provide substantial reassurance to various publics that they are not in danger of nuclear war, that nuclear accidents are unlikely, or that their safety is in no danger, once the question arises? This notion may contribute to our understanding of the consistent denial by government of risks to the public from nuclear testing, the stocking and transporting of nuclear weapons, nuclear power production, the proliferation of nuclear devices throughout Western Europe, and the removal and storage of toxic wastes (see Hilgartner, Bell, and O'Conner, 1983: pt. 4).

On the other hand, when one deals with the control of present events, one is attempting to manage their existence, to set acceptable standards and levels of risks, and to work toward compliance. Known and identifiable risks are made visible, and policy seeks to be reactive or responsive to these risks.

There are thus two policymaking contexts. They contain a different horizon of attention which focuses on certain types of events in the world, makes them real, isolates them from other events, attributes to them causes and consequences, and advances them for control or solution. In the case of anticipated events, one is developing what might be called prospective policy and, in the case of ongoing events, responsive policy. It follows then that treating one sort of event with the "wrong" sort of policymaking will result in confusion. It is not clear that both seek the same outcomes.

Furthermore, if one takes up anticipated events, one may possess a quite different agenda if the aim is (1) to reduce the number of errors, or (2) *increase the reporting of errors* (within the power-production system), or (3) manipulate public views of the costs and risks associated with such errors. These require different strategies. Increased internal controls, safety checks, reporting requirements, and the investigation of plans, rules and regulations, and quality assessment procedures are much needed. Such checks may increase the rate of reported violations and the social costs of nuclear power production. The reduction of risks and errors and the construction of safety systems and the like speak to objective events framed in "machine language" and the logic of engineering. The reduction of public fears, concerns, and existential dread speaks to subjective meanings framed in hermeneutic language and the logic of social relationships. Strategies based on maximizing the reduction of errors may not increase public confidence and vice versa.

Policy will little increase public confidence if the public feels it will be invaded by an invisible, pernicious, and destructive force that is cultivated, protected, and loosed by the state.

Summary

The present chapter has argued that the model of regulatory policy-making borrowed from neoclassical economics inadequately captures many features of social regulation and is poorly equipped to capture the substantive character of regulation of nuclear power generation. The eleven features listed cohere to form a regulatory arena which resembles that for other collective goods yet is at once unique. The unique character of nuclear power regulation, a result of the character of nuclear power itself, derives from its existential potential for producing dread, eroding well-being, and undermining faith in the future and the continuity of generations. It maintains an association with nuclear weapons and nuclear war. One solution would be to abandon this form of power production, close the plants, dispose of the radioactive cores, and write off another human quest for perfection. Failing that course of action, different forms of policy-making would appear to be required for the events and scenes associated with the regulation of nuclear power production. Anticipatory policy may frequently be formulated without the sort of self-conscious reflection that academics value as "rationality." It may not be seen as "anticipatory" in the terms used here. Perhaps even the distinction between solving or coping with the present event and anticipating future events is not as clean as one would like. One may provide the model for the other. Their mutual entanglement is apparent in policymaking practice.

Notes

1. A classic economic approach to social regulation is found in Richardson, Ogus, and Burrows (1982).

2. Simon (1957) has been very critical of the conceptual puppet man, the rational, self-interested actor who processes information regardless of its character and source, responds to events regardless of their scope and existential features, and lacks a personal biography or persona. Simon and others have viewed these as contributing to bounded rationality, or to limits upon otherwise information-based rational decisions. In this sense Simon could be viewed as biased in terms of information. The key problem is "un-

certainty," which captures such a range of human coping patterns and sets them aside, suggesting that, if one defines a situation as one in which a decision is to be made, one could find that "certainty" characterizes some such decisions. What is unanalyzed is the "ground" against which data became a "figure," or the tacit assumptions made regardless of, or prior to, the assembling of facts to make a decision.

3. I am unfairly characterizing this literature. Changes are apparent in recent publications such as Gusfield (1981), Diver (1980), Paris and Reynolds (1983), and Feldman, forthcoming. These words argue for an interpretive dimension of policymaking and against an "assembly-line metaphor" of logical and cumulative incremental rationality in social policy. The work of Perrow has been particularly impressive albeit somewhat overstated and provocative (1983, 1984).

4. Vogel attempts to account for the quite different strategies or approaches to the regulation of air quality with reference to cultural similarities and differences. These differences are located in "cultural" norms rewarding compliance, cooperation, deference, and tacit acceptance of authority in Britain; in contrast, American culture exhibits an "adversarial nature."

5. "Costs" are named as a cause, but the present political context is so volatile that many nuclear-powered generators seem unlikely to be built in America even if costs can be met. There is an irony here. If the Three Mile Island incident had not occurred, nuclear power plants might have continued to be built, and the risk of accidents, being an additive function, would have increased. The threat to the consumer would have grown even *if costs had diminished.*

6. This policy was sidestepped by President Reagan when he announced his intention of selling nuclear reactors to the Chinese (April 1984). Two of his chief advisers and cabinet members, Schultz and Weinberger, are former executives of the San Francisco–based company, Bechtel, which has been seeking to sell nuclear reactors to the Chinese since 1981 ("The Future of Nuclear Power in Britain," ITV special, London, January 1983).

7. It is impossible to determine empirically the sources of the large cost increases associated with the building of nuclear power plants. Whether they were created by mismanagement, corruption, inept engineering, actuarial juggling (the assigning of high costs to gain high profits, as in other defense spending), or public protests cannot be determined because only the power companies and engineering firms possess the data. A neutral state has little data on which to assign benefits, but costs are produced routinely for the press.

8. Perrow (1983), making different assumptions, claims that these are a central concern in "human factors engineering."

9. See, for example, previous work in this tradition by Gusfield (1963, 1981), Edelman (1964, 1971), Manning (1977, 1980), Hawkins (1984), and Rock (1986).

10. See Allison's (1971:33) model of the rational actor, based in large part on the economic theory of the firm.

11. The absence of information, the need to estimate a parameter in its absence, and extrapolation and prediction procedures all lie beyond the scope of this chapter. On these questions, see Cohen (1964).

12. Police work, for example, is assumed to be based upon information (see Manning, 1977, 1980, for criticism of this view). Close examination of drug law enforcement in several American cities, however, revealed that information relevant to regulating drug markets, such as number of users, rates of use, number of dealers, the size of the market (volume of transactions), and "demand" and supply indexes – in other words, the impact of various strategies of enforcement or changes in the procedural or substantive law – were not systematically gathered and analyzed. Relevant information that was gathered, such as the prices of drugs, the location of users and dealers, and the use of valid and useful informants, was not maintained centrally or analyzed. It resided in the private case files, memories, and lore of the detectives (see Manning, 1980:55–67). Policy governing enforcement was understood by participants but was not articulated, formalized, or written. It could be described as orchestrated on the basis of tacit, implicit meanings (compare Gusfield, 1975).

13. Such extrapolation has been accomplished in nuclear safety engineering by means of risk trees, which set out points of decision and associated costs (see below).

14. These might be considered hypotheses, since little data is available on how regulations are *actually* enforced in Britain and in America. It is possible that two quite different frames of reference are involved in creating standards, where deterrence seems to be the aim, and in enforcing rules, where compliance is sought (see Reiss, 1984). Comparisons of regulation must thus take into account "culture" as well as the frame of reference.

15. This is called "top-down processing" (Tysoe, 1984) or a mentalist view of decisionmaking (see also Broadbent, 1984). That is, I am assuming that there is a notion of the expectations of machines, gauges, events, outcomes, and states which is based upon experience. This notion is often visualized as an image with which actual or perceived events are contrasted. People develop mental pictures which provide the nest into which informational eggs (signs) are placed. It is difficult to establish, as Wittgenstein and Malcolm have shown, what these pictures are, since they can be reconstructed only on the basis of observed behavior or personal experience.

16. This tendency for benign language to be applied to matters atomic seems related to the obvious danger to human life that they have always been known to represent. Thus, Hilgartner, Bell, and O'Conner (1983) have argued that NUKESPEAK, the language of banal safety, has emerged. It is used with reference to horrendous death by frying, disintegration, radiation, or genetic destruction, for example when we speak of "megadeaths" or

the results of "clean, surgical strikes"; it is also evident when we call bombs with the potential of extinguishing the species "nuclear devices." By edging toward the unthinkable with laundered terms, so the argument goes, one avoids the factual reality of the threat and costs.

17. For an extension of this argument about the uses of information, see Feldman and March (1981).

18. The Three Mile Island incident caused a restructuring of NRC procedures. The commission has been very stringent in its scrutiny of applications for reopening and opening since late 1982. Perhaps nuclear regulation will, like other social agencies, be subject to crisis and crackdown, or a waxing and waning of enforcement (Becker, 1963; Cohen, 1972; Lindesmith, 1965). It could be suggested that these "moral panics" are a function of changes in public trust and agency legitimacy rather than changes in actual risk to the public of radioactive waste, malfunctioning generators, or carcinogenic agents released into the air.

19. Global theories which attempt to explain the pattern of relationships obtaining between agencies and those they regulate are rather crude, untestable speculations. It is perhaps necessary to examine lower levels of articulation and interdigitation which might be located by a study of the assumptions and the vocabularies of motives used by the members of the regulatory matrix.

20. Perhaps because the building of fission and fusion reactors was from the beginning linked to national security and shrouded in secrecy (Hilgartner, Bell, and O'Conner, 1983: chap. 5) with the intention of rapidly developing the technology, there has been little concern regarding public health questions raised about exposure to radiation associated with testing, exploding, and building nuclear devices. In fact, the American pattern has involved lies, deceit, manipulation, the withholding of information, and the denial of the risks of nuclear developments of all kinds. Evidence is only now being revealed of the consequences of the open air testing of nuclear devices upon civilians in Australia and the United States in the 1950s (Hilgartner, Bell, and O'Conner, 1983).

21. The question does arise, of course, why it has *not* become so. The various costs and the like have never been independently established. Private enterprise has been allowed to make a profit at every point in the process.

22. Many of the debates in the nuclear safety field surround not questions of fact but the interpretation of facts, for example, the estimation of risks to humans, given animal risk figures, the probability of certain sorts of malfunctioning that have never occurred, the number of deaths from bombs of sizes that have never been exploded, and so on (see Hilgartner, Bell, and O'Conner, 1983: chap. 10). It is, in short, not a matter of gathering additional facts.

23. The only other disaster of this type is the explosion of a Russian nuclear installation in the Urals. Only scanty evidence and reports are avail-

able (see Hilgartner, Bell, and O'Conner, 1983: chap. 9). (Chernobyl occurred after this was in press, but the general points are dramatically illustrated by the aftermath of this latest tragedy.)

References

Aldrich, H., and J. Pfeffer. 1976. "Environments of Organizations." In *Annual Review of Sociology,* ed. A. Inkeles, J. Coleman, and N. Smelser, pp. 79–105. Palo Alto, Calif.: Annual Reviews.

Allison, G. 1971. *Essence of Decision.* Boston: Little, Brown.

Barton, A. 1969. *Communities in Disaster.* New York: Doubleday.

Becker, H. S. 1963. *Outsiders.* New York: Free Press.

Broadbent, D. 1984. "The Psychology of Risk." Lecture presented at Wolfson College, Oxford, autumn term.

Burke, K. 1968. *Rhetoric of Motives and a Grammar of Motives.* Cleveland: Meridian Books.

Burns, T., and G. M. Stalker. 1961. *The Management of Innovation.* London: Tavistock.

Cherry, Colin. 1978. *On Human Communication.* 3d ed. Cambridge, Mass.: MIT Press.

Cicourel, A. 1968. *The Social Organization of Juvenile Justice.* New York: John Wiley.

Cohen, J. 1964. *Behaviour in Uncertainty.* London: George Allen and Unwin.

Cohen, S. 1972. *Folk Devils and Moral Panics.* London: Palladin.

Culler, J. 1975. *Structuralist Poetics.* Ithaca, N.Y.: Cornell University Press.

Dawson, F. G. 1976. *Nuclear Power: Development and Management of a Technology.* Seattle: University of Washington Press.

Dewey, J., and A. Bentley. 1949. *Knowing and the Known.* Boston: Beacon Press.

Diver, C. 1890. "A Theory of Regulatory Enforcement." *Public Policy* 28: 25–99.

Eco, U. 1976. *The Theory of Semiotics.* Bloomington: Indiana University Press.

———. 1983. *Semiotics and the Philosophy of Language.* London: Macmillan.

Edelman, Murray. 1964. *Symbolic Uses of Politics.* Urbana: University of Illinois Press.

———. 1971. *Politics as Symbolic Action.* Chicago: Markham.

Emery, F. E., and E. L. Trist. 1960. "Socio-Technical Systems." In *Management Science, Models, and Techniques II,* ed. C. W. Churchman and M. Verhulst, pp. 83–97. London: Pergamon.

Erikson, K. T. 1976. *Everything in Its Path.* New York: Simon and Schuster.

Feeley, Malcolm. 1970. "Coercion and Compliance: A New Look at an Old Problem." *Law and Society Review* 4 (May): 505–19.

Feldman, M. S. Forthcoming. *The Invisible Mind: Order Without Design.* Palo Alto, Calif.: Stanford University Press.

Feldman, M. S., and J. G. March. 1981. "Information in Organizations as Sign and Symbol." *Administrative Science Quarterly* 26 (June): 171–86.

Ford, D. 1981a. "Three Mile Island I: Class Nine Accident." *New Yorker,* 6 April: 49–119.

———. 1981b. "Three Mile Island II: The Paper Trail." *New Yorker,* 13 April: 46–109.

Garfinkel, H. 1967. *Studies in Ethnomethodology.* Englewood Cliffs, N.J.: Prentice-Hall.

Goffman, Erving. 1969. *Strategic Interaction.* Philadelphia: University of Pennsylvania Press.

———. 1974. *Frame Analysis.* New York: Harper and Row.

Guirard, P. 1975. *Semiology.* London: Routledge and Kegan Paul.

Gusfield, J. 1963. *Symbolic Crusade.* Urbana: University of Illinois Press.

———. 1975. "The (F)utility of Knowledge?: The Relation of Social Science to Public Policy Toward Drugs." *Annals* 417 (January): 1–15.

———. 1981. *The Culture of Public Problems.* Chicago: University of Chicago Press.

Hale, P., and M. Perusse. 1977. "Attitudes to Safety: Facts and Assumptions." In *Safety at Work,* ed. J. Phillips, Oxford: SSRC/Centre for Socio-Legal Studies, Wolfson College.

Hawkins, K. 1984. *Environment and Enforcement: Regulation and the Social Definition of Pollution.* Oxford: Clarendon Press.

Hawkins, K. O., and J. M. Thomas, eds. 1984. *Enforcing Regulation.* Boston: Kluwer-Nijhoff.

Hilgartner, S., R. Bell, and R. O'Conner. 1983. *Nukespeak.* Harmondsworth, Middlesex: Penguin Books.

Hirschman, A. 1970. *Exit, Voice, and Loyalty.* Cambridge, Mass.: Harvard University Press.

Kagan, R. 1984. "Regulatory Enforcement Styles in the United States." In *Enforcing Regulation,* ed. Hawkins and Thomas.

Kanter, R. M. 1977. *Men and Women of the Corporation.* New York: Basic Books.

Kidder, T. 1982. *The Ghost of a New Machine.* New York: Bantam Books.

Leach, E. R. 1976. *Culture and Communication.* Cambridge: Cambridge University Press.

Lifton, R. 1969. *Death in Life.* New York: Vintage Books.

———. 1983. "Indefensible Weapons." Massey Lecture, CBC #1, October.

Lindesmith, A. 1965. *The Addict and the Law.* Bloomington: Indiana University Press.

Lipsey, M. 1980. *Street-Level Bureaucracy.* New York: Russell Sage.

Louch, A. R. 1969. *Explanation and Human Action.* Berkeley and Los Angeles: University of California Press.

Lowrance, W. W. 1976. *Of Acceptable Risk: Science and the Determination of Safety.* Los Altos, Calif.: William Kaufmann.

Lyman, S., and M. Scott. 1970. *The Sociology of the Absurd.* New York: Appleton Century Crofts.

Manning, P. K. 1977. *Police Work: The Social Organization of Policing.* Cambridge, Mass.: MIT Press.

———. 1980. *The Narcs' Game.* Cambridge, Mass.: MIT Press.

———. 1982a. "Queries Concerning the Decision-Making Approach to Police Research." In Legal Psychology Division, British Psychological Association, *Proceedings,* pp. 52-63.

———. 1982b. "Organizational Work." *British Journal of Sociology* 33 (March): 118-39.

Meyer, J., and C. Rowan. 1977. "Institutionalized Organizations: Formal Structure as Myth and Ceremony." *American Journal of Sociology* 83 (October): 340-63.

Meyer, J., and W. R. Scott. 1983. *Organizational Environments: Ritual and Rationality.* Beverly Hills, Calif.: Sage.

Mills, C. Wright. 1940. "Situated Action and Vocabularies of Motives." *American Sociological Review* 5 (December): 904-13.

Oi, W. 1977. "On Socially Acceptable Risks. In *Safety at Work,* ed. J. Phillips. Oxford: SSRC/Centre for Socio-Legal Studies, Wolfson College.

Olson, Mancur, Jr. 1970. *The Logic of Collective Action.* New York: Schocken Books.

Paris, D. C., and J. F. Reynolds. 1983. *The Logic of Policy Inquiry.* London: Longman.

Perrow, C. 1983. "The Organizational Context of Human Factors Engineering." *Administrative Science Quarterly* 28:521-41.

———. 1984. *Normal Accidents.* New York: Basic Books.

Reiss, A. J., Jr. 1984. "Selecting Strategies of Social Control over Organizational Life." In *Enforcing Regulation,* ed. Hawkins and Thomas, pp. 23-35.

Richardson, G., A. Ogus, and R. Burrows. 1982. *Policing Pollution.* Oxford: Oxford University Press.

Rock, P. E. 1986. *A View from the Shadows.* Oxford: Oxford University Press.

Samuelson, P. 1954. "The Pure Theory of Public Expenditure." *Review of Economics and Statistics* 36 (November): 387-90.

Schell, J. 1982. *The Fate of the Earth.* New York: Avon Books.

Schelling, T. 1963. *The Strategy of Conflict.* New York: Oxford University Press.

Simon, H. 1957. *Administrative Behavior.* New York: Free Press.

——. 1969. *Sciences of the Artificial.* Cambridge, Mass.: MIT Press.

Terreberry, S. 1968. "The Evolution of Organizational Environments." *Administrative Science Quarterly* 12 (March): 509–613.

Turner, B. 1977. "The Origins of Disaster." In *Safety at Work,* ed. Phillips.

Tysoe, M. 1983. "The Psychology of Nuclear Accidents." *New Society,* 31 March: 505–07.

——. 1984. "The Psychology of Plane Crashes." *New Society,* 8 March: 361–63.

Veljanovski, C. 1982. *The New Law and Economics: A Research Review.* Oxford: SSRC/Centre for Socio-Legal Studies, Wolfson College.

Vogel, D. 1986. *National Styles of Regulation: Policy in Great Britain and the United States.* Ithaca, N.Y.: Cornell University Press.

Weick, K. 1979. *The Social Psychology of Organizing.* 2d ed. Reading, Mass.: Addison-Wesley.

——. 1980. "Loosely-Coupled Systems: Relaxed Meanings and Thick Interpretations." Unpublished, Cornell University, Ithaca, N.Y.

Wilson, J. Q. 1968. *Varieties of Police Behavior.* Cambridge, Mass.: Harvard University Press.

——. 1978. *The Investigators.* New York: Basic Books.

II

The Agency Decisionmaking Process:
Rule-Making Procedures and
Enforcement

Regulatory policymaking involves not only the selection of rules which define legislative goals and objectives but also confrontation by the agency of basic issues concerning methods for implementing policy objectives and the design of procedures to be followed with constituency groups that seek to influence substantive policies. These problems are analyzed in three case studies in part II.

One of the principal constraints on policymaking relates to the way in which agency officials interpret the more pragmatic but none-theless real economic concerns of those to whom policies are intended to apply; policymaking in regulatory agencies reflects these tensions (and in law is sometimes required to do so). This theme is prominent in the first essay of part II, Barry Boyer's analysis of the relation-ship between legal procedures for policymaking and the various constituency groups of the Federal Trade Commission (FTC). Regulatory policy is also, of course, tied to larger political and economic changes. Boyer points to the larger political influences which have recently shaped FTC policy, observing, for instance, that Congress, the White House, and the courts all seemed united in urg-ing greater activism from the agency in the 1970s.

Robert Rabin's study focuses on how internal agency politics and coalitions of various decisionmakers influence policy choices about implementation and enforcement. When the Environmental Protec-tion Agency (EPA) attempted to regulate the chlorofluorocarbons (CFCs) emitted from certain manufacturing products, a conflict emerged between two departments in the agency; each was commit-ted to a different enforcement policy. Like Boyer's study, Rabin's analysis highlights the role of political climate in shaping regulatory policy outcomes. Rabin recounts how, after the change of government in 1980 together with the prevailing mood of antiregulatory senti-ments and new scientific information caused the projected impact of CFC emissions on the ozone layer to be revised downward, the EPA simply withdrew its proposal to regulate.

The third essay in part II, Errol Meidinger's study of the emergence in the EPA of an enforcement policy based upon a "market mechanisms" philosophy, focuses on professional ideology's influence on enforcement policy within the agency. Meidinger describes how a group of professional entrepreneurs was able to impose a particular view of enforcement. His analysis demonstrates how a prominent, recently devised strategy (in this case market incentives) gains impetus when people share interpretations both of the way policy should be designed and implemented and the policy's perceived relevance for a legitimate and responsible role for government in environmental problems.

4

The Federal Trade Commission and Consumer Protection Policy: A Postmortem Examination

Barry Boyer

DURING THE PAST decade, there has been a major shift in the direction and emphasis of efforts to reform regulatory policymaking. The reforms of the early 1970s were based upon a concept of interest representation that sought to increase access to the policymaking process for underrepresented interests such as consumers and to rationalize and judicialize policy formation so that the positions advocated by participating interest groups would have to be taken seriously (for example, Stewart, 1975). By the 1980s, the goal of interest representation in adversary policymaking proceedings had been largely abandoned as a failure, and in its place there had arisen a widespread belief that procedures for the formulation of policy through a process of negotiation, or consensus building, within the regulatory agencies—"reg neg," as it had come to be known—were the best hope for avoiding rule-making gridlock and creating sound public policy (for example, Harter, 1982; Bingham, 1986).

The Federal Trade Commission (FTC) occupied a key position in this shift of goals and methods for policy formation. In the early 1960s, the FTC was generally regarded as a success story of regulatory revitalization. In response to sharp criticism from a Nader study group and from the American Bar Association, the commission had seized the initiative to formulate national consumer protection policy through aggressive use of its rule-making powers. In 1975 Congress confirmed the FTC's power to issue binding rules backed by stiff penalties. This statute, known as the Magnuson-Moss Act, represented the state of the art in regulatory reform. It prescribed a novel "hybrid rule-making" procedure[1] which was praised by a leading legal commentator as "some of the best thinking" about the judicialization of administrative policymaking (Davis, 1978:551), and it also contained an early prototype of the "regulatory analysis" requirement that became the centerpiece of reform efforts in the Carter and Reagan administrations.[2] Armed with this new authority, the FTC launched an ambitious agenda of proposed rules designed to root out abuses in consumer credit transactions, hearing aid and used car sales, vocational school promotions, funeral arrangements, television advertising for children, and other fields as well. There were almost two dozen major rules in all.

Within five years, the Federal Trade Commission's consumer protection policymaking program had been reduced to ashes. Congress had stepped in to impose a series of new restrictions on the agency's rule-making power, including a legislative veto of final rules (FTC Improvements Act, 1980). During the 1980s, the Reagan administration systematically replaced the FTC's activist leadership with appointees who were committed to the proposition that the agency should refrain from interfering with market forces unless there was clear evidence both of market failure and of the agency's ability to correct that failure without introducing additional distortions. The rules that were able to survive this close economic scrutiny were typically much pared down from the ambitious policies that had been proposed in the 1970s, and new initiatives were virtually nonexistent.

In medicine, an autopsy can provide valuable insights into the reasons why an organism died and can thus suggest possible pathways for prevention and cure. The same principle may apply to failed regulatory agencies. A critical reexamination of the FTC's fall may be particularly appropriate at this time because a simplistic and misleading folklore of regulatory policymaking seems to be growing out of the agency's experience.

Two recent books apply an outdated and useless version of the venerable capture theory[3] to explain the FTC's difficulties, reaching radically different conclusions. Michael Pertschuk, who presided over the demise of the agency as chairman in the late 1970s, is largely unrepentant in the lectures reprinted under the title *Revolt against Regulation* (1982). In his view, the FTC of the 1970s represented a brief, inspiring interruption of "the universally acknowledged capture of the regulatory agencies by the regulated" (p. 19). As the agency shook off its long dormancy and began to act with the vigor and independence that the public interest demanded (pp. 90–91), the forces of business rose up to reassert their hegemony over the defenseless commission:

> By 1974 the foundations had been laid for a political mobilization effort by business of a scope and breadth for which only the industrial mobilization of World War II provides a sufficiently heroic, if extreme, analogy. . . . Horizontally among firms within industries, vertically within companies, structures of political coordination and cooperation have proliferated, from the chief executives of the major industrial and financial firms politically united in the Business Roundtable to the 2,700 local congressional action committees of the Chamber of Commerce, which make up a network of close personal friends and supporters of congressmen and other political leaders. [Pp. 56–57]

Fueled with the money contributed by unsavory political action committees, this business conspiracy revolted against regulation in the public interest and led the Congress and the media in a "stoning" of the FTC, according to Pertschuk. By the 1980s, the recapture of the commission by probusiness interests was virtually complete. The veterans of the consumer movement, bloody but unbowed, retreated from the centers of power to wait for "a resurgence of popular demand that business be made to serve the public interest" (p. 156).

Bernice Rothman Hasin tells a similar story of conspiracy and capture in *Consumers, Commissions, and Congress* (1987) but with the roles reversed. In her version, Pertschuk and his cronies from the Nader-dominated New Class were the illegitimate captors of the Federal Trade Commission. Vaguely socialist, and therefore hostile to traditional American economic and social values, these alien forces managed to seize control of the FTC during the 1970s (pp. 4, 124–27). Ignoring the desires of the people and their elected representatives in Congress, the New Class consumerists singlemindedly pursued their agenda of structural transformation of the American economy (pp. 219). The capitalist system was forced to defend itself against this attack by the anticorporate forces and to rally the American people in defense of a free market economy. Ultimately, the usurpers were driven out by a newly elected Congress more responsive to the real needs of the American people.

The ways in which these two narratives cancel each other out illustrate the weak explanatory power of capture theories: any regulatory policy that one dislikes can be attributed to capture, and political opponents can be denounced as the captors. In this sense, capture "theory" is more of a rhetorical device than an analytical one. But if it is widely accepted, capture theory can also become a self-fulfilling prophecy. For the true believer in capture theory, regulatory policymaking begins and ends with finding a way to seize the reins of power by getting the right people into positions of authority within the relevant agency. Concern with rational techniques of policy analysis, organization theory, managerial skill, and opportunities for consensus building all become marginal. The only thing that matters is the opportunity to catch the political wave of the moment and ride it as far and as fast as possible.

This kind of simple capture theory ignores the possibility that things might have been otherwise with a different approach or a different set of techniques. In other words, the failure of the FTC may have reflected a failure of policymaking rather than a failure of politics. If so, then trying to achieve reform of agency policymaking solely at the political level may be both inefficient (because political change may be harder to achieve than changes in policymaking techniques) and ultimately unsuccessful. At the least, the possibility that the commission could have avoided some of the reversals and lost opportunities of the late 1970s deserves examination.

Before we can address the issue of whether the FTC committed avoidable errors in policymaking, we must make some initial assumptions about how the policy process works or ought to work. A primary dimension of this conceptual framework, especially for an agency which has had as much political visibility as the FTC, is the extent to which policymaking should to be regarded as a rational, analytical process rather than as a political or consensus-seeking activity. Robert Reich, who headed the FTC's Office of Policy Planning during the turbulent times of the late 1970s, has argued that the agency was whipsawed between two "warring critiques" of regulation. On the one hand, the FTC was faulted for not being politically responsive to its constituencies. On the other, it was attacked for failing to develop an adequate analytical base for its decisions, which usually meant that its data and reasoning regarding the economic effects of a proposed rule were inadequate. In Reich's view, these two warring critiques are fundamentally inconsistent because they imply different assumptions about the nature of the decisionmaking process (Reich, 1979). Ultimately, one or the other must prevail,[4] or presumably a kind of regulatory gridlock will result.

Reich is undoubtedly correct in noting that the FTC was faulted for being both analytically sloppy and politically obtuse. However, the two critiques are not as inconsistent as he suggests. Except in the largely hypothetical world of rational-comprehensive decision-making (Simon, 1960), regulatory policymaking is only partly determined by data gathering and analysis. Rational techniques of policy analysis may attempt to encompass a greater or lesser range of relevant factors (Carley, 1980), but in the end analytical inputs must be reconciled with considerations of political feasibility and desirability. Moreover, even when a policymaking decision is expected to be predominantly rational, it will often be based on "ordinary knowledge" – casual empiricism and common sense – rather than on formal research such as economic modeling or opinion surveys (Lindblom and Cohen, 1979). Since much ordinary knowledge is socially constructed through processes that may be broadly political (Meidinger, 1987), the boundaries between rationality and political responsiveness will often be blurred or nonexistent.[5]

Moreover, the experience of the FTC during the 1970s suggests that the two kinds of failures may spring from common roots. If one looks at the framework of incentives affecting the agency's policy-making (Sabatier, 1977) – the web of resource constraints, legal directives, technical competencies, normative preferences, and social processes within the bureaucracy – several related factors seem to have paved the way for the FTC's downfall. Some of these incentives originated outside the agency, in relationships that the FTC had with formal oversight bodies and constituencies and in the feedback it received from the marketplace. Others related primarily to forces within the agency, such as ideological and disciplinary orientations, careeer incentives, and bureaucratic constraints. In the aggregate, they help to explain how the Federal Trade Commission found itself in an untenable position, and they also suggest that the story might have taken a different turn.

Failures of Rationality

The concept of rationality in policymaking has a variety of meanings. In the legal tradition, "reasoned decisionmaking" usually refers both to the data or evidence that policymakers rely upon in making a particular decision and to the process of reasoning and articulation that they must follow in moving from raw data to finished policy. To meet the test of rationality, a decision must be based on reasonable factual support and must have a defensible rationale. However, these requirements shift from one decisionmaking context to another and also vary over time. During the 1970s, the legal and institutional norms governing this aspect of FTC policymaking were extremely ambiguous.

Before it began to issue industrywide rules, the FTC's consumer protection activities focused almost entirely on the prosecution of individual firms engaged in deceptive sales practices. The evidentiary standards that had evolved in these case-by-case adjudications were extremely lax (Gellhorn, 1969). When the commission charged that a particular advertising claim or representation was deceptive, for example, it did not have to demonstrate by reliable empirical evidence such as surveys that the ad had actually deceived significant numbers of consumers. Similarly, the commission did not have to introduce expert opinions showing that the representation had the capacity or tendency to deceive consumers. Anecdotal testimony about particular transactions or occurrences was sufficient, and in some cases the reviewing courts permitted the FTC to base cease-and-desist orders on even less evidence: dictionary definitions of the literal meanings of the words used by the seller, or the agency's largely unarticulated expertise in consumer behavior.

The FTC also had the power to prohibit "unfair" acts or practices affecting consumers, but the requirements for proving unfairness were even less defined than those relating to deception. The Supreme Court's 1972 decision in *FTC* v. *Sperry & Hutchinson Company* compared the commission's unfairness jurisdiction to the broad discretionary powers of a court of equity and concluded that the agency could consider general public policy values in defining what is unfair rather than performing a detailed technical or economic analysis. Since there was very little authority before *S&H* on the meaning of unfairness, it was unclear what had to be proved to demonstrate unfairness, or what kind of evidence (if any) was needed to prove it.

On the other hand, by the mid-1970s when the Magnuson-Moss Act confirmed the FTC's rule-making power, there was reason to believe that this tradition of deference to the presumed rationality of the commission's decisions might be eroding. Industrywide rule making was fundamentally a different enterprise from case-by-case adjudication. Instead of attacking one or two firms with marginal ethics and marginal power, the agency was taking on a whole segment of industry, good companies as well as bad. Moreover, the industries that the agency proposed to regulate with its new rule-making power were no longer the traditional hard-core consumer ripoffs inflicted by chinchilla salesmen, pyramid sales plans, and door-to-door encyclopedia sales. The FTC of the 1970s went after some of the pillars of the economy, including food advertisers, credit grantors, clothing manufacturers, and a host of semiprofessionals such as optometrists, funeral directors, and hearing aid salespersons. Because of the greater sweep of these kinds of rules, and the more serious consequences of errors in judgment, the agency might well be expected to gather better and more extensive evidence before deciding to issue a binding rule.

Another cautionary signal could have been read in the legal and intellectual currents of the time. The Magnuson-Moss Act exemplified the wave of so-called hybrid rule-making statutes and judicial decisions that evolved in the 1970s. The common feature of hybrid rule making was the insistence that agencies improve the rationality of their policymaking processes. Various means were adopted to assure this heightened rationality, ranging from more intensive judicial review of the data and rationale supporting policy judgments to more open, adversary procedures that would give interested persons an opportunity to challenge the factual basis for proposed rules. Cost-benefit analysis was emerging as a general framework for organizing the evaluation of policy proposals. Underlying all of these requirements, however, was a general loss of faith in both the expertise and the neutrality of regulatory agencies (Stewart, 1975; De-Long, 1979). Competence in policymaking would no longer be assumed; instead, it would have to be demonstrated, publicly and on the record.

Despite these cautionary signals, the FTC failed to come to terms with the requirements of rationality until it was too late. Part of the reason was that the agency was also receiving some powerful conflicting signals. Moreover, the procedural structures of rationality made the process so cumbersome and loaded with inertia that it was difficult to turn, once it was headed in a particular direction (Boyer, 1983).

FORMAL OVERSIGHT BODIES

Like other federal regulatory agencies, the FTC is formally accountable to the Congress, the White House, and the courts. Throughout most of the period in question, these overseers generally either

ignored the issue of quantity and quality of support for agency decisionmaking or sent signals to the FTC suggesting that low-quality
data were adequate or desirable for this kind of rule making.

Congress   The Magnuson-Moss Act itself sent a rather garbled
message about the desired rationality of FTC policymaking. It created an elaborate procedural structure for rational decisionmaking,
including hearings with cross-examination and reasoned decisions
based on the evidence of record; but it incorporated so many qualifications and exceptions to these procedural rights that it was difficult
to determine what opportunities to participate had actually been
given or whether they would be meaningful. Substantively, the statute directed the FTC to consider not only the unfairness or decep-
tiveness of the practices being challenged but also their prevalence
and economic effect. However, it provided no guidance on how to
weigh these potentially conflicting factors or what evidence should
be collected – other than the cryptic directive that the evidence be
"substantial." Reviewing courts might be expected to give some content to the rationality requirements of the statute, but the judicial
review provisions were so garbled that a bemused court summarized
them by saying: "In short, (1) we must review the whole record,
(2) the record is explicitly defined to include the statement of basis
and purpose, yet (3) we are explicitly forbidden to review the statement of basis and purpose 'in any respect'" (*American Optometric
Association* v. *FTC* 1980:905). Thus, instead of providing detailed
guidance, the basic statute presented a series of puzzles about the
role of rational analysis in FTC policymaking.

Legislative oversight through committee hearings and informal
contacts often serves to fill the gaps left by legislation. The Congress
engaged in considerable oversight activity regarding the FTC during the 1970s, but the signals emerging from the oversight process
shifted rapidly from one extreme to the other. In the two years after
passage of the Magnuson-Moss Act, Congress seemed to be prodding the agency toward an expansive, aggressive interpretation of
its new powers. In 1976 when the commission was issuing a blizzard
of rule-making notices under the news statute, Congress's investigative arm, the General Accounting Office, praised the FTC for its competence and vigorous pursuit of the public interest (*Washington Post,*
October 3, 1976). At about the same time, congressional oversight
committees were prodding the FTC to move ahead quickly with the

rule-making proceedings that had been stalled while the agency revised its rules of practice to incorporate the new statutory procedures. Memories of the painful congressional oversight hearings that had taken place a few years earlier when Ralph Nader's study group and the American Bar Association had criticized the FTC for being slow, timid, and overly solicitous of business interests were still relatively fresh at that time. Against this background, it is not surprising that the few checks on agency discretion in the Magnuson-Moss Act were regarded more as minor irritants than as a legislative warning to proceed with caution. The commission thought it had a congressional mandate to be, as Chairman Pertschuk (1982) later described it, a truly independent regulatory agency.

The White House White House involvement in FTC affairs during this period was less visible but also supportive of vigorous consumer protection programs. Since the "revitalization" of 1969–70, presidential appointees to the commission had generally been ambitious, activist, and proconsumer. These qualities were mirrored in the FTC's middle-echelon political leadership and in the career staff. While there were some indications in the Nixon and Ford administrations that the White House had mixed feelings about the FTC's increasingly tough enforcement posture, there was little overt effort to slow down the pace of activity. The FTC's budget steadily increased, and the president's consumer adviser had testified in support of the rule-making powers in the Magnuson-Moss Act. Through the 1970s, there was no visible concern within the executive branch regarding the quality of data and analysis used to support FTC rules.

This support from the executive branch faded rapidly when the Reagan administration took office. The White House promptly appointed new agency leadership, and the top officials at the FTC soon began expressing strong views about the quantity and quality of data needed to support consumer protection policies.[6] However, the Reagan administration's attempts to require more data and analysis as a prerequisite for administrative policymaking may actually have undermined the usefulness of rational analysis. For example, the perception rapidly spread that "the process [of regulatory analyses] was intended not to make social regulation more cost-effective and coherent, but to serve as a political filter" (Eads and Fix 1984:136; see also Morrison, 1986). In other words, the Office of Management and Budget's insistence on rationality was designed not to improve regulation but to prevent it or weaken it in accord with the administration's antiregulatory philosophy. This politicization of rational policy analysis probably lessened its authoritativeness and utility; at the least, it probably undercut the already weak demand for honest analysis of the need for and effects of policy initiatives.

Judicial Review While rational policy analysis might be expected to play a marginal role in the political branches, the courts should have been better equipped and motivated to exercise quality control over the FTC's analytical operations. They stood outside the realm of politics and operated in a tradition that valued rational evaluation of evidence and argument. Moreover, by the late 1970s, reviewing courts had developed a relatively large array of hybrid rulemaking docrines to assure that agencies generated good data, applied appropriate analytical methodologies, and responded to substantive critiques of their proposed policies (for example, DeLong, 1979; Gellhorn and Boyer, 1981:255–65). The elaborate and ambiguous procedures created by the Magnuson-Moss Act, along with the statute's cryptic judicial review provisions, provided ample doctrinal justification for courts to review the analytical basis of the FTC's consumer protection policy in some depth. However, the courts reviewing trade regulation rules not only failed to create a strong incentive for high-quality data and analysis; in some respects, they seemed to reward poor empirical analysis.

The failure of reviewing courts to demand high-quality analytical work, and a reasonable process for generating that analysis, can be illustrated by three of the early rules promulgated under the Magnuson-Moss Act. The first rule to reach the courts dealt with sales abuses by proprietary vocational schools. By the time the final rule reached the commission and the courts, there were three major differences between the agency staff supporting the rule and the industry opponents relating to the rule's analytical basis. One concerned the statute's requirement that the commission consider the "prevalence" of the practices it found to be unfair or deceptive – in this case, high-pressure sales tactics and false claims about earnings or job opportunities. The commission relied heavily on a few "horror stories" from former vocational school sales representatives, fragmentary data about student dropout rates, and anecdotal evidence by former students to conclude that the practices were widespread. The industry claimed that these data were unreliable when they were extrapolated to the industry as a whole and that it would have been feasible for the agency to generate good data by conducting a survey of former students.

The second substantive dispute centered on the statutory requirement that the commission consider the economic effect of its proposed rule. The key provision was the primary remedy adopted by the FTC, a requirement that the vocational schools grant a pro rata refund to any student who failed to complete a course of study. The schools claimed that this requirement would be prohibitively costly because they had to incur many of their expenses for hiring teachers and procuring equipment at the outset of a particular course. If students had an unqualified right to cancel and receive a pro rata refund at any time, some schools could be forced to absorb substantial costs. Neither the FTC staff nor the industry had produced much reliable evidence on this point, and the presiding officer remarked in his report on the hearings that the economic effect of the rule was unknown.

The third major issue related to the fairness of the procedures used to analyze the large masses of data collected in the rule-making record. The basis of the industry's objection was that the only officials in a position to canvass the rule-making record in detail, the staff attorneys, had become advocates fighting to uphold the rule. The officer who presided at the hearings was impartial, but he had access to only a part of the record. This challenge to the fairness of the process was supported by a detailed statistical and substantive analysis of the record material that the staff had cited in their final report to the commissioners. It also corresponded to the observations of those close to the hearings; as one FTC official remarked, "it is simply not realistic to expect a staff of inexperienced attorneys battling with the hardened mercenaries of the Washington bar to maintain the posture of being the only neutral parties in a highly charged proceeding."

The Second Circuit Court's decision reversing the rule (*Katharine Gibbs School, Inc.*, v. *FTC*, 1979) was remarkable for addressing none of these important questions about the rationality of the rule in any detail. Instead, the court seized upon a statutory technicality and found that the commission had failed to "define with specificity" the practices it had found to be unfair or deceptive in the text of the rule rather than in the accompanying "statement of basis and purpose."

The second FTC rule to reach the courts, dealing with price advertising of eyeglasses, offered a marked contrast to the loose theories and proof standards used in the vocational schools proceeding. This rule had a tight theoretical basis, grounded in economic models: state bans on the price advertising of eyeglasses would cause the price of glasses to be higher and more "dispersed" (less tightly clustered around the mean). The proceeding had also generated some "hard" empirical information relevant to the issue. Several social scientists who had conducted studies of price dispersion, some relating to the eyeglass market, had testified and submitted copies of their data to the rule-making record.

Unfortunately for the commission, while its staff was gathering and analyzing these data, the Supreme Court undermined much of the rule by holding that price advertising was protected by the constitutional right of free speech (*Bates* v. *State Bar of Arizona,* 1977). Nevertheless, the commission decided to promulgate the rule, largely because of the risk that states would impose affirmative disclosure requirements on eyeglass advertisers that would reduce or effectively prohibit price advertising. The staff had reviewed state laws on eyeglass advertising, finding that "a substantial number . . . have enacted disclosure requirements that are so demanding or so vague" as to discourage advertising and that a number of other states were considering such affirmative disclosure requirements.[7] Thus the commission put stringent limits on state affirmative disclosure laws.

The District of Columbia Circuit took the opposite position. It found that the Supreme Court's *Bates* decision had rendered most of the rule "unnecessary" (*American Optometric Association* v. *FTC,* 1980). According to the court, the rule's affirmative disclosure requirements lacked adequate factual support because they rested solely on expert opinion testimony.[8] "There is by now," Judge McGowan wrote, "considerable evidence as to the conduct of the states under *Bates* which makes it unnecessary for the Commission to rely on the speculations of a few witnesses." Presumably, the agency was being faulted for not reopening the rule-making proceeding when *Bates* was decided; however, it is not clear exactly what kind of evidence the court thought that the FTC should have collected beyond what was already in the record.

The third decision on judicial review involved the funeral practices rule, regarded by many observers as a weakly supported rule. As initially proposed, the funerals rule sought to ban a wide range of practices, ranging from embalming corpses without permission to displaying cheap caskets only in garish colors.[9] By the time it reached the courts, only the more significant provisions remained, focusing primarily on disclosure of price information. In the course of its long progress through the FTC, the funerals rule had generated a massive record. The Fourth Circuit Court noted with some awe that it contained 20,000 pages of prehearing comments and investigative material, 15,000 pages of hearing transcripts, 4,000 pages of exhibits, and more than a thousand posthearing comments. This tally was about as close as the court came to substantive analysis of the rational basis for the rule. Evidently treating the weight of the evidence as a literal test, the judges summarily proclaimed the evidence "more than adequate." Objections to the fairness of the procedure were dismissed with equally cursory consideration,[10] and the rule was affirmed (*Harry and Bryant Company* v. *FTC*, 1984).

These opinions, and others relating to the judicial review of FTC rules,[11] suggest that the courts are unwilling or unable to conduct substantive review of the analytical basis for policy analysis when the agency has not focused analysis on a manageable set of key issues. The opinions reflect scant understanding of the issues, much less a sophisticated appraisal of the data that would help to resolve those issues in a reasonable way. Nor is it clear, when the records are as massive and disorganized as they were in the funeral practices proceeding, that the courts should become deeply involved in the nuances of data and analysis. At most, as Judge Bazelon suggested in the *Ethyl* case, they might serve as policemen of the process, assuring that interested persons at least had an opportunity to present their views (*Ethyl Corporation* v. *Environmental Protection Agency*, 1976). But this limited role will, by itself, not create a very strong demand for improvements in rational analysis.

Thus the FTC's experience suggests that the governmental institutions responsible for overseeing administrative policymaking will not exert a very powerful demand for rational analysis. Indeed, in some respects they may create a demand for anecdotes and horror stories or for "adversary studies" that can be used to support a political position already taken.

REALITY CHECKS

An important influence on policymaking discretion is the kind of feedback that an agency receives from prior policy decisions. When the impact of decisions is likely to be substantial, immediate, and objectively determinable, the agency can be said to have a strong reality check; it will get both the necessary information to adjust policy and a strong incentive to use it because the consequences of decisions will be highly visible. Often, however, reality checks may be skewed in a particular direction. Agencies controlling price and entry in an industry may generally err on the side of protecting regulated firms because widespread failures of service will be immediately apparent, while overcharges or inefficiencies will not (Noll, 1971). Similarly, an agency such as the Food and Drug Administration (FDA), which has the responsibility for protecting the public from dangerous or ineffective drugs, may be more concerned about the risk of approving a drug that can cause death or injury than about the possible harm from keeping a beneficial drug off the market unnecessarily (Peltzman, 1973); failures of the first type will be quickly detected, while those of the second will be hard to identify.

A notable feature of the FTC's policymaking during the 1970s was the absence of any reliable reality check on most areas of consumer protection. The general shift from case-by-case adjudication to industrywide rule making contributed to this trend because a series of cases can provide incremental feedback on policy initiatives, whereas a general rule offers the opportunity to "clean up" abuses in a particular industry once and for all. Many of the rules proposed by the commission during this period fit this model, as they sought to eradicate a wide spectrum of questionable sales practices within the target industries.

Beyond the form of policymaking, however, is the uncertainty that pervades consumer protection decisions. Apart from the hardcore consumer frauds, where a trail of cheated customers might expose the failures of FTC enforcement, the effects of either an overly timid or an excessively zealous policy would be subtle and difficult to identify with confidence. This was apparent in proceedings where the agency was amending an existing rule or building upon a base of experience with different regulatory policies at the state level. Despite substantial expenditures for empirical studies of these existing consumer protection policies, the results were invariably inconclusive or conflicting. Often, the results of a particular study seemed to depend more on the identity of the interest group funding it than upon the actual state of the world. In Lindblom and Cohen's terminology (1979:42–43), the social science studies that were available to the agency were not "authoritative" in the sense of being either scientifically conclusive or generally accepted as determinative of policy questions. By regulating in a field where policy needs and impacts were so debatable, the FTC was largely free of the disciplining effects of reality checks.

CONSTITUENCY CHECKS

While the actual effects of a regulatory policy are often difficult to measure, the perceived impacts on organized constituency groups rarely are. The interactions between an agency's staff and its constituency groups can take a variety of forms and can serve many purposes. One important category of interaction, bargaining and related consensual techniques for seeking a compromise solution, is discussed separately below. Even in a purely reasoned process of deciding on the merits, however, an agency can engage in several kinds of contact with constituencies such as a regulated industry or a consumer group. These contacts are likely to affect the agency's information base, its perceived need for additional data, and its chances of obtaining more information.

One of the most common forms of contact grows out of the accumulated experience of the agency staff, either as employees of regulated firms or as regulators scrutinizing the industry's operations over a period of years. In either case, the prolonged exposure should sensitize the agency staff to the details of how the industry functions, to the nature and extent of the abuses that occur, and to the kinds of remedies the industry is able to live with. A continuing course of dealing also creates informal channels of communication which may be more accurate and efficient than formal public hearings or written submissions.

In the FTC of the 1970s, there were very few such informal contacts and exchanges of information. One reason for the absence of informal relationships was reaction to the conventional wisdom regarding the "capture" of the agency. Inspired by the Nader and American Bar Association reports that had criticized the agency for being insufficiently aggressive on behalf of the consumer, the Nixon administration had initiated a thorough housecleaning of the FTC. As a result, very few of the professionals and policymaking officials who had been employed at the FTC when the Nader report was issued in 1969 were still working there when the period of intensive rule making began in 1975. The few "old hands" who did survive in the

Bureau of Consumer Protection were mostly assigned to serve as presiding officers at the rule-making hearings, where they were subjected to limits on ex parte contacts that inhibited any informal contact with constituency representatives.

Most of the new people had come from places other than private industry; the lower levels of staff were recruited primarily from the law schools and university economics departments, while the higher-level officials came predominantly from academia or other branches of government. Thus they had relatively little direct exposure to those they would regulate, and the revitalized FTC's proactive enforcement strategy minimized their opportunities for informal, nonadversarial contact during their tenure with the agency.

A second general way in which constituency ties can influence an agency's information base for policymaking is through investigative contacts – agency requests for information, or voluntary provision of it, during the preliminary stages when a proposed rule is taking shape. The investigations leading to the 1975–80 wave of rule making were a diverse lot, but for the most part there was little systematic attempt to contact representatives of the target industries informally. In a few proceedings, staff resorted to the subpoena power early and often, which generated huge collections of marginally useful paper and considerable resentment within the industries. In other proceedings, staff consulted only with "friendly" segments of the target industry who might benefit from the proposed rule, and in others they avoided investigative contacts with industry altogether, relying primarily on experts and published sources. Both approaches created hostility and suspicion within the target industry. Later, the agency revised its staff directives to provide that attorneys conducting a rule-making investigation should systematically consult with all constituency groups affected by a proposed rule. By that time, however, more than a dozen rules had moved beyond the investigative stage. Staff has thus missed an opportunity to get some potentially useful information from regulatory targets not only about the technical details of their businesses but also about the nature and intensity of their objections to an evolving rule.

A final type of constituency feedback in a rule-making proceeding is material submitted for the public record, such as written comments, testimony, motions papers, and technical reports. These formal filings may be less enlightening than informal contacts, because they are public positions taken in an adversarial process where tactical considerations will likely compel the advocates to shade their facts and positions. The extent to which advocacy techniques submerge useful communication of factual information and constituency preferences will depend upon a variety of factors; however, the FTC's experience suggests that one of the most crucial may be whether a constituency group believes that it has a reasonable chance to convince the agency that it should modify its initial proposal. As Sabatier (1978:400) has observed, "Resources are not expended [to gather and present technical information] when value divergence [between the agency and the constituency group] is either nil or substantial, as the former produces trust and the latter, despair." In the proceedings studied, industry targets had several reasons to be skeptical about their chances of changing the agency's mind.

One factor which may have played a role in several of the proceedings studied was the general climate of suspicion and hostility between FTC staff and industry counsel. The lack of prehearing contacts, coupled with a widespread perception that the FTC staff attorneys were remote and arrogant, probably inhibited candor in many industry submissions. This factor alone would probably not have deterred industry spokesmen from presenting technical information if it had been clear that the quality of technical analysis in the record would influence the final agency policy decision—in the legal vernacular, if there had been a reasonable shot at "winning on the facts." In other agencies, such as the Environmental Protection Agency or the Occupational Safety and Health Administration, the parties usually argue their policy positions in highly technical terms, backed by empirical data, despite frequent personal or institutional conflicts between the agency and its constituencies. At the FTC, as noted above, there was no consensus about the importance of technical information in the policymaking process. Since the commission was unwilling to confine its own discretion by articulating precise legal theories of unfairness or deception or by establishing proof standards indicating what kinds of evidence would be determinative on particular issues, a rule opponent might well be wasting time and money, or even digging its own grave, by presenting empirical information. The FTC might simply hoist the industry spokesman on his own petard, as it had done several years earlier in the mail order merchandise rule making. In that case, a trade association opposing the rule had gathered data purporting to show that the problem addressed by the rule, failure to deliver ordered merchandise promptly, was not widespread in the industry. The commission had responded by concluding that even the low levels of abuse claimed by the industry were sufficient to support the rule. In the absence of clear ground rules as to how much consumer deception or unfairness was needed to warrant regulation, a rule opponent could find himself proving the FTC's case for the rule by documenting conditions in the marketplace.[12]

Since addressing the issues on the merits held such limited prospects for success, a rule opponent might reasonably decide that its best chances for winning lay elsewhere: trying to goad the agency into committing procedural errors, or adopting a purely negative strategy of putting the agency to the test on every conceivable issue, or trying to bring political pressure to bear through the Congress. All of these strategies were evident in the proceedings studied. As the political controversy over the commission's rule-making program fed the growing climate of hostility between the FTC and its business constituencies in the late 1970s, the FTC staff in many proceedings became even more isolated from contracts with industry and even less likely to give credence to any information or analysis that the industry might provide. The depth of this division between staff and industry was perhaps best illustrated in the hearing aids proceeding, where staff prepared a posthearing report arguing that virtually every major witness who had testified against the rule lacked credibility or was incompetent. An antirule trade association responded by charging that the staff's characterization of opposing witnesses was "at best unprofessional for any attorney and totally inexcusable for attorneys representing the Federal government."

IDEOLOGY AND TECHNICAL TRAINING

When legal standards give agencies broad discretion, the characteristics of the people involved in the decisionmaking process – their prior training and experience, their personal beliefs and values – can influence the kind of information the agency seeks and the techniques it uses to evaluate available data. In turn, these personal attributes may be systematically propagated in the bureaucracy through patterns of recruitment and socialization. During the mid-1970s, FTC personnel generally had several attributes which made it unlikely that they would engage in systematic empirical analysis or formal modeling when formulating consumer protection policy.

During the 1970s, the FTC was almost exclusively a lawyers'

agency. The people who investigated industries, developed rules, conducted hearings, and made decisions were overwhelmingly lawyers by profession. Since most lawyers are trained to deal with individual cases rather than with aggregate statistical patterns, and to concentrate on winning the case rather than on finding the underlying realities, the FTC's legal staff and supervisory personnel would not be naturally inclined to approach rule making as a technical fact-finding exercise. There were some economists on the FTC staff, but they were primarily concerned with antitrust rather than with consumer protection. The commission had virtually no survey research expertise other than what could be purchased from contract consultants. Thus it was not equipped to deal adequately with quantitative data that might illuminate general industrywide patterns of conduct. This deficiency became painfully apparent in proceedings such as credit practices, where legal staff had been given relatively free rein to use the subpoena power during the investigation. The credit staff collected some 200,000 pages of consumer account files relating to collection practices during its investigation, but it failed to set up any systematic sampling technique to assure that these documents reflected widespread practices. Later a survey research consultant was hired to try to draw statistical inferences from this material, but defects in the original data gathering made the results questionable.

As previously noted, the staff was also generally inexperienced in business practices. This lack of experience was partly a function of youth, since many had been recruited directly from law school; to a significant extent, however, it was also a product of the personal ideologies that staff lawyers brought to the agency. As the revitalized FTC became known as an activist agency, it attracted people who were dedicated to the cause of consumer protection and who were correspondingly suspicious of business practices and motivations. This ideology was fostered by the agency's recruitment policy, which put a premium on experience in a consumer organization or similar public interest group.[13] Occasionally an attitude of hostility or distaste toward business surfaced in public documents, as in the following excerpt from the funeral practices staff investigative report:

> The need for protections for funeral buyers is particularly acute because the funeral director plays two conflicting roles. His public relations image emphasizes his duties as a professional serving people at a time of particular desperation. His economic self-interest puts him in a different role: he is a

salesman of goods and services . . . and, if he wants to prosper . . . , he must move his high profit lines.

This conflict is exacerbated because the image of disinterested professionalism makes the funeral director a more effective merchandiser. The more the public accepts the professional role, the less it will inquire, shop, or bargain, and the greater the opportunity for high mark-ups, unnecessary services, and unscrupulous practices. Consequently, the industry tends to promote the professional image and fight anything that would interfere with it.

Agency staff who begin the proceedings with this attitude will probably not be inclined to seek out information tending to show that the rule is really unnecessary. At the same time, the staff's disdain will hardly encourage industry to be candid or cooperative. As one of the industry witnesses in the funeral proceeding noted, the "very damning language" of this initial staff report "left those of us in the industry who would like to have assumed a more moderating position in a bad position. If we supported the FTC position we were in essence forced to admit *all* the charges, and if we did not wish to admit them (they are, at least in my area, exaggerated), were forced to support the [trade association leading opposition to the rule], whose position, I feel, is unrealistic." The funerals staff may have been extreme in the obviousness of its dislike for the industry, but it was not unique.

CAREER INCENTIVES

The FTC of the 1970s was not a classic "revolving door" agency; its personnel did not shuttle to and from the regulated industry. Nonetheless, its key employees typically had a relatively short tenure in the agency. In the Washington job market of that time, talented lawyers at both the entry-level staff attorney positions and at the policymaking levels such as bureau director or commissioner could expect to move on within a few years to rewarding positions in major law firms, other government agencies, academia, or public interest organizations. In James Q. Wilson's terminology (1980:374–75), the FTC was dominated at the staff level by "professionals" who defined their status by reference to the practicing bar's standards of competence, while it was controlled at the leadership levels by "politicians" who sought to build careers in elective or appointive office outside the agency. The relatively few "careerists" who identified their careers and rewards with the agency were assigned to serve as presiding officers in the rule-making proceedings, and they were largely ignored when major policy issues arose.

This career pattern created several disincentives to the careful consideration of empirical data about the justification for rules and the consequences of proposed regulations. With a short-term perspective, agency personnel could be expected to think in terms of relatively quick payoffs; anything that would delay decisions (as systematic rational analysis usually does) would be disfavored. Moreover, since few staff members or higher-level officials would be around during implementation of the new policies, there was a high premium on initiation of projects rather than on following them through to a successful conclusion. Someone else would have to live with the consequences of a bad decision.

An FTC official who expected to be looking for another position in the near future might also have an incentive to develop broad, innovative rules rather than narrow, incremental policy changes. A novel rule provision, a new theory, or rule that restructured the target industry could enhance the proponent's reputation and hence his marketability. As one industry witness in the hearing aid rule making noted, "It is not inconceivable that the careers of the staff counsels [sic] will be forwarded if the 'new law' parts of the proposed regs are approved by the Commission. How, then, could it be expected that their purpose be any other than to see the regs [adopted]?" Paradoxically, these perverse incentives would be strongest for the most ambitious, talented, and influential FTC people, who would have the richest opportunities to advance their careers by fattening their résumés and moving on to new positions.

BUREAUCRATIC CONSTRAINTS

In addition to the personal values of the FTC staff and leadership, bureaucratic incentives influenced the nature and quality of information that the FTC generated in its policymaking process. Organizational considerations, for example, probably limited the use of economic analysis in rule making. The economists were in separate units such as the Bureau of Economics and the Office of Policy Planning and Evaluation which were usually not involved in the initial development of rules. Thus they entered the process after a proposal had developed a certain momentum within the Bureau of Consumer Protection, and they usually found themselves in the position of criticizing the staff attorneys' work product for inadequate economic analysis. This role was hardly calculated to make the staff attorneys who controlled the proceedings receptive to economic evidence, nor could it be expected to generate enthusiasm among the FTC economists for participating in consumer protection rule making.

When supervisory personnel managed to bridge these two cultures and seek more careful theoretical and empirical analysis of proposed rules, they were frustrated by resource constraints and production norms that made it difficult to delay a proceeding long enough to gather the additional information. One assistant bureau director summarized the multiple frustrations of the middle-management official who tried to push for better technical analysis in the face of bureaucratic production norms, resource limitations, ideological imperatives, and personnel constraints:

> At one time I was running seven major programs, including four rulemaking proceedings, with a total of $10,000 in contract money and 18 attorneys, the most senior of whom had three years' experience. [I thought that] the quality of work leading up to the proposed rules was not good, at least not when judged from the viewpoint of someone interested in analysis of the consequences of policy decisions rather than in abstract legal analysis. Even if we had been able to persuade the Commission that a massive increase in non-legal resources (i.e., contract money) was necessary—and as of 1975 this was impossible for assorted bureaucratic and intellectual reasons—and even if the OMB and the Congress had agreed, a request for such resources in the summer of 1975 would not have resulted in their becoming available until the fall of 1976, and the results of any work done with these resources would probably not have been available until mid-1977. I thought then . . . that the Commission should have stopped in its tracks, . . . used the statute in a couple of small experimental hearings, and geared up to do the job right. At the time, however, this was totally contrary to the views of both the top of the agency . . . and the staff attorneys, who had been raring to go and resented even the delay imposed while we waited for the statute and then drafted the rules of practice [implementing the new procedures].
>
> . . . Ultimately, the strategy I developed . . . was to let [one rule] go forward; I had to have something on the road to rapid completion, the staff was rabidly opposed to any delay, and I thought that the rule was narrow enough and focused enough that the sprawling approach [i.e., "throw the whole thing wide open in oral hearings and hope that enough solid information came in"] might work. I also let [a second rule] go forward as rapidly as the staff could push it, largely because I thought it was a bad rule and I wanted to give the staff so much rope that they could not claim to have been mistreated. [A third rule] was held up for almost two years until we were able to scrape up contract money to do some economic studies. . . .

> Finally, [the fourth rule] was an effort to do a rulemaking proceeding right
> from the start, with a specific and limited theory, . . . serious attention to
> the type of evidence needed, etc.

Even in situations where the agency leadership sought to improve the analytical basis for proposed rules, the search was thus bounded by a series of practical limitations.

For a variety of reasons, then, the FTC's capacity and incentive to generate systematic information about its proposed rules seemed relatively low. Alteration of the incentive structure might have made the key actors more receptive to the use of empirical data about the need for or effect of the policies under consideration, but it does not necessarily follow that greater reliance on economic or behavioral analysis would have improved the content of policy or avoided political problems. Even when participants made a determined effort to grapple with the factual underpinnings of proposed rules, the sheer bulk of material dumped into the records – sometimes totaling hundreds of thousands of pages – tended to drown the relevant and useful in a sea of trivia. One consumer group representative acknowledged this "needle-in-a-haystack" problem in her final oral presentation to the commissioners:

> There have been questions about what the record shows and what the record doesn't show. The record at this point consists of some 45,000 pages. If we had brought copies here, it would cover the table and possibly obscure most of us. There's no way in this kind of hearing that I can point to specifics in the record, nor can most of the people here claim to have read the entire record.

To avoid this kind of problem, the agency needed to have in place both an intellectual foundation for rational analysis – a clearly articulated definition of the kinds of information it needed to make an informed decision – and a mechanical system for compiling and analyzing its records that helped to separate useful data from marginal or worthless material. The FTC had neither.

Only at the very end of the process, when the rules returned to the commissioners for final promulgation, did it begin to become apparent what issues they considered the most important. The commissioners seemed primarily concerned with the practicalities of enforcing any rules that they might adopt and with finding ways to replace detailed "command-and-control" regulations with self-enforcing market incentives. The hearing records rarely addressed these concerns in any detail. As a result, the commissioners were forced to rely on "ordinary knowledge" – common sense and lawyers' rule-of-thumb policy judgments. Over time, these concerns might have been internalized in bureaucratic routines, and fact gathering might have become more focused. However, this possibility was foreclosed by the political firestorm that broke over the FTC, terminating most of its policymaking initiatives.

The question remains as to whether rational, empirically based policy analysis is cost justified in a program such as consumer protection rule making. Tactically, raising the "burden of proof" – the quantum of data and analysis needed to support a particular policy – is often an effective way to defeat a policy initiative, and this theme has been played out repeatedly in American administrative law. It was evident in the New Deal debates over the proper role of judicialized procedures and findings of fact,[14] and it has persisted into contemporary practice through the environmentalists' use of the National Environmental Policy Act to block construction projects[15] and the business community's support for regulatory analysis requirements. It is possible that a move toward more empirical data and analysis would simply have made the FTC's consumer protection policymaking slower rather than better.

Some support for this hypothesis can be found by considering the conclusions that the FTC's presiding officers drew about the utility of the empirical studies that were introduced into the hearing records. As previously noted, the presiding officers were generally experienced attorneys who maintained a substantial measure of impartiality. They also had the opportunity to hear and question the witnesses who were presenting formal analyses related to the proposed rules and to consider the material carefully when they were preparing their detailed written reports.

Even in hearings where relatively sophisticated economic and behavioral studies were introduced, however, the presiding officers found them inconclusive. In the credit practices proceeding, for example, the presiding officer's report canvassed five major empirical studies of the economic effects of limiting creditors' remedies and concluded that "all suffer from theoretical and methodological defects; and as a result, the studies do not enable one to predict with any degree of certainty the actual economic effect of the proposed rule." Similarly, in the ophthalmic goods rule, a substantial body of economic literature and record evidence addressed the question of how advertising restrictions affected the dispersion of prices paid by consumers. Nevertheless, the presiding officer noted that "all of the surveys are imperfect" and that "a first-class study of the market structure of this industry would be a very difficult, time-consuming task costing into the six-digit figure range." Even then, he concluded, "the first-class study would doubtless be questioned by other experts."

Clearly, rational policy analysis would not have been a panacea for the FTC even if it had been produced in greater quantity and quality and had been used much more effectively than it was during the late 1970s. This conclusion is perhaps not surprising, since the agency had no real tradition of reliance on systematic social inquiry during policy formulation and had scant institutional capacity for generating and using it. Over time, the situation might have changed as a body of usable knowledge accumulated and as agency personnel developed the skills needed to collect and analyze data. External constituencies and overseers might have followed the agency's lead as it became apparent that careful analysis could affect the content of policy.

Before this more optimistic scenario could develop, however, the FTC would have needed a different political environment and a different set of relationships with its prime constituencies. In this respect, rational inquiry can be regarded as a part of the process by which reality is socially constructed in particular fields of regulation. If the contending factions define their relationship as a zero-sum game in which the overriding goal is to capture the reins of power and impose one's views on the other players, then rational analysis will likely be deployed as another weapon in that struggle, as it was in the Reagan administration's use of regulatory analysis. On the other hand, if regulation is viewed as an arena in which the parties jointly search for improved solutions to mutual problems, then empirical analysis can be used as a means of examining and redefining these mutual interests. Thus the FTC's failures in the field of rational analysis may be less significant than their failures to generate a working consensus in support of their policy initiatives.

Failures of Consensus

Regulatory negotiation, or "reg neg," has generated a considerable literature in recent years, much of it designed to identify situations and techniques that will foster bargained resolutions of regulatory policy issues (for example, Administrative Conference of the United States, 1987). However, this focus on the engineering of negotiated policies overlooks the possibility that there are less visible but still interactive ways of seeking consensus on regulatory policy. Charles Lindblom (1965) provides a detailed typology of the forms of "partisan mutual adjustment" that may take place among the participants in a government decisionmaking process. His categories include familiar techniques such as bargaining or logrolling and also adaptive strategies, in which one decisionmaker does not seek a direct response from another but rather adjusts his own position in anticipation of its effects on another interested party. Efforts to manipulate the other party into assent may be direct or indirect, and they may be tacit or overt. Through these processes, Lindblom asserts, government decisions achieve a form of rationality or coordination superior to any that could be imposed by a centralized decisionmaker.

The FTC's experience illustrates that these forms of mutual adjustment are neither simple nor inevitable. In developing its proposed rules, the FTC evidently made minimal use of the tactic that Lindblom (1965:33) calls "calculated adjustment," in which the decisionmaker "does not wholly avoid adverse consequences" for another interest group but "nevertheless adjusts his decision out of consideration for adverse effects" on the other. Instead, many of the commission's proposed rules attempted a wholesale restructuring of sales practices in the target industries, with little regard for costs or compliance difficulties. When representatives from the regulated industries made overtures to open settlement negotiations, these attempts were generally rejected. Instead, the FTC simply tried to impose its will on the target industries, and in most instances it fell far short of this goal.[16] These appear to be several reasons why the commission failed to adjust its policies to the objections voiced by the rule targets. In broad outline, they parallel the factors influencing the FTC's limited use of technical information.

FORMAL OVERSIGHT BODIES

In addition to prodding the FTC into action on its proposed rules, the Congress and the reviewing courts during the early 1970s seemed to be sending the FTC a message that negotiation or accommodation with the regulated industries was either suspect or illegitimate. The key congressional committees apparently adopted the Nader report's assumption that voluntary compliance or policy compromises through bargaining were at best ineffective means of protecting the public and ought not to be encouraged.

The congressional committee hearings and reports leading up to the passage of the Magnuson-Moss Act, which span three congresses, contain voluminous material about the scope of the FTC's policy-making discretion and the need for judicialized procedures and court review of rules to provide a check against bureaucratic arbitrariness. However, there was negligible consideration of the possibility that legal requirements imposing judicial procedures and demanding greater evidentiary support for rules might inhibit the commission's ability to accommodate contending interests. Throughout the early 1970s, Congress gave the agency little encouragement, if any, to work out some accommodation with the industries it regulated.

The courts were even more explicit in discouraging consensual approaches to policymaking. Through such cases as *Home Box Office* v. *FCC* (1977), they threatened to reverse agency rules which were based on a negotiated outcome acceptable to the regulated industry. In response to these decisions, the commission issued rules of practice banning many kinds of ex parte contacts in its rule-making proceedings. Thus regulated parties could communicate with the commissioners during the several years that a rule was pending only through the rule-making record or through the political process.

FEEDBACK AND THE PACE OF POLICY CHANGE

Prior decisions can provide the agency not only with information about the practical impact of its policies but also with feedback about their political acceptability. If the agency has misread the political climate, or the capacity of the regulated industry to modify its practices, the resulting controversy may cause it to be more cautious the next time around. As a result, it may be motivated to explore the possibilities of explicit or tacit mutual adjustment with the aroused constituencies. Through a combination of circumstances and choice, the FTC largely lost the ability to make such adjustments in the 1970s.

One dimension of the pace of change is the scope of the policy that the agency is considering. Once the FTC decided that an industry like funeral homes should be regulated, it could have followed either of two general strategies. It might adopt an incrementalist approach, trying to remedy a few serious problems first, with the expectation of revising or expanding the regulations in a few years, or it could adopt a once-and-for-all strategy of trying to clean up all known or suspected abuses in one giant proceeding. While examples of both approaches can be found in the FTC's rules during this period, many of the proposed regulations seemed to exemplify the once-and-for-all approach. This approach not only foreclosed the possibility of incremental adjustment over time but also made it less likely that industry spokesmen would be willing to consider accommodation. When the proposals threatened a wholesale restructuring of industry practices, the conflict became a life-or-death struggle rather than a case of reasonable disagreement over marginal practices.

Another aspect of the pace of policy change is the number of major initiatives pending at any one time. If a program of policymaking is spread sequentially over a period of years, the agency will have a chance to apply knowledge gained in one field to other areas and will be able to seek mutual adjustment as it learns from experience. The FTC took the opposite approach of launching all of its major policy initiatives within a short period of time. In the early years of the decade, the commission had opened a large number of industrywide investigations with little apparent attempt to set priorities or to develop a long-term plan of action.[17]

Many of these investigations were culminating in staff proposals for rule making at about the time that Congress was moving to amend the rule-making procedures. They were held in abeyance for months or years while the Magnuson-Moss Act was passed and internal procedures were developed to implement it. By this time, the staff attorneys who had developed the rules were extremely impatient to proceed with the public hearings, and the commissioners for the most part obliged them. As a result the stakes increased enormously, it became impossible for the commission to learn from experience, and the widespread impression that the FTC was an agency out of control, indulging in an orgy of overregulation, was fostered.

CONSTITUENCY RELATIONSHIPS

The literature on regulatory negotiation places considerable emphasis on the importance of a rough balance of power between the agency and the target industry as a precondition for successful negotiated rule making. For example, Philip Harter (1982:48) notes that a precondition to meaningful bargaining over regulatory policy is the participants' perceptions of countervailing power. That is, a party is not likely to seek compromise solutions unless he believes that his adversary can inflict unacceptable sanctions – such as cost, delay, harassment, or political pressure – if he tries to dictate a result.

The FTC's failure to bargain or otherwise to reach a mutual accommodation with its constituencies can be explained in part as the agency's failure to adapt to a shifting political environment that restructured the power relationships surrounding the agency. The commission's primary supporting constituency, the consumer movement, was fragmenting and losing influence in the mid-1970s (Nader, 1975). At the same time, the nature of business opposition to regulation in general and to the FTC in particular was changing. The business community was mobilizing a serious political counteroffensive to the wave of social regulation enacted in the early 1970s and was making the FTC a prime target. When the FTC proposed nearly two dozen major rules within a few months, it gave credibility to these opposition groups and mobilized supporters for their efforts. With many powerful opponents and a few weak friends, the FTC was in no position to dictate results without fear of reprisal. By the time the commissioners realized that the agency's situation was precarious and tried to trim back the rules, it was too late for conciliatory gestures to have any effect.

This description is accurate as far as it goes, but it does not address the reasons why this agency, at this time, was so out of tune with its constituencies. If we view the relationship between regulator and regulated purely as a matter of power, it is possible, if not likely, that cooperation will develop even among mutual antagonists with little direct contact. For example, Robert Axelrod (1984) has described the elaborate forms of cooperation that emerged between the contending armies in the trench warfare of World War I and has developed the theory that cooperation will often prove superior to conflict even when the antagonists are trying to maximize their own gain in a situation where there is no face-to-face bargaining and no central authority to impose a solution.

The circumstances defined by Axelrod as generating cooperation, referred to as an "iterated prisoners' dilemma," can help to illuminate some of the reasons why the FTC failed to achieve basic cooperation with its constituencies. In many respects, the conditions that Axelrod considers necessary for cooperation did not exist during the intensive rule making of the late 1970s. The prisoner's dilemma analysis applies when the payoffs for cooperation are greater than the payoffs for defection or recalcitrance. In many respects, the personal and organizational payoffs facing the FTC did not appear to meet that requirement in the late 1970s. Moreover, it was not clear to the agency at that time that its relationship with the regulated industries was "iterative," or composed of a series of similar transactions in which each party would have more or less equivalent opportunities to harm the other. Instead, the parties often acted more like "gypsies" who had the ability to exit from the game before the next round and could therefore escape retaliation.

In retrospect, these appearances of freedom from the prisoner's dilemma may have been illusory. From the FTC's perspective as an institution, at least, it seems plausible that the payoffs for cooperation would have been greater than the payoffs it ultimately received for its intransigence. However, the framework of prisoner's dilemma can help to illuminate the reasons why the potential payoffs for cooperation seemed so minimal at that time.

IDEOLOGY AND TECHNICAL TRAINING

The activist, proconsumer beliefs of many FTC staff members probably influenced their perception that there were no payoffs for cooperation and this may have inhibited the search for satisfactory mutual adjustments. Many of them seemed to regard consumer protection issues as matters of moral right, with the result that attempts at compromises or tradeoffs would be viewed as selling out principles rather than as a method of developing sound policy. Recruitment and socialization within the agency did little to moderate this viewpoint, especially after the FTC had become politically embattled. Apart from willingness, many FTC staff attorneys may have lacked the technical ability to conduct successful negotiations. Like most young lawyers, they had negligible formal training in the techniques of negotiation and bargaining, and their experience at the agency did little to fill this void. Thus they might well have concluded that they were less likely to achieve an acceptable outcome through negotiation than through litigation.

CAREER INCENTIVES

The personal career interests of the FTC staff and the interest group representatives participating in the rule-making proceedings may have created some disincentives to cooperation. Reich (1981:84) suggests that the contentiousness of contemporary regulatory practice is partly a function of "the behavioral norms and institutional incentives of the professionals who specialize in communicating between government and business" – the lawyers, lobbyists, public relations experts, trade association staffs, and others who made their living representing private interests before the regulatory bureaucracies. According to Reich, these intermediaries need conflict to justify their services, and they are highly skilled at increasing and prolonging the conflict inherent in many fields of regulation. Thus the payoffs for the individual actors may be different from the payoffs for the institutions they represent or from the payoffs for society as a whole.

In the FTC proceedings studied, there was little direct evidence that intermediary groups were consciously provoking confrontation. Furthermore, as previously noted, some of them tried to begin negotiations even when the proceedings were highly polarized. However, it did seem to be true that the intermediary organizations tried to play to their own professional strengths; the trial lawyers on all sides often sought to treat the proceedings as a prosecution of the industry, while the lobbyists focused on mobilizing political pressure, for example. In an amorphous proceeding, the intermediaries' attempts to move the decisionmaking process closer to their own field of expertise could be justified not only as a method of making their services more useful but also as a means of winning for their clients.

In addition, the high cost of representing an interest in the FTC hearings, which frequently ran to several hundred thousand dollars, made it necessary for the intermediary spokesmen to raise a lot of money quickly from their constituents. An effective way to do so was to persuade them that the FTC was out to destroy the industry, perhaps by unethical or questionable means (Cartwright and Boyer, 1984).

On the FTC side, the short-term perspective of most staff lawyers made them act like gypsies with little incentive to pursue cooperative mutual adjustment. If the proponents of the rules could expect to move on to other jobs or at least to regulation of other industries in the near future, they would not be overly concerned about alienating industry members or private sector intermediaries because they would not be likely to deal with them again. In addition, finding a successful compromise solution to a policy conflict would probably give the agency lawyer a less useful credit on the résumé than a successful fight to the finish through public hearings and judicial review. Bargaining is typically a low-visibility process, at least outside the circle of those who are party to the dealing, and credit for a successful outcome is therefore less easily gained. Moreover, negotiating skills generally seemed to be less highly valued than litigation skills in the legal job market of the time.

PROCEDURAL CONSTRAINTS

The fact that the Magnuson-Moss Act required the FTC to make rules through a relatively formal, public, and judicialized process also seemed to inhibit mutual adjustment. After the hearing process had begun, the only people who could approve and implement a consent settlement – the FTC commissioners – were isolated from the unfolding proceedings. Rules typically took four or five years to progress through the public hearing and posthearing stages before they were ready for final commission action, and during this period there was no easy opportunity for the commissioners to intervene or to monitor the issues. Rules against ex parte contacts insulated them from direct dealings with constituency groups or with congressmen who became concerned about the direction of the commission's consumer protection policymaking (Boyer, 1982).

When the rules eventually did return to the commissioners for final action, it became apparent that the agency leaders were willing to make fairly substantial concessions to meet industry's objections. By then, however, the political pressure to rein in the FTC was irresistible; the time when mutual adjustment might work had passed, at least for these rules. In this respect, the process diverged markedly from the model of the iterated prisoner's dilemma, where parties have regular, frequent interactions and opportunities to respond promptly to the actions taken by their adversaries.

Conclusions

Unless one subscribes to the comforting simplicities of traditional capture theory, the FTC's policy misadventures of the 1970s stand as a disturbing monument to missed opportunities and reforms gone wrong. In many respects, the FTC was the best and the brightest of a generation of revitalized regulatory agencies, and its effective demise marks the end of an era. Certainly its fall casts doubt on the efficacy of the conventional wisdom of the 1970s. Neither the recruitment of a talented staff, nor its zealous commitment to the agency's mission, nor elaborately crafted legal procedures, nor the trappings of rational policy analysis were sufficient to save the Federal Trade Commission from an ignominious end. Instead, these reforms seemed to contribute to the agency's self-destructive tendencies.

If there is an escape from alternating between the regulatory extremes of mindless activism and enforced torpor, the FTC experience suggests that it must be based on a more systematic and careful understanding of the incentives that are at work within the agencies. Both improved use of rational analysis, and the emergence of cooperative relationships between agencies and their constituencies, may depend upon a variety of incentives. Many of these incentives are socially constructed or socially reinforced and thus become part of the culture of bureaucracies such as the FTC (Meidinger, 1987). Moreover, that culture can be "engineered" to achieve a balance among differing viewpoints and differing policy preferences (Mashaw, 1983). From that culture may come something that has a reasonable claim to the name of bureaucratic justice (Mashaw, 1983) or something like the FTC of the 1970s – a regulatory disaster by almost any standard.

Notes

1. The term "hybrid rule making" is used to describe administrative rulemaking procedures which fall somewhere between the polar models established by the Administrative Procedure Act of 1946. The simplest and most common APA process for formulating general rules is called "notice and comment" rule making; as the name suggests, the agency merely publishes a draft of a proposed rule or policy statement and allows interested persons to file written comments. At the opposite extreme is formal "rule making on a record," which requires use of trial procedures such as oral hearings with witness testimony and cross-examination, an impartial presiding officer, and a decision based solely on a hearing record. For general discussions of the evolution of hybrid rule making, see Hamilton (1972); Davis (1978: 448–634); Scalia (1978).

2. A regulatory analysis is generally a cost-benefit analysis of a proposed rule or policy. Provisions requiring agencies to prepare a regulatory analysis for major policy initiatives vary considerably with respect to questions of methodology, such as whether all costs and benefits should be quantified or how extensively agencies should canvass alternatives to a proposed action. See, for example, National Environmental Policy Act of 1969, and Ex-

ecutive Order No. 12291 (1981). For general discussions of regulatory analysis requirements and their enforcement by the Office of Management and Budget, see Morrison (1986), and DeMuth and Ginsburg (1986). The FTC's rule-making statute, the Magnuson-Moss Act, required the agency to include in its final statement of basis for a rule an analysis of the prevalence of the deceptive or unfair practices covered by the rule as well as an assessment of the costs of the rule (taking into special account the costs to consumers and small businesses).

3. Capture theory generally holds that agencies become "captives" of the industries they are supposed to regulate and formulate policies that will serve the interests of the industry rather than protecting consumers or the public. Early variants of capture theory were developed by Samuel Huntington (1952) and Marver Bernstein (1955). Capture theories figured prominently in the ideology of the Nader-inspired public interest movement of the 1970s; see, for example, Lazarus (1974).

4. Reich (1979:42) posits that the political responsiveness critique will prevail "where the benefits of regulation are narrowly focused while the costs are spread more widely and thinly" because "those who enjoy the benefits will know that they can rely on the political process to guard them." Conversely, he sees the rationalist economic analysis critique as prevailing when the "benefits of regulation are apt to be spread widely and thinly over the population while the costs initially fall on a smaller group" because "those who bear the costs will assume they cannot look to the political process to guard their interests." This kind of constituency analysis does not fit the FTC's situation very well, since the business constituencies that the agency threatened with its proposed policies ultimately proved most influential in the political process.

5. As Charles Lindblom (1965:15) has noted, interactive problem-solving techniques designed to achieve an acceptable adjustment of interests can also be defended as rational systems which efficiently marshal and evaluate relevant evidence. Similarly, increased opportunities for public participation in administrative proceedings, which serve the goal of political acceptability, may also be justified as a way of generating a better analytical base for regulatory decisions (Boyer, 1981). On the other hand, rational analysis can be used in a purely political fashion, to justify or defend decisions made on other grounds. See, for example, Sabatier (1978:396); Eads (1981); Sohn and Litan (1981); Eads and Fix (1984:135–38).

6. In 1982, Timothy Muris, director of the FTC's Bureau of Consumer Protection, argued that the commission should refrain from issuing a rule unless the "best available evidence"—usually surveys and expert opinion testimony—demonstrated that the practices covered by the rule were widespread, and that "the rule will likely remedy the problems . . . in [such] a way that the benefits of the rule exceed its costs" (Muris, 1982a; see also 1982b, 1982c). At about the same time, the FTC's new chairman, James C. Miller

III, testified in congressional hearings that he favored raising the standards for proof of deception (Anonymous, 1982:267).

7. Quotations not otherwise attributed are taken either from field research conducted in 1975–79 or from the records of FTC proceedings conducted during that period.

8. The ambiguity of the court's message about the quality of evidentiary support needed to uphold a trade regulation rule is emphasized by one of the provisions of the eyeglass rule that the D.C. Circuit Court upheld. The provision in question required that eye examiners release a copy of the lens prescription to the customer. In evaluating the evidentiary support for this provision, which it characterized as "considerable," the court relied on a blanket citation to the staff report on the rule, and "an example, perhaps extreme but nonetheless illuminating" – in other words, a single anecdotal "horror story" (*American Optometric Association* v. *FTC*, 1980:916).

9. The prohibition on displaying cheap caskets only in garish or pallid colors (which presumably would induce purchasers to buy more tasteful and expensive caskets) generated a variety of amusing but rather unenlightening anecdotes at the hearing, including the following exchange between staff witness Jessica Mitford, author of a book criticizing American funeral customs, and counsel for one of the funeral directors' trade associations:

> COUNSEL: [Assume that] John Jones dies of a kidney disease. He is jaundiced. His wife is looking at a casket with an interior that will bring out the jaundiced condition. Should [the funeral director] suggest other caskets which would make a more aesthetic picture for the wife and the members of the family?
> MITFORD: Well, I like the idea of the matching casket, the jaundice-colored one. . . . I mean, if I died of jaundice, I would rather have the jaundice-colored casket for myself. Just so with scarlet fever.

10. The funeral practices rule was one which FTC Chairman Pertschuk specifically mentioned when he admitted in congressional testimony that "some FTC staff members had pursued a 'vendetta' against certain industries, had been 'hostile to evidence and witnesses that went against the staff's recommendations,'" and had utilized tactics which had "justifiably caused animosity" (Kramer, 1979). Nevertheless, the court summarily rejected the industry's procedural objections to the fairness of the hearings (*Harry and Bryant Company* v. *FTC*, 1984:997–98).

11. For example, as discussed in the text below, in the credit practices rule the FTC staff had gathered a huge amount of material from credit company files but had not used any sampling techniques to assure that the material collected in any way represented the universe of consumer credit transactions. The presiding officer found that all of the empirical studies introduced at that hearing had significant flaws that made it impossible to rely on them to predict the economic effects of the rule. Brushing aside the

industry's objection to the factual basis for the rule, the reviewing court stated: "Petitioner's argument harbors a misconception about the nature of the Commission's cost-benefit analysis. Petitioners would require that the Commission's predictions or conclusions be based on a rigorous, quantitative economic analysis. There is, however, no basis for imposing such a requirement" (*American Financial Services Association* v. *Federal Trade Commission,* 1985:986).

12. The Fourth Circuit Court continued this tradition of using the industry's evidence of lack of abuse to find that there is sufficient evidence of abuse in the funeral practices litigation. In considering a rule provision requiring funeral directors to pass along rebates and similar financial incentives to the consumer, the court noted, "The record indicates that in California alone, twelve percent of all funeral directors in an industry-sponsored study *acknowledged* that they impose mark-ups on cash advance items or receive a rebate from the supplier which is not returned to the consumer" (*Harry and Bryant Company* v. *Federal Trade Commission,* 1984:1,000).

13. In an interview conducted shortly after he became chairman of the Federal Trade Commission in 1977, Michael Pertschuk stated: "What I basically did [in recruiting] was to look for people with two sets of qualifications — unquestioned professional qualifications and a strong history of public interest involvement and advocacy" (Cohen and Demkovich, 1977:855).

14. James Landis, in his 1938 Storrs lectures on the administrative process, argued that regulation would be hamstrung if agencies were required to make detailed findings of fact on a formal record:

> The ultimate judgment of the administrative [agency] rests on considerations that evolved out of a wide range of experience and observation and out of its study of [the industry]. . . . To require this range of evidence to be reduced to findings of fact is as equally unrealistic as to impose a requirement upon legislatures that specific findings of fact must be a prelude to the passage of legislation. [Landis, 1938:149]

A decade later, Louis Jaffe (1949:473) noted that "the basic and perennial demand for an adequate rationalization of judgment" was expressed in demands "for 'findings,' for 'reasons,' for a 'theory.'"

15. The National Environmental Policy Act requires agencies to prepare an environmental impact statement before undertaking major actions which may have a significant effect on the environment. The impact statement must evaluate alternatives to the proposed action and must systematically canvass the environmental costs and benefits associated with each alternative. Perhaps the best example of the way these rational-comprehensive decision-making requirements can be used to block disfavored action is in the licensing of nuclear power plants; see, for example, Cook (1980) and Ebbin and Kasper (1974). Critics have charged that such environmental review provi-

sions have been used to block development in other contexts as well (for example, Frieden, 1979).

16. In Lindblom's terminology (1965:33–34), an agency decision to propose a relatively narrow rule may represent a "calculated adjustment" in which "X does not wholly avoid averse consequences for Y but nevertheless adjusts his decision out of consideration for adverse effects on Y." Alternatively, it might represent an overture to seek "manipulated adjustment" through, for example, bargaining ("induc[ing] responses from each other by conditional threats and promises") or "partisan discussion" ("X and Y induce responses from each other by effecting a reappraisal of each other's assessment of the objective consequences of various courses of action"). Instead, the FTC's basic approach seemed closer to what Lindblom (1965:77) calls "authoritative prescription" – a form of adjustment that occurs "(a) when a person receives an authoritative message from another; (b) when he then adopts it as the basis for decision or action; and (c) when his grounds for doing so are that [the commands] ought to be obeyed without his subjecting them to independent evaluation in terms of his own criteria of judgment." Lindblom suggests that authoritative prescription rarely exists in its pure form.

17. The FTC attempted to establish an effective system for setting priorities in the wake of the Nader report's criticism of the agency's failure to plan (Cox, Fellmeth, and Schultz, 1969); the Office of Policy Planning and Evaluation was established in the early 1970s. However, that office had not succeeded in creating a credible role for itself in the commission's consumer protection work when the events described in the text took place.

References

Administrative Conference of the United States. 1987. *Sourcebook: Federal Agency Use of Alternative Dispute Resolution.* Washington, D.C.: Office of the Chairman.

Anonymous. 1982. "Commissioners Disagree on Proposals to Redefine Deception Under FTC Act," 43 *BNA Antitrust and Trade Regulation Report* 267.

Axelrod, Robert. 1984. *The Evolution of Cooperation.* New York: Basic Books.

Bernstein, Marver H. 1955. *Regulating Business by Independent Commission.* Princeton, N.J.: Princeton University Press.

Bingham, Gail. 1986. *Resolving Environmental Disputes: A Decade of Experience.* Washington, D.C.: Conservation Foundation.

Boyer, Barry B. 1983. "'Too Many Lawyers, Not Enough Practical People.'" 5 *Law and Policy Quarterly* 9.

―――. 1981. "Funding Public Participation in Agency Proceedings: The Federal Trade Commission Experience." 70 *Georgetown Law Journal* 51.

Carley, Michael. 1980. *Rational Techniques in Policy Analysis.* London: Heinemann Educational Books.

Cartwright, Bliss, and Barry Boyer. 1984. "Mobilizing Friends and Foes in Administrative Proceedings." 6 *Law and Policy* 451.

Cohen, Richard E., and Linda E. Demkovich. 1977. "Pertschuk―Moving Quickly to Cast the FTC in His Own Mold." *National Journal,* June 4, 1977, p. 853.

Cook, Constance Ewing. 1980. *Nuclear Power and Legal Advocacy.* Lexington, Mass.: Lexington Books.

Cox, Edward, Robert C. Fellmeth, and John E. Schultz. 1969. *"The Nader Report"on the Federal Trade Commission.* New York: Richard W. Baron.

Davis, Kenneth Culp. 1978. *Administrative Law Treatise.* 2d ed. vol. 1. San Diego, Calif.: K.C. Davis.

DeLong, James V. 1979. "Informal Rulemaking and the Integration of Law and Policy." 65 *Virginia Law Review* 257.

DeMuth, Christopher C., and Douglas H. Ginsburg. 1986. "White House Review of Agency Rulemaking." 99 *Harvard Law Review* 1075.

Diver, Colin S. 1981. "Policymaking Paradigms in Administrative Law." 95 *Harvard Law Review* 393.

Eads, George. 1981. "Harnessing Regulation: The Evolving Role of White House Oversight." *Regulation,* May/June 1981, p. 19.

Eads, George, and Michael Fix. 1984. *Relief or Reform? Reagan's Regulatory Dilemma.* Washington, D.C.: Urban Institute Press.

Ebbin, Steven, and Raphael Kasper. 1974. *Citizen Groups and the Nuclear Power Controversy.* Cambridge, Mass.: MIT Press.

Frieden, Bernard J. 1979. *The Environmental Protection Hustle.* Cambridge, Mass.: MIT Press.

Gellhorn, Ernest. 1969. "Proof of Consumer Deception before the Federal Trade Commission." 17 *Kansas Law Review* 559.

Gellhorn, Ernest, and Barry B. Boyer. 1981. *Administrative Law and Process in a Nutshell.* St. Paul, Minn.: West.

Hamilton, Robert W. 1972. "Procedures for the Adoption of Rules of General Applicability: The Need for Procedural Innovation in Administrative Rulemaking." 60 *California Law Review* 1276.

Harter, Philip J. 1982. "Negotiating Regulations: A Cure for Malaise." 71 *Georgetown Law Journal* 1.

Hasin, Bernice R. 1987. *Consumers, Commissions, and Congress: Law, Theory, and the Federal Trade Commission, 1968–1985.* New Brunswick, N.J.: Transaction Books.

Huntington, Samuel P. 1952. "The Marasmus of the ICC: The Commission, the Railroads, and the Public Interest." 61 *Yale Law Journal* 467.

Jaffe, Louis L. 1949. "Administrative Findings; or, The Ameer in America." 34 *Cornell Law Quarterly* 473.

Kramer, Larry. 1979. "Pertschuk Admits Vendetta By Former Staffers at FTC." *Washington Post*, Oct. 6, 1979, p. D-9 col. 4.

Landis, James M. 1938. *The Administrative Process*. New Haven, Conn.: Yale University Press.

Lazarus, Simon. 1974. *The Genteel Populists*. New York: Holt, Rinehart and Winston.

Lindblom, Charles. 1979. "Still Muddling, Not Yet Through." 39 *Public Administration Review* 517.

———. 1965. *The Intelligence of Democracy: Decision Making through Mutual Adjustment*. New York: Free Press.

———. 1959. "The Science of Muddling Through." 19 *Public Administration Review* 154.

Lindblom, Charles, and David K. Cohen. 1979. *Usable Knowledge: Social Science and Social Problem Solving*. New Haven, Conn.: Yale University Press.

Mashaw, Jerry L. 1983. *Bureaucratic Justice*. New Haven, Conn.: Yale University Press.

Meidinger, Errol. 1987. "Regulatory Culture: A Theoretical Outline." 9 *Law and Policy* 356.

Morrison, Alan B. 1986. "OMB Interference with Agency Rulemaking: The Wrong Way to Write a Regulation." 99 *Harvard Law Review* 1059.

Muris, Timothy J. 1982a. "Memorandum to Commission Regarding Care Labeling Rule Amendments. May 25, 1982." Washington, D.C.: Federal Trade Commission.

———. 1982b. "Memorandum to Commission Regarding Food Rule Phase I, May 17, 1982." Washington, D.C.: Federal Trade Commission.

———. 1982c. "Rules without Reason: The Case of the FTC." *Regulation*, September/October 1982, p. 21.

Nader, Ralph. 1975. "Consumerism: A Coalition in Flux." 4 *Policy Studies Journal* 31.

Noll, Roger G. 1971. *Reforming Regulation*. Washington, D.C.: Brookings Institution.

Peltzman, Sam. 1973. "An Evaluation of Consumer Protection Legislation: The 1962 Drug Amendments." 81 *Journal of Political Economy* 1049.

Pertschuk, Michael. 1982. *Revolt against Regulation: The Rise and Pause of the Consumer Movement*. Berkeley: University of California Press.

Reich, Robert B. 1979. "Warring Critiques of Regulation." *Regulation*, January/February 1979, p. 37.

———. 1981. "Regulation by Confrontation or Negotiation?" *Harvard Business Review*, May/June 1981, p. 82.

Sabatier, Paul. 1978. "The Acquisition and Utilization of Technical Information by Administrative Agencies." 23 *Administrative Science Quarterly* 396.

———. 1977. "Regulatory Policy-Making: Toward a Framework of Analysis." 17 *Natural Resources Journal* 415.

Scalia, Antonin. 1978. "Vermont Yankee: The APA, the D.C. Circuit, and the Supreme Court." 1978 *Supreme Court Review* 345.

Simon, Herbert A. 1960. *Administrative Behavior.* New York: Free Press.

Sohn, Michael, and Robert Litan. 1981. "Regulatory Oversight Wins in Court." *Regulation,* July/August 1981, p. 17.

Stewart, Richard B. 1975. "The Reformation of American Administrative Law," 88 *Harvard Law Review* 1669.

Weingast, Barry R., and Mark J. Moran. 1982. "The Myth of Runaway Bureaucracy: The Case of the FTC." *Regulation,* May/June 1982, p. 33.

Wilson, James Q., ed. 1980. *The Politics of Regulation.* New York: Basic Books.

LEGAL REFERENCES

Administrative Procedure Act (1946). Codified in 5 U.S. Code Secs. 551–559, 701–706, 3105 7521, 5372, 3344.

American Financial Services Association v. Federal Trade Commission. 767 F.2d 957 (D.C. Cir. 1985).

American Optometric Association v. Federal Trade Commission. 626 F.2d 896 (D.C. Cir. 1980).

Bates v. State Bar of Arizona. 433 U.S. 350 (1977).

Ethyl Corporation v. Environmental Protection Agency. 541 F.2d 1 (D.C. Cir. 1976) (en banc).

Executive Order 12291. 46 F.R. 13193 (February 19, 1981).

Federal Trade Commission Improvements Act (1980). 94 Stat. 374, codified in 15 U.S. Code, various secs.

Federal Trade Commission v. Sperry & Hutchinson Company. 405 U.S. 233 (1972).

Harry and Bryant Company v. Federal Trade Commission. 726 F.2d 993 (4th Cir. 1984).

Home Box Office, Inc., v. Federal Communications Commission. 567 F.2d 9 (D.C. Cir. 1977), cert. denied, 434 U.S. 829 (1978).

Katharine Gibbs School, Inc., v. Federal Trade Commission. 612 F.2d 658, 627 F.2d 481, 628 F.2d 755 (2d Cir. 1980).

Magnuson-Moss Act (1975). Codified in 15 U.S. Code Secs. 57a–57c.

Mail Order Merchandise Rule. 40 F.R. 49492 (October 22, 1975), codified in 16 Code of Federal Regulations Part 435 (1981).

National Environmental Policy Act (1969). Codified in 42 U.S. Code Secs. 4321–4347.

5

EPA Regulation of Chlorofluorocarbons: A View of the Policy Formation Process

Robert L. Rabin

O N O CTOBER 7, 1980, the Environmental Protection Agency (EPA) issued an advance notice of proposed rule making indicating that the agency was seriously considering further regulation of chlorofluorocarbons (CFCs), a chemical substance suspected to be the agent of an especially pernicious, imperceptible form of environmental degradation. Only two years earlier, a governmental ban on using CFCs as a propellant in aerosol spray cans had appeared to meet public safety concerns. Notwithstanding this recent effort, the EPA announced that the hazards associated with CFCs loomed larger than ever and raised the prospect of new regulatory action. Moreover, the agency indicated that, if additional controls were to be imposed, it was seriously considering a marketable-permits system— an economic incentives approach that had been much discussed in the literature but which remained untested in the rough-and-tumble world of regulatory reform.[1]

The major objective of this essay is to offer some insights into the policy formation process at the EPA. After discussing the hazards posed by CFCs, I will indicate the scope of the regulatory issue by surveying the principal uses of the chemical and noting the extraterritorial dimensions of the problem. I will then describe the major regulatory options that were available to the EPA and will attempt to demonstrate why the agency reached the conclusion that, if further controls were to be undertaken, the most promising strategy was a marketable-permits approach. We will thus ultimately look behind the advance notice of proposed rule making in an effort to understand the key variables that led the agency to propose additional regulatory action through an innovative regulatory strategy.

Ozone Depletion: The Theory and Its Consequences

Chlorofluorocarbons are a family of chemical substances with a wide variety of industrial, commercial, and consumer uses. Beginning in 1974, scientists warned that one of the great virtues of CFCs – their chemical stability – might also be a critical vice. Unlike most other chemical compounds containing chlorine, which break up in the lower atmosphere, CFCs appear to remain intact as they rise slowly to the stratosphere (the region of the atmosphere ten to fifty kilometers above the earth's surface). In the stratosphere, ultraviolet radiation causes them to decompose, freeing the chlorine atoms, which, in turn, destroy ozone through further catalytic reactions.

The destruction of any substantial portion of the so-called ozone shield in the stratosphere would be cause for substantial concern. The ozone layer limits the amount of damaging ultraviolet radiation that reaches the earth's surface – radiation within the spectrum harmful to human and other organic cellular matter. While the level of stratospheric ozone varies under natural conditions, it is subject to imperfectly understood dynamic forces of creation and destruction which maintain a relative level of equilibrium. If the ozone depletion theory is accurate, this equilibrium is jeopardized by the continuing chemical invasion.

Note, then, that the scientific side of the CFC scenario has two distinct aspects. The ozone depletion theory itself indicates the stratospheric effects that are likely to result from continued release of CFCs into the atmosphere. The theory generates real concern only when it is linked to a growing body of scientific research indicating that damaging ultraviolet radiation has potentially harmful impacts on human and other organic cellular life.

The government has relied heavily on the National Academy of Sciences (NAS), both to validate the theory and to assess its impact on living organisms. The initial NAS findings were reported in 1976–77. Shortly thereafter, the Clean Air Act Amendments of 1977 directed EPA to sponsor further research, report to Congress, and regulate unreasonably dangerous impacts on stratospheric ozone.[2] A year later, in 1978, came the aerosol ban.[3]

Students of the regulatory process might well have predicted a period of inattention, or at least benign neglect, after this flurry of activity. Not so, however, in the case of CFCs. With the continuing congressional mandate to sponsor research and to report, the EPA turned once again to the NAS for further scientific evaluation. By early 1980, the agency had new data in hand suggesting that the depletion problem was even more serious than previous studies had indicated.[4]

NAS estimated that, at 1977 levels of CFC release, the ozone layer would eventually be depleted by 16.5 percent and would reach one-half of the estimated steady-state depletion within thirty-five years (error range of ±11.5 at a 95 percent confidence level).[5] Moreover, should CFC release continue to grow at the estimated rate of 7 percent annually, the NAS projected a 75 percent likelihood that ozone depletion would eventually exceed 30 percent of 1977 levels.[6]

Regarding biological harm, the scientists discussed an array of findings.[7] Skin cancer is the principal type of direct harm to human beings associated with damaging ultraviolet radiation. On the basis of an evaluation of epidemiological data, nonmelanoma skin cancer – the nonfatal but disfiguring variety – would be expected to increase by about 5 percent for every 1 percent increase in ozone depletion. If stratospheric ozone were in fact to be depleted by 16.5 percent, this incidence ratio of four to one would translate into several hundred thousand more cases of nonmelanoma skin cancer in the United States alone. The relationship between malignant melanoma skin cancer – which is frequently fatal – and damaging ultraviolet radiation is less clear, but is sufficiently well established for the NAS to have predicted several thousand additional cases per year (based on an incidence ratio of about two to one).

The harm anticipated to other biological systems is similarly a function of cellular damage, observed in controlled and open-field experimentation. Although the data were far from conclusive, it appeared that a wide variety of plants, including such staple crops as sugar beets, tomatoes, and corn, would be seriously affected. Similarly, a number of marine organisms which are critical links in the biological food chain – anchovies, crab, and shrimp larvae, for example – appeared to have a very low tolerance for increased doses of damaging ultraviolet radiation. Finally, the NAS described the potential "greenhouse" effect, or contribution to the warming of the

earth's atmosphere, that might result from a continuing increase in
the level of heat-absorptive CFCs in transit to the stratosphere.

The Market for Chlorofluorocarbons: Growth and Diversification

In addition to the continuing scientific work, the EPA also sponsored
research by the Rand Corporation on the economic consequences of
broad-based CFC regulation. Because CFCs are nontoxic, nonflam-
mable, and chemically inert and score very high on thermal energy
absorption, the Rand report perhaps unsurprisingly indicated that
demand was growing steadily – and would continue to do so for the
next decade at least.[8] Overall, Rand estimated a 7 percent growth
rate in U.S. production.[9]

Most striking, though, was the variety of uses to which CFCs
were being put, even with aerosols out of the picture. CFCs serve
as a blowing agent in both flexible methane foams (used in bedding,
furniture, automobile seats, and carpeting) and rigid polyurethane
foams (used as an extremely efficient means of insulation for build-
ings and mobile refrigeration units). Furthermore, and an indication
of their versatility, they are a widely used blowing agent in non-
methane foams (polystyrene sheet products, which are fabricated into
foam trays, cups, egg cartons, and fast-food wrappers). In addition,
because of their exceptional thermodynamic qualities, CFCs are employed as the refrigerant in automobile air conditioners, industrial
and commercial air conditioners, and home refrigerators and freezers.
They are also an important solvent. In particular, they are highly
valued by electronics and aerospace industries as a precision clean-
ing agent for printed circuit boards, for scientific instruments, and
in a variety of contamination-controlled environments.

Obviously, not all of these product areas were growing at the same
rate. And as might be expected, the feasibility of product substitu-
tion for CFCs varies from one use to another. Other characteristics
of the CFC market that are critical to risk/growth projections de-
serve mention too, even if they need not be spelled out here: (1) different members of the CFC family – with corresponding differences in
ozone depletion potential – are used in various end products; (2) some
uses of CFCs involve immediate emission, while others contribute
to the "bank" of CFCs trapped until the end product is destroyed;
and (3) some CFCs contain hydrogen atoms, which appear to decrease the ozone-depleting potential significantly (both the NAS

and Rand excluded these nonhalogenated CFCs from their primary analyses).

What seemed crystal clear, however, was that the admirable properties of CFCs had created a competitive edge in many fields of use — a preference that they were not about to lose. Rand projected aggregate U.S. emissions by 1990 at more than double the existing level, with flexible foams, solvents, and rigid foams growing at an especially dramatic pace — well in excess of the estimated overall increase of 7 percent annually.

Thus the economic data underscored the import of the scientific findings. If the NAS's main conclusion — 16.5 percent depletion at steady-state 1977 emission levels — was reasonably accurate, the biological impact of continuing uncontrolled growth in CFC use would be devastating. Viewed in this context, the EPA's responsibility under the Clean Air Act to consider further regulatory action seemed clear. The critical question was what form the action might take.

The Process of Policy Formation

AGENCY DECISIONMAKING STRUCTURE

Typically, the main responsibility for proposing new EPA regulations resided in the "substantive" program offices: Air and Waste Management, Water and Hazardous Materials, and Toxic Substances (OTS). In the case of CFCs, the lead role had been assigned to Toxic Substances when the aerosal ban was imposed. And, with the assumption of that responsibility, OTS came to expect future regulatory efforts also to fall within its jurisdiction. Like all the other program offices, OTS carefully guarded its authority from "outside" usurpation.

In this environment, the Office of Planning and Management (OPM) — which had cross-cutting authority to suggest regulatory reform efforts within the bailiwick of any program office — was, quite naturally, viewed with considerable suspicion by the substantive offices. As might be expected, OPM staff were regarded as "overly theoretical," as "planning types" who lacked hands-on familiarity with the technical details of existing programs and the subtleties of long-standing personal relationships.[10]

In order to initiate reforms, then, the OPM had to tread carefully, seeking to share program responsibility without antagonizing the substantive program personnel. During the 1977–80 period, the office benefited greatly from the close personal relationship between its top official, the OPM assistant administrator, and the agency chief, the EPA administrator. Nonetheless, the administrator could not afford to alienate the assistant administrators in charge of substantive program offices, even if he had been predisposed to do so, and as a consequence the OPM needed to develop independent strategies that created leverage for exercising power in areas where it had strong views on programmatic reform.

One such strategy was exemplified by the Rand contract. By using OPM research funds, even before the aerosol ban, to finance a long-term major economic impact study of CFC regulation, OPM was able, in effect, to buy a piece of the action. Almost certainly the study would yield data of major importance to the agency. Moreover, by instructing Rand to focus on economic incentive strategies (discussed below), OPM was able to introduce its own policy preference as a serious agenda item for the agency.

As a consequence, OTS was unable to exercise singular authority over CFC regulation. Only by cooperating with OPM could it play some role in shaping the questions that Rand would address and thereby gain access to preliminary data – as it was generated – indicating the "latest word" on the potential effects of EPA regulation. Strong pressures thus developed to cooperate with OPM and share responsibility for related CFC activity.

At the same time, however, OTS jealously guarded its ultimate authority to write any new regulations governing CFC emissions. Its suspicions regarding OPM's motives on this score were provoked by the fact that there was a genuine difference of opinion between the regulatory philosophy in the two offices on the direction that any new regulatory initiative should take. Like the other substantive offices, OTS was accustomed to approaching regulatory problems through traditional command-and-control regulation.[11] In contrast, OPM was determined to promote economic efficiency goals through greater reliance on rules featuring market incentives whenever feasible.

In order to understand this difference better, we need to survey briefly the principal regulatory options that were available and the agency constituencies supporting each of them.

REGULATORY OPTIONS

It would have been feasible, of course, for the EPA to have chosen a traditional regulatory option. Following its earlier course, the agency could simply have imposed another product ban. But to do so would have been to rely on a very crude tool. Surely, it would be arbitrary to ban emissions of the product whose share of the CFC market most closely approximated the projected 7 percent growth increment solely on the grounds that such overall market growth was the agency's regulatory target. If instead the agency were to impose a ban through the use of traditional criteria – that the product or products selected were, on some basis, deemed to be "inessential" – the usual economic efficiency arguments would apply: why impose a collective judgment that a designated product is inessential rather than adopt a quota and allow the market to determine the shifts in demand? Politically as well as economically, there seemed to be no persuasive reason for pursuing this option. Within the agency, there was no discernible sentiment for another product ban.

Another option would have been to rely upon classic command-and-control regulations. There were many precedents. From the outset, the Clean Air Act has been implemented principally through federal and state regulations setting performance and design standards for various classes of polluters.[12] With respect to CFCs, the Rand report provided candidates for traditional regulations: recovery and recycling standards could be set for some flexible and rigid foam manufacturing; equipment standards could be established for solvent applications; and product substitutes could be mandated for certain refrigeration uses. While OTS never squarely endorsed a command-and-control strategy, key OTS officials showed considerable reluctance to abandon the customary approach.

Nonetheless, a strong case could be made against traditional regulatory standards. First of all, Rand concluded that some of the most important uses of CFCs – including auto air conditioners and building insulation – would not be touched by technology-based standards under the existing state of the art. Second, adoption of all currently feasible standards would have had a limited overall impact on emission reductions because, according to Rand, the rate of growth in CFC use would be diminished but growth would continue nevertheless. Finally, Rand's cost projections were consistent with what economists would expect: mandatory controls within the range of feasibility turned out to involve about double the compliance costs of a comparable level of control implemented through an economic incentive approach (the marketable-permits system discussed below). The reason for this disparity is that mandatory controls do not ordinarily reflect the most cost-effective means of achieving a target level of control. The agency has neither the data on production costs nor the ability to set selective standards that would be required to establish economically efficient limits.

For all of these reasons, the OPM was strongly opposed to the use of traditional command-and-control regulatory standards. Indeed, the office had been instrumental in working out a variety of economic incentives approaches, within the existing structure of the Clean Air Act, which constituted attempts to make air pollution control regulations more sensitive to market forces.[13] Concomitantly, an important reason that the OPM funded the Rand study was to generate a full-scale comparative analysis of the economic consequences of traditional regulations and a marketable-permits approach.

The OPM's policy views were not lost on OTS officials. Along with reservations about economic incentives options, the OTS feared that endorsement of such an approach might mean relinquishing to the OPM – in view of its economic expertise – the program office's traditional leadership role in framing agency regulations.

The third major option available to EPA, then, was an economic incentives approach. As mentioned above, in recent years the agency had experimented with such measures – principally under the Clean Air Act. Much was being written about bubbles, offsets, and the banking of emissions reductions – strategies designed to achieve greater economic efficiency in controlling air pollution.[14] Despite a great deal of discussion, however, a marketable-permits system had yet to be implemented. For a variety of reasons, the OPM viewed CFC regulation as an excellent candidate for the maiden venture.[15]

In contrast to the other regulatory control options, a marketable-permits system would allow the agency to exercise precise control over the aggregate output of CFCs. A quota could be set, imposing a target level of emissions, and a corresponding number of permits would then be issued for the use of CFCs. The permits could be written in terms of a standard permit pound, based on chlorine content, the ozone-depleting constituent of CFCs. Trading in permits, once issued, could be openly allowed among users of the various types of CFCs. Since chlorine content varies among types of use, those products dependent on CFCs that had a greater ozone-depleting potential presumably would incur a correspondingly greater cost of materials.

The basic objective of the permits system, obviously, would be to allocate the costs of scarcity through a market mechanism to the uses that are most highly valued, thereby substituting a private system of resource allocation for agency determinations of either "essentiality" or feasible design standards. Such a system fit perfectly into the prevailing regulatory philosophy at the OPM: to find ways of maximizing the value of industrial output under any given set of environmental controls.

THE PROCESS OF DECISION

OTS recalcitrance was matched by industry skepticism. Because a marketable-permits system was untested and potentially expensive, major chemical manufacturers and users were uneasy. More fundamentally, they maintained the position that *no* further regulation was necessary under the prevailing circumstances of scientific uncertainty. These arguments, presented to the OTS by the chemical manufacturers in a series of informal meetings, bolstered the position taken there that the agency should think twice about further regulatory action – especially if it were to involve a new regulatory approach.

In the midst of this ongoing debate, in December 1979, the NAS reports were published, indicating graver risks to the stratospheric ozone layer than had previously been expected. The agency came under renewed pressure, at a minimum, to propose new regulations for comment and discussion.[16] Still, the designated work team from the OTS and the OPM moved cautiously, in an atmosphere of mutual suspicion. At every step, the question of who was in charge surfaced. When the Rand study group submitted its preliminary draft, many hours were spent haggling over whether the OTS or the OPM would take the lead in analyzing and aggregating the interagency comments that were to be transmitted back to Rand. At a later point, when the Rand group made its formal presentation, tensions arose over the agenda for the meeting. Each office feared that the other would use the occasion to establish its own hegemony over the forthcoming regulatory effort. When a CFC work group was established – principally an exercise in window dressing, meant to signal "activity" on the CFC front to outsiders (both in the EPA and in other agencies) – considerable jockeying for position occurred, as both offices strove to give the appearance of being in charge. If industry representatives appeared at the agency, haggling took place over the composition of the EPA group at the meeting.

In this atmosphere, very little progress was made until outside events forced a joinder of issue. In mid-April 1980, the deputy administrator was scheduled to attend an international CFC meeting in Oslo, where the participating countries were expected to indicate their official views. In early March, the OTS and the OPM were suddenly told that they had one month to prepare a decision memorandum to the administrator (and deputy administrator), indicating the executive position of the United States on CFC emissions. Under the pressure of an external deadline, the Oslo meeting, it thus became essential for the agency to take a position that it could support publicly.

As might be expected, however, the principal concern of the administrator was not with the means of implementing a decision to impose new CFC regulations. On the contrary, the issue of regulatory design – traditional versus economic incentives, which had been the preoccupation of both the OTS and the OPM – was of distinctly secondary interest to the administrator. The tail had been wagging the dog. In Oslo, the key questions about U.S. policy would be whether the EPA considered new regulatory controls warranted and, if so, at what level they should be imposed. The OTS and OPM analysts, pressing ahead to devise a regulatory approach, had for the most part assumed that new regulatory controls were needed and had largely ignored the issue of how stringent those controls should be.

Interestingly, once these critical issues had been directly confronted, they were in fact resolved with far less disagreement and debate than the secondary questions of regulatory design. In large part, a consensus was reached with greater ease because of the absence of deeply felt philosophical differences comparable to the sharply divergent views on the regulatory design issue. However complex the threshold questions about the need for further regulation, they did not divide the agency on ideological lines.

Nonetheless, the issues of whether and how much to regulate involved highly debatable substantive considerations. In addition to scientific uncertainty about the ozone depletion theory, the issue of whether to regulate was greatly complicated by the fact that CFC emissions recognize no national boundaries. Scientists believe that a pound released on the other side of the globe is potentially as damaging to the ozone layer above the United States as a pound released here. And the data on worldwide use suggest the magnitude of the problem; as indicated earlier, extraterritorial emissions were estimated to be growing at 9 percent annually.

This growth rate had to be interpreted in conjunction with another salient fact. The United States accounted for about a third of total world emissions – a substantial percentage but by no means a controlling one from an environmental perspective. Working with these and related figures, EPA calculated that the difference in eventual steady-state ozone depletion if the United States immediately reduced its emissions by 70 percent, compared with a failure to take any action – assuming in both cases that 1990 emission levels, once reached, were maintained indefinitely – would amount to a reduction from only 32 percent to 26 percent in stratospheric ozone depletion as long as the rest of the world did not enact controls. In short, if the magnitude of the problem was correctly perceived, international action would be essential.

In view of these major obstacles, once EPA policy analysts focused on the issue of whether regulation was warranted (shortly before the April deadline for the decision memo), they were faced with three threshold options: wait and see, no growth, and substantial reductions. At the time, the first option was rejected without substantial disagreement. The reasoning was that, while unilateral U.S. action would achieve only a limited impact, a total failure to act could easily contribute to a reciprocal response abroad. However it might be phrased, a wait-and-see approach would signal a lack of genuine concern – to domestic CFC industries and foreign producer nations alike. Moreover, European producers, accounting for roughly another third of total emissions, had taken at least some action in response to the earlier U.S. ban. They agreed to a partial ban on aerosols, a freeze on overall production capacity, and a commitment to discuss further emission reductions in formal meetings.

Still, there was no immediate prospect of genuine international cooperative effort, and as a consequence, the agency also rejected the substantial reductions option as a present strategy. A consensus quickly emerged that it might well backfire, lulling foreign producers into thinking that the problem had been diminished by unilateral U.S. action to the point where it could be ignored for a while.

Recognizing these considerations, the decision memo – and later the advance notice of proposed rule making – proposed a short-term freeze at current production levels, linked to substantial reductions in the future when corresponding steps were taken by foreign producer countries (assuming, obviously, that the ozone depletion theory maintained its credibility).

Interestingly, in devising a politically pragmatic approach for dealing with the tangled world of international politics, the agency sidestepped the need to commit itself to an analytically supported figure on "acceptable" ozone depletion. A moment's reflection on the earlier discussion of risks and benefits should be sufficient to demonstrate the boldness it would take to assert that, say, an ozone depletion level of 2 percent, as distinguished from 5 percent or 8 percent, was *the* appropriate target. On the benefits side, the scientific data on human and nonhuman consequences of ultraviolet radiation, let alone the calibration of the ozone depletion theory itself, are so imprecise that any quantitative monetary estimate of the avoidable harm would be a sham. Similarly, the estimated economic costs of various levels of CFC control are based on industry projections that constitute sheer guesswork about market responses to contrived scenarios. Indeed, Rand was unwilling to supply even the roughest projections at levels of control departing in any significant measure from current patterns of CFC use.

Cost-benefit analysis would thus have yielded a target figure for acceptable ozone depletion based largely on the illusion of precise information. To complicate matters even more, it is by no means evident that an emissions reduction target should be based on a cost-benefit methodology. Like pollution control generally under the Clean Air Act, the statute appears to anticipate a more limited role for economic considerations in determining the appropriate level of CFC emissions. The agency is to "take into account the feasibility and the costs" of further regulatory controls when ozone depletion "may reasonably be anticipated to endanger public health or welfare."[17] The language parallels that in other parts of the Clean Air Act provisions where the costs of regulation are to be taken into account but are not precisely balanced against anticipated health risks.

Clearly, the agency is afforded minimal guidance in deciding what is an acceptable level of risk by such a standard. The vague statutory mandate thus undoubtedly bolstered the agency's inclination to set a level of control – a production freeze at existing levels – that would simply keep the current situation from worsening and to postpone indefinitely the perplexing problem of establishing and justifying an "acceptable tolerance."

By the time that the OTS and the OPM had reached agreement on a production freeze as the optimal level of control, divisiveness over the strategy of implementation had diminished considerably.

The staff economists in OTS who were assigned actual responsibility for working with OPM analysts on the decision memo became increasingly bold about challenging the traditionalist sentiments of their supervisors. Command-and-control adherents in OTS were thus increasingly isolated. As the decision memo moved through a number of drafts and work meetings, the analysts stubbornly pressed the advantages of a marketable-permits design and the shortcomings of other alternatives. At the same time, they used the close rapport between the administrator and top OPM policymakers to reemphasize the agency's general commitment to economic incentives approaches. When the decision memo was finally sent to the administrator, various options were included – in order to "save face" within OTS – but a clear preference was expressed for the marketable-permits strategy. Afterward, the same approach was incorporated into the advance notice of proposed rule making. Within the agency, at least, the opposition to the reform proposal had been put to rest.

Regulatory Design: Some Final Thoughts

Clearly, the threshold question facing the EPA was whether further controls on CFC emissions were warranted. Relying on the available scientific data, the agency reached a preliminary decision – incorporated into its October 1980 advance notice of proposed rule making – that further regulation was justified.[18] In response, the agency received approximately 2,000 comments, mostly negative and primarily from producers and users of CFCs. Meanwhile, there was a change in leadership at the EPA after the presidential elections – which led to a sharp break with the past. An antiregulatory mood prevailed. At the same time, new scientific information appeared, leading to a temporary downward revision in the projected impact of CFC emissions on the ozone layer.[19]

It is difficult to say what role each of these factors played in the ultimate withdrawal of the regulatory proposal.[20] For present purposes, the question has only limited importance. I have attempted to describe the process of policy formation that led to the proposal of a rather bold regulatory reform, a ceiling on CFC use through a highly innovative implementation strategy – the marketable-permits approach. In this final section, I offer some thoughts, from an administrative perspective, on the strengths and weaknesses of the marketable-permits approach as a technique for implementing environmental controls. In doing so, I will continue to ground my comments in the CFC context.

In my view, there is a great deal to be said for the marketable-permits approach. First, it would create incentives for cost-justified technological controls on CFC emissions and for consumer shifts in demand to close substitutes for CFC-using products. Neither of these incentives is necessarily a by-product of command-and-control regulation. On the contrary, while a permits approach would lead CFC users to invest in control equipment or a substitute precursor product only if that option would be cheaper than reliance on CFCs—consequently affecting each CFC user differently, depending on its costs of production—a traditional regulatory standards approach would impose the same control requirements on every CFC user in a designated industrial category, irrespective of cost considerations for the particular firm.

In addition, a marketable-permits system would be relatively easy to enforce compared with a command-and-control system. Under the latter, an enforcement scheme would likely rely upon investigation and inspection techniques to ensure compliance with design and process standards. Because of the large number of industrial users, even a carefully designed system of audits and random spotchecks would probably involve substantial agency resources. In comparison, a marketable-permits system could be enforced principally by requiring that the five domestic producers of CFCs maintain adequate records of their sales.

Another advantage would be the greater flexibility that the system would give the agency in reacting to future developments. Consider the possibility that, at some future time, either scientific data or international political developments might make it advisable to adjust the domestic level of emissions. At that point, *any* agency response would probably be hotly contested. But adjustments in the flow of a permits pipeline would be less likely to be disruptive—both economically and politically—than having to reconsider design standards or selective bans.

From the EPA's standpoint, a marketable-permits approach had a much better chance of getting a decent trial on CFCs than in most other areas. For one thing, there would have been the significant benefit of operating in an area uncluttered by the dense tangle of statutory provisions and implementing regulations that so frequently ensnares efforts at regulatory innovation. Every venture under the

Clean Air Act must accommodate itself to this jungle. In contrast, apart from the aerosol ban, there was no regulatory framework for CFCs and, consequently, no built-in obstacles to a permits scheme.

In addition, the massive cloud that overhangs effective regulation of CFCs – the worldwide scope of the problem – had its silver lining on the domestic side: a nationwide trading market as contrasted with the limited regional and local markets that often undermine the effectiveness of air-quality control trading schemes. Finally, the very nature of CFCs is a distinctive attribute from an economic incentives standpoint. Unlike air pollutants that are an unwanted secondary consequence, a by-product of industrial processes, CFCs are an end product of a manufacturing process. As a result, the measurement problems that frequently plague proposals for pollution-related economic incentives – by making it unclear whether genuine emission reductions have been realized – would be virtually nonexistent in dealing with CFCs.

Most reform measures generate their own problems, and the marketable-permits system is no exception to the rule. One difficulty concerns the basic question whether the system would be implemented through an auction or an allocation scheme – a decision that the EPA left open in its proposal because of the difficult political and conceptual issues. Under an auction scheme, the EPA would sell off permits in a market that might be unrestricted or that could be limited to producers, to industrial users, or in a variety of other ways. Circumscribing the participants could cause problems at the political level; for example, the question could arise (largely hypothetical, in my estimation) as to whether environmental groups would be able to buy up permits in order to achieve greater than mandated limitations on emissions. Collusion is another possibility. Conceivably, large-scale participants might attempt to reap monopolistic profits from the permits market. But such practices seem highly unlikely, in view of the number of prospective participants and the profusion of uses to which the permits would be put.

If an auction system were chosen, other problems would arise as well. Because the EPA would generate revenues from the auction of permits, a legal question of statutory authorization arose. My own view was that the case law allowed the agency to collect funds as a secondary consequence of a regulatory scheme implemented principally as a control measure under the broad language of Section 157 of the Clean Air Act, but the issue was not free from doubt.[21]

Most critical of all, however, if the Rand study was correct, was the possibility that the auction revenues might be so large as to cause serious political and economic repercussions. While Rand estimated compliance costs at about half those imposed by "feasible" mandatory controls, it concluded that the transfer payments generated by purchase of the needed permits would be massive—more than $1.5 billion over a ten-year period even if emissions limits were at the relatively modest level equivalent to achievable cutbacks under feasible command-and-control regulations. Note that these transfer payments, unlike compliance expenditures, are not a real resource cost; they are simply a transfer of revenues from one set of pockets to another, from the purchasers of CFC permits to the government. For this very reason, the politics of implementation could be complex and controversial.

Similar knotty problems would have been encountered if the EPA had selected an allocation scheme. At the outset, the transfer payments problem reappears, posing a dilemma over distribution of the permits. If allocation were to producers, they would pocket the wealth created by property rights in a scarce resource which they would be supplying to CFC users. A serious equity issue obviously arises. On the other hand, if allocation were directly to CFC users, the transfer payments would probably be drastically reduced. As long as the allocation reflected historical patterns of usage, trading among these end-product assemblers—which would be the exclusive source of explicit transfer payments—would probably be relatively limited in the initial round. But allocation to users (whose numbers are in the thousands and whose claims to special equitable consideration would be staggering) might well create an administrative nightmare.

Without a doubt, these distributional issues raise serious problems. And the details of implementation are not insignificant: would the permits, for instance, be for a limited term, a single year, or some intermediate life? This question alone is inextricably related to the distributional issues just raised. Nonetheless, while the agency would have been obligated to give careful consideration to these questions if the advance notice had been transformed into a proposed regulation, there is no reason to think the problems are insoluble.

Similar caution would have to be exercised in defining the parameters of the system. On the domestic side, there is a "second-best" concern, to use economic jargon.[22] If the permits system raised the price of CFCs as compared with riskier unregulated product substitutes, it may be that no regulation would be better than a partial scheme. And some of the chief substitutes for certain CFC uses do pose problems of toxicity and flammability. So the issue has more than merely academic interest.

On the international side, there are questions of how imports and exports would be handled. Exports represent one dilemma. If they are restricted by a permits scheme, will foreign producers simply step into the breach, nullifying the impact of regulatory control at the cost of domestic producers? Imports pose another problem. Would they be incorporated into the permits system, subjected to a separate allocation, or treated otherwise? Fortunately, because of transportation cost constraints, both imports and exports accounted for a relatively small percentage of domestic production and use. Again, however, the issues required serious further consideration.

In the final analysis, there were no easy answers to the problems posed by CFC emissions. The ozone depletion theory is not unassailable; a measure of scientific uncertainty will continue to exist in the near future at least. The reactions of foreign nations to various options that the United States might have exercised could not be predicted with great confidence. And each of the regulatory control strategies that the EPA might have employed was open to debate. Under the circumstances, it is perhaps surprising that the agency moved as decisively to a preliminary decision as it did – even if the internal process of policy formation reveals the somewhat haphazard impact of personalities and outside events.

Notes

1. On economic incentives approaches, see generally F. Anderson, A. Kneese, P. Reed, R. Stevenson, and S. Taylor, *Environmental Improvement through Economic Incentives* (Baltimore: Johns Hopkins University Press, 1977).

2. See Clean Air Act Amendments of 1977, 42 U.S. Code, secs. 7450–59.

3. *Federal Register* 43 (March 1978), 11501.

4. National Academy of Sciences, *Stratospheric Ozone Depletion by Halocarbons: Chemistry and Transport* (Washington, D.C.: NAS, 1979).

5. Ibid., p. 1.

6. Ibid., pp. 174–78.

7. National Academy of Sciences, *Protection Against Depletion of Stratospheric Ozone by Chlorofluorocarbons* (Washington, D.C.: NAS, 1979).

8. *Economic Implications of Regulating Chlorofluorocarbon Emissions from Nonaerosol Applications* (Santa Monica, Calif.: Rand, 1980).

9. Ibid.; data obtained by the EPA from the Chemical Manufacturers' Association at about the same time indicated a probable 9 percent growth rate in foreign production.

10. This was in contrast to the substantive program offices, where scientists and engineers were prominent among the decisionmakers. OPM was staffed largely by economists and public management professionals.

11. On command-and-control regulation, see Anderson et al., *Environmental Improvement.*

12. For a critical overview, see Pedersen, "Why the Clean Air Act Works Badly," *Univ. of Pa. Law Review* 129 (1981), 1059.

13. For discussion and citation of numerous references, see F. Anderson, D. Mandelker, and A. Tarlock, *Environmental Protection: Law and Policy* (Boston: Little, Brown, 1984), pp. 263–69.

14. Ibid.

15. For an earlier discussion of the CFC marketable-permits strategy, see Rabin, "Ozone Depletion Revisited: EPA Regulation of Chlorofluorocarbons," *Regulation* 5 (March/April 1981), 32f. seq.

16. Much of this pressure was anticipatory or self-generated. Although the NAS findings were widely publicized, no organized lobbying or litigation group monitored developments in the ozone depletion area with the intensity that was afforded to pesticides or sulfur dioxide emissions. Indeed, industry provided the most consistent source of political pressure on the CFC issue – principally the Chemical Manufacturers' Association and the CFC producers. Nonetheless, the ozone depletion issue involves the type of risk – namely a potentially catastrophic instance of irreversible harm – that often triggers ad hoc political activity with relatively short lead time for agency response.

17. See Clean Air Act Amendments of 1977, sec. 157 (b).

18. See "EPA Advance Notice of Proposed Rulemaking, Ozone-Depleting Chlorofluorocarbons: Proposed Production Restriction," *Federal Register* 45, no. 196 (1980), 66726–34.

19. By 1981, the reaction rate data indicated that the NAS estimate might need to be revised downward to 7–12 percent steady-state depletion at then current emission levels. See Engelmann, "A Look at Some Issues before an Ozone Convention," *Environ. Policy and Law* 8 (1982) 49, 50, which reports on findings published in October 1981, by the Coordinating Committee on the Ozone Layer of the United Nations Environmental Programme. Even earlier, however, shortly after the Reagan administration assumed control, the EPA decided against further action on the advance notice of proposed rule making.

In 1987, the tide appeared to turn strongly in favor of further regulation. With the published findings of a "hole" in the ozone layer over Antarctica, public concern was aroused. Federal officials began to press, once again, for a freeze on emissions at current levels. See "Chlorine Found at High Level over Antarctica," *New York Times,* 10 March 1987, p. 13. Late in 1987, a 31-nation treaty was negotiated (with U.S. participation) that would initially stabilize CFC emissions and then gradually reduce them to half of 1986 levels. The most recent projections suggest that even with successful implementation of the treaty, substantial ozone depletion will occur within the next few decades. See "Even with Action Today, Ozone Loss Will Increase," *New York Times,* 20 March 1988, p. 1.

20. It bears notice, however, that the withdrawal of the CFC initiative was one of a wide variety of recently adopted health and safety regulations that were overturned at the outset of the Reagan administration. See generally Rabin, "Federal Regulation in Historical Perspective," *Stanford Law Review* 38 (1986), 1189, 1315–26.

21. Compare Federal Energy Administration *v.* Algonquin SNG, 426 U.S. 548 (1976), with National Cable Television *v.* U.S., 415 U.S. 336 (1974).

22. For general discussion of the second-best problem, see Lipsey and Lancaster, "The General Theory of Second Best," *Review of Economic Studies* 24 (1956), 11.

6

The Development of Emissions Trading in U.S. Air Pollution Regulation

Errol Meidinger

D URING THE PAST decade the legal-administrative framework by which air pollution is regulated in the United States has undergone a significant change. In the early 1970s the framework was founded on a detailed system of uniform rules. Emissions limits were set and applied to categories of pollution sources in discrete administrative proceedings. Starting in the mid-1970s and continuing to the present, the system has been gradually transformed through a series of related regulatory initiatives into one that allows considerable *trading* of pollution allowances among polluters. Under the "emissions trading" programs, emissions limits may now effectively be set by polluters themselves, through market and internal transactions. The rise of emissions trading represents a significant transformation of applied regulation and may suggest future currents of regulatory change in other areas.

This chapter reviews the development of emissions trading, proposes an explanation, and suggests some potential implications. Perhaps its central arguments are in the proposed explanation. The adoption of emissions trading can be explained partly by the complex, highly detailed nature of prior Clean Air Act regulation, partly by the cost-savings market mechanisms offer, and partly by efforts of regulatory agencies to preserve their legitimacy in a period of recession and conservative public opinion trends. But these factors are not sufficient to explain the persistence of the market mechanism movement in the face of substantial obstacles. A key force in the process has been the development and spread of a distinctive *regulatory culture*. Promoted primarily by recent graduates of law and public policy programs, this culture emphasizes that: (1) while *science* is critical to understanding the impacts of regulatory policies, it cannot form the basis for choosing them, (2) regulatory decisions are inherently and necessarily merely *compromises* among contending interests, (3) the goal of the regulatory agency is thus a *stable,* predictable *framework* within which the pull and haul of interests can take place and through which compromises can be implemented, and (4) the content and legitimacy of regulatory policies should be based as much as possible on the interests and compromises of *private parties.* While the success of this orientation seems attributable in significant part to the inherent complexity of air pollution regulation, which limits effective discourse to a very small group of experts, and to the organizational location of the regulatory entrepreneurs promoting it, it is simultaneously connected with larger ideological tendencies and a general belief in markets in American society.

At present it remains difficult to evaluate the significance of emissions trading. While it might be a desirable development for purposes of implementing agreed-upon pollution control goals, it also raises two significant problems. First, mechanisms like emissions trading may imply severe limits for the practice of politics, that is, for the creation and articulation of collective values with which to choose social goals. Second, they may serve to obscure the distributional implications of policy choices. Before making these arguments, however, it is important to provide some background on market mechanisms, traditional regulation, and the Clean Air Act. (Readers familiar with this information may wish to go directly to the section explaining emissions trading.)

THE CONCEPT OF MARKET MECHANISMS

The market mechanisms concepts which provide the underpinnings for the emissions trading program involve two basic ideas. The first is that the allocation of pollution control should be inversely related to its costs. Thus polluters for whom pollution control is cheap should reduce emissions greatly and polluters for whom control is expensive should reduce them little or not at all. Accordingly, then, as if a market allocated pollution, any given level of pollution control would be achieved at the lowest feasible total cost of society (as paid by polluters and reflected in the costs of the products and services they provide to society).

Second, the pollution control to be carried out should not exceed the price society is willing to pay. At some point the cost of additional pollution control will exceed the value of the amenities that members of society are willing to give up for it, and at this point no more pollution control should occur. At this optimal point, no one would be willing to trade anything she has (or could get with the same amount of resources) to obtain any further pollution control. In the jargon, the marginal cost of increased pollution control would equal the marginal benefit. At this point, too, the price of pollution control would hover until tastes changed, pollution control grew cheaper, or something else happened to alter either the cost or the value of pollution control.

The problem with this market ideal is that there is no good way of ascertaining the price of pollution control. There is not, and cannot be, a market for pollution control. We cannot go to a store and buy pollution control as we can buy, say, a hamburger. It would do me little good to go to a polluter and pay for a reduction in emissions of ten pounds of sulfur dioxide per year. Not only would I derive little actual benefit from the reduction, but I would share any benefit with a multitude of other people who paid nothing for it. Moreover, any other polluter could increase emissions and wipe out the benefits for which I had paid. Then, too, pollution costs lives and years of lives, and lives are very difficult to price. Finally, it is not at all clear that people should have to pay to avoid pollution; a strong market argument can be made that they should be paid if they must suffer it.

Nonetheless, even if the market cannot be used to decide how much pollution there should be, it does not follow that the market cannot be used to decide who should have the privilege of creating whatever level of pollution society will tolerate. American regulatory discourse has focused on two means of so using the market—emissions charges and marketable permits. Emissions charges would require polluters to pay a fixed price for every unit of pollution emitted. Assuming that polluters are economically rational, they would pay only those emissions charges that are lower than the cost of pollution control; they would therefore reduce emissions until the unit cost of further reductions exceeded the unit tax. And of course, controls would be concentrated among polluters for whom reductions are cheapest and emissions among those for whom reductions are most expensive, thus minimizing the total social cost of pollution control.

Marketable permits would seek the same end in a slightly different fashion. Instead of taxing all emissions, permits would be required for all emissions. Only a limited number of permits would be available. Therefore, those polluters for whom emissions controls are most expensive would buy up the permits, while those for whom controls are least expensive would reduce emissions. Each form of market mechanism has intrinsic advantages and disadvantages which I need not discuss here.[1] The important point is that before the emissions trading program, an effort to create marketable permits, neither mechanism had been attempted in the United States or had even been seriously discussed in the policy arena. To understand why, and to understand the forms which have actually been attempted, it is necessary to place the market mechanism debate in historical context.

THE REGULATORY BACKDROP: TRADITIONAL ECONOMIC REGULATION

The idea of regulation as we understand it today implies a social world divided into state and economy, a world in which the state "intervenes" in the economy to achieve certain goals which the economy is not achieving on its own. While the conception of separate economic and political spheres is less than two centuries old, the extensive use of state regulation in the United States is only about half that age. In the last third of the nineteenth century, after a long period of widely proclaimed laisser-faire policy, the relative incomes of farmers and many other laborers underwent a steady, long-term decline, while the fortunes of the railroads, grain interests, and later the oil and steel interests skyrocketed (for example, Hughes, 1977; Reiter and Hughes, 1981). Not surprisingly, calls for regulation to "curb the abuses" of the free market grew louder and more widespread as the successive social waves of the Greenback, Granger, and Populist movements crested.

The social compromise that had been sketched out by the turn of the century and became a veritable regulatory archetype during the New Deal was what is now often called "economic regulation." It involved creating an expert agency to oversee a sector of the economy, for example, the Interstate Commerce Commission (ICC) for heavy transportation, the Federal Power Commission (FPC) for energy, the Civil Aeronautics Board (CAB) for aviation, or the Federal

Communications Commission (FCC) for radio and television.[2] To be sure, they each had their particular problems and peculiar statutory structure, but they shared broad patterns of authority and assumptions. Most were to be independent agencies subject to minimal legislative or executive interference. All were to be staffed by experts, who were to examine the problems of their sectors objectively and to promulgate rational solutions. These solutions were to be implemented through regulatory control of entry into the industry and of prices charged for services. Thus the public would be charged only "reasonable" prices, but the regulated industry would have the comfort of knowing that it would receive a "fair rate of return" and protection from "destructive competition." The agencies were given substantial discretion to determine what these terms meant and were generally asked simply to regulate in the "public interest."[3]

With the exception of occasional scandals over one form of graft or another, these traditional agencies lived a comfortable life from the New Deal through the late 1950s, when significant doubts began to shadow the model of the independent regulatory commission. The doubts came from many directions. Such scholars as Marver Bernstein (1955) found the agencies getting old and rigid, caught in past ways of doing things, unattuned to new information. He and others saw the agencies as having been "captured" by the industries they were supposed to regulate, as having at heart not the public interest but the interests of the railroads, power companies, airlines, and so on (for example, Huntington, 1952; McConnell, 1966). Conservative economists portrayed agencies either as fostering cartels whose moderate monopoly profits kept industries stable and laborers content while overcharging consumers (for example, Stigler, 1956; Kamerschen, 1966) or as so overregulating industries as to cause inadequate profits, underinvestment, and inadequate supply (for example, MacAvoy, 1962).

At the same time, the agencies were coming to be seen as insensitive to values outside the narrow confines of industrial commodity production. The FPC, for example, was compiling a record of disdain for the costs of environmental degradation that would be notable by today's standards. The same is true of the Nuclear Regulatory Commission. Moreover, the 1960s, perhaps in part because of the agencies' poor records, brought a steady, inscrutable decline in public willingness to trust expertise. At the same time, congressional staffs were growing rapidly and filling with experts able to follow the activities of agencies at relatively close range. Finally, the last half of the decade saw an explosion of distrust in government and in "the system" (an interlinked network of government and large corporations) as a result of the Vietnam War. Environmental degradation, too, came to be seen as having assumed crisis proportions. In this milieu the Clean Air Act (CAA) was born.

SOCIAL REGULATION AND THE CLEAN AIR ACT

The 1970 U.S. Clean Air Act probably ranks as one of the more complicated statutes yet produced by a modern industrial state. The reason is in part that air pollution is a very complicated problem, and in part that the act was created in a climate of great distrust of both agencies and industries.

Social Regulation Structurally, the CAA falls in a paradigm which has come to be called (mostly at the instance of economists) "social" regulation. It differs from traditional economic regulation in several ways. First, rather than regulating a particular sector of the economy, the agency regulates a particular type of problem across sectors (see Weidenbaum, 1980). Second, rather than regulating entry, services, and prices, it regulates particular production practices both within firms and across sectors. The regulatory agency is then primarily responsible not for allowing fair rates of return to particular types of firms but, for example, for controlling pollution in society at large. Third, the implementing agency is typically located within the executive branch rather than being given formally independent status. While the difference between regular executive agencies and independent commissions is not as clear or significant as the labels might suggest, the choice of the executive form reflects a rising presumption that agencies should be subject to established channels of political authority. Fourth, however, the agency is also subjected to a *new* channel of political authority: parties other than regulatees are given rights to participate in agency proceedings, obtain judicial review of agency decisions, enforce agency-set standards on regulatees, and, in many cases, force the agency to promulgate standards or act in other specified ways.[4]

Although this chapter will not explore the implications of these expanded "third-party," or "private" rights of action in any depth (but see Boyer and Meidinger, 1986), it is important to understand that they involve not just expanded rights of participation but also ex-

plicit substantive requirements to which the new interests may hold
the agency. Very roughly, these standards can be divided into two
forms: scientific criteria and action deadlines. Because of high levels
of scientific uncertainty, definitional ambiguities, and the like, scientific criteria have in practice allowed considerable standard-setting
discretion, but they have also acted as constraints.[5] Action deadlines,
while generally not specifying actual outcomes, have also acted as
constraints on agency discretion by (1) reducing agency control over
agenda setting and (2) forcing agencies to take action (which is then
judicially reviewable) in circumstances where political pressures, scientific uncertainties, or simple inertia would otherwise prevent or
delay it.

While the above features reflect significant structural departures
(*contra* Lowi, 1984), the CAA also showed important continuities with
traditional regulation. Two of the most important were heavy reliance on administrative expertise and use of uniform, categorical rules
as basic regulatory building blocks. The development of emissions
trading greatly reduces reliance on uniform rules. To understand this
change, it is helpful to understand the key provisions of the CAA.

The Clean Air Act

National Ambient Air Quality Standards. The CAA decided the
basic question of how much pollution is to be allowed by directing
the newly created Environmental Protection Agency (EPA) to set
nationwide *ambient air quality standards* (NAAQS) for major, widespread pollutants having adverse effects on public health or welfare.
In essence these NAAQS set limits on the total concentrations of
selected pollutants allowed in the atmosphere over any given period
of time. "Primary" NAAQS were to be health based and sufficiently
stringent to prevent new injury or aggravation of preexisting injury
even to unusually sensitive members of society. "Secondary" NAAQS
were to prevent other negative effects on public welfare, such as diminished soil or water productivity. The primary NAAQS requirements were interpreted as prohibiting EPA from considering the
costs of attainment in setting them; thus the utilitarian tradeoff
analysis of how much pollution should be allowed was explicitly rejected in favor of an absolute, health-based standard.[6] Moreover, the
agency did not have open discretion to consider which pollutants
would be subject to NAAQS. The detailed terms of the CAA required
it to promulgate standards for the six "criteria" pollutants on which

some technical data had already been compiled under predecessor statutes and to do so within 120 days of CAA enactment. The agency managed to meet that feverish deadline, but in the subsequent years only one new ambient standard has been promulgated (for lead, under court order) and only one has been significantly revised (although revision of two others should soon be complete).[7] The CAA has many similar discretion-limiting and action-forcing requirements.

State Implementation Plans. The nature of the NAAQS meant that particular locales might be "in attainment" with regard to some ambient pollutants and "out of attainment" with regard to others. In theory, it was up to the states to devise plans ("state implementation plans," or SIPs) for bringing nonattainment areas into attainment and for preventing attainment areas (also called "prevention of significant deterioration," or PSC, areas) from sliding more than a set increment toward nonattainment.[8] But they were to do so under significant federal constraints. First, the CAA set a 1975 deadline for attainment of most primary NAAQS; construction of major new pollution sources or modifications was prohibited where it would jeopardize meeting the deadline. (The deadline was generally not met and was moved back.)[9] Second, the states were to develop SIPs and submit them for EPA approval within nine months of the promulgation of NAAQS. To be approved, the SIPs had to meet manifold requirements, including (1) specific "emissions limitations, schedules, and timetables for compliance," (2) monitoring and data gathering programs; and (3) assurances of adequate state personnel, funding, and legal enforcement authority. The clear intent of the statute was that states should carry out their regulatory activities by the use of emissions limitations and control equipment requirements for particular sources and classes of sources.

Third, two major types of new sources were to be subject to uniform federally set standards; states could be more stringent if they wished but not less.

Federal New Source Performance Standards. Major new *stationary* sources, and major modifications to existing ones, were to be subject to categorical emissions standards promulgated by the EPA. These new source performance standards (NSPS) were to be tailored to particular categories of sources and to be set at emission levels based on "application of the best system of emission reduction which . . . the Administrator determines has been adequately demonstrated." Unlike the NAAQS, they could reflect cost considerations, but because they were to be uniform for all sources in a given category, only estimated *average* costs would be reflected. In setting these NSPS, and especially in reviewing state emissions regulations in SIPs, the EPA tended to favor quite detailed regulations, with limits set for each individual emission point (often a particular subprocess) in a manufacturing complex rather than for the complex as a whole. The same was generally true of standards set by states for types of stationary sources not directly covered by EPA standards. Such detailed regulations, it was apparently believed, would make emissions limits clearer and easier to enforce.

Federal Mobile Source Standards. New *mobile* sources (cars, trucks, airplanes, and so forth) were to meet standards directly set by Congress. Partly in response to the cozy relationship that the old line agencies were seen to have developed with major regulated industries, Congress gave the EPA very little discretion with regard to setting automobile standards. Rather, it specified in the statute what emissions reductions were to be achieved over what period of time (although these deadlines were later relaxed in several cases).

The CAA's focus on uniform, detailed, source-specific emissions regulation is inconsistent with the forms of market mechanism regulation outlined above. The basic framework of the CAA therefore makes it difficult to allow individual sources to implement emissions controls most consistent with their particular cost structures. Despite this formidable structural constraint, the EPA has over the past decade made very significant headway toward transforming the CAA from a categorically uniform, detailed emissions-limit framework to a marketable-permits framework. This movement may be a remarkable demonstration of the agency's ability to create discretion where none was intended. At the same time, as will become evident below, it seems possible that the very creation of the market mechanism framework may significantly curtail the EPA's ability to marshal and exercise discretion in the future.

THE RISE OF MARKET MECHANISMS IN CAA REGULATION

The Academic Discussion The conceptual foundation for market mechanisms in pollution control had been sketched out in the largely hypothetical speculations of economists decades before the passage of the CAA. Indeed, as early as 1862 John Stuart Mill noted that, "if from any revolution in nature the atmosphere became too scanty for the consumption, . . . air might acquire a very high marketable value." Pigou had developed an elaborate argument for using pollution taxes to equilibrate "private" and "social" costs by the 1920s. The modern era in resource economics as applied to "fugitive" resources like air arguably began with an elegant analysis in 1954 by H. S. Gordon of fisheries as common property resources. That study was initially followed by a small number of comments and minor studies, and then in the early 1960s by R. H. Coase's extremely influential article in which he argued that private bargaining will eliminate externalities in a far larger class of cases than is commonly believed, and that government intervention is therefore much less often justified than is commonly believed.

Significant battle lines had thus been drawn in the general terrain of the then-reigning welfare economics. Accordingly, when the physical environment came to be widely perceived as a serious and growing problem in the last half of the decade, a wide-scale debate ensued. The debate was framed in terms of the relative desirability of emissions charges, marketable permits, private bargaining, and traditional regulation for handling pollution problems. By the end of the decade, emissions charges had, perhaps not surprisingly in light of the developed economic literature on taxation as a policy instrument, emerged as the alternative most favored in the literature. Traditional regulation, again not surprisingly, was the least favored alternative, since it relied on directives rather than incentives. And while most economists had come to believe that systematic state intervention was necessary to handle air pollution problems, a small but hardy band continued to assert the superiority of private bargaining. Marketable permits had received little serious attention at this time. They seem to have been viewed as an intriguing but somewhat eccentric and uninspiring alternative.[10]

The Statute   The economics debate and literature had very little influence on the design of the CAA. The possibility of effluent charges was raised in the 1971 debates over proposed federal water pollution control legislation, but the Clean Water Act eventually imitated the CAA's use of uniform emissions controls and detailed regulatory procedures. Very fragmentary evidence suggests that this choice reflected the views that it would be morally wrong to allow people to "pollute for a fee" and that a charge system would be harder to implement than an emissions control system.

In any event, at the genesis of the CAA, the concepts of narrow discretion, uniform rule regulation and market mechanism regulation stood in a complex but only partly antagonistic relationship to each other. Although it was true that the chosen system of regulation reflected distrust of "private" economic decisionmaking, while the alternative made such decisionmaking a central tenet of faith, it was also true that both conceptions reflected a deep-seated distrust of administrative discretion and sought to maximize the predictability of the EPA's regulatory activities to the greatest possible degree. As things are working out, a marketable-permits system seems to be rising from the regulatory cracks of the narrow discretion, uniform rule system. Many important details of the process are obscure, and even what is reasonably well known is too involved to recount here, but the general contours of the process are easy enough to map.[11]

The Early Bubble Policy.   The first concrete move toward transforming the framework apparently came only a year after the CAA went into effect, when the smelting industry and several officials in the Nixon administration proposed to use what eventually became known as the "bubble" concept. The basic idea of the bubble concept is that a given plant with any number of discrete emissions points should be envisioned for regulatory purposes as existing under a bubble with a single hole in the top and that the only issue of interest to regulators should be the total emissions coming out of it. The smelters used this concept to argue that they should not be subject to the strict new NSPS emissions limitations for major plant modifications if the total quantity of pollutants coming out of the bubble did not increase. They thus hoped to avoid installing costly new control equipment for plant expansions or improvements simply by decreasing emissions at other points in the plant. The proposal was strongly opposed by the Office of Air Programs and Enforcement, which was responsible for administering the NSPS program, as an effort to evade the clear requirements of the act. The proposal looked vulnerable as a legal matter for this reason and also because it seemed to undercut the "technology-forcing" purposes of the CAA (see Levin, 1982). The issue was put on a back burner for several years, but in 1975 the EPA partially adopted the smelting industry's proposal when it revised the NSPS regulations governing smelters to allow the use of bubbles for modifications of existing sources but not for construction of new ones. The EPA's adoption of the NSPS bubble was eventually reversed in a quite critical and rather confusing set of opinions by the District of Columbia Circuit Court of Appeals.[12] Bubbles not involving NSPS requirements were later approved for use in attainment areas.[13] But meanwhile the market mechanism concept had cropped up in different form under a separate CAA rubric.

The Early Offset Policy. As 1975 approached it became increasingly clear that virtually no major nonattainment areas would succeed in meeting the deadline for coming into attainment. The CAA provided that no major new stationary sources or major modifications could be allowed where they would jeopardize attainment by that deadline. The possibility of a real, immediate conflict between environmental protection and economic growth thus began approaching reality; since most urbanized areas were nonattainment for some pollutants, the CAA would preclude any significant industrial growth in them. The EPA responded by proposing the "offset" policy, which would allow major new stationary sources or modifications in industrial areas if they met three requirements. They must: (1) provide for an emission reduction ("offset") from an existing source in the area greater than the increase in emissions due to their moving into the area, thus achieving economic growth simultaneously with a net improvement in local air quality; (2) use control equipment producing the "lowest achievable emission rate" (LAER) for the type of industrial process involved;[14] and (3) ensure that all their other emissions sources in the area were in compliance with applicable emissions limits.

The next year Congress essentially ratified this innovative and rather unauthorized gambit in the Clean Air Act Amendments of 1977,[15] and it extended the attainment deadline for most primary standards to 1982. Although Congress ratified the offset policy, however, it also left the states the option of achieving growth in nonattainment areas simply by ordering added cutbacks among existing sources, and thereby creating room ("growth allowances") for new sources under the declining total emissions curve for the area. Thus the states have the option of using either market or regulatory means to allow new source growth in nonattainment areas.

The Move to a Generalizable Emissions Trading Policy During the Carter Administration. The offsets and bubble policies formed the cornerstones of what would become a unified policy approximating the marketable-permits model explicated a decade earlier by J. H. Dales (1968) and other economists. Both techniques of course allowed emissions to be "transferred" from less valuable uses to more valuable ones (bubbles allowing them within a plant and offsets between plants).[16] The 1977 amendments to the CAA ratified and elaborated those policies. Moreover, the Carter administration had come into office, and several of its key officials made the development of market-oriented regulatory techniques a high priority. Development of the emissions trading initiatives continued on both the conceptual and operational levels. In 1978 the EPA ruled that modified sources in NAAQS attainment areas (but not new or reconstructed sources) could "net out" of best available control technology requirements by reducing existing emissions at least as much as they expanded new emissions.[17] In 1979 the agency promulgated regulations allowing a somewhat constrained form of bubbling for both existing and new sources in nonattainment areas. It also authorized states to allow the "banking" of emissions reductions. Thus sources might reduce emissions at one point in time, "deposit" them in the "bank," and use them later, either in the same plant (a bubble extended over time) or in another plant (an offset extended over time).[18]

Two years later, after having changed course on the question several times, the agency proposed to authorize "netting" in nonattainment areas.[19] Netting involves a form of bubble quite similar to that originally proposed by the smelting industry but would allow the modifying source in a nonattainment area to avoid not only certain control technology requirements (LAER and not NSPS) but also new source *review* requirements by so reducing existing emissions as to "net out" of review of new ones. In other words, a polluter would not even have to go through the lengthy federal review process to prove that its new emissions qualified for a bubble exemption; state preconstruction review would still apply for the determination and quantification of such exemptions. At about the same time, the EPA approved the use of a "generic" bubble policy, which would authorize states to allow existing source bubbles so long as they met certain previously approved criteria without amending their SIPs, and thereby undergoing EPA review, for each case.[20]

Emissions Trading During the Reagan Administration. Although the Reagan administration swept out of the EPA some of the key Carter-era emissions trading proponents, a number of important staff-level advocates remained at the agency. With some fits and starts due primarily to changes in leadership at the top level, they continued building the emissions trading initiatives into a general program. The operational issues became increasingly complex and need not be detailed here. At the conceptual level they were organized largely in terms of how many "safeguards" (the language of the skeptics) or "obstacles" (the language of the proponents) were to be placed on the trading mechanisms.

The first Reagan EPA administrator, Anne Gorsuch Burford, seems initially to have resisted the trading proposals (perhaps because they were seen as a product of the Carter administration). Eventually, however, she gave considerable play to trading. A frequently revised internal document which had been titled "Controlled Policy Trading Statement" in mid-1981 eventually emerged from the agency as a proposed "Emissions Trading Policy Statement" (ETPS) in April of 1982.[21] The change of title was taken by many observers to signify the agency's increasingly permissive attitude toward trading. Although the document contained many changes of language and emphasis, however, in overall treatment emissions trading remained little changed from earlier drafts. The statement attempted to define a common currency of sorts, the emission reduction credit (ERC), and to provide a unified name for the process, emissions trading (quaintly abbreviated ET), aimed at crystallizing a new, unified framework. It tried to establish some general, cross-program criteria for ERCs: they must be (1) "surplus," (2) "enforceable," (3) "permanent," and (4) "quantifiable." Although much of the policy statement was devoted to defining these requirements, they remained relatively vague.

On the whole, the draft ETPS was quite liberal in encouraging trading. But widespread failure by the states to meet the 1982 attainment deadlines combined with the political travail of the Gorsuch administration to prevent its quick finalization. When William Ruckelshaus replaced Gorsuch about a year after the ETPS original publication, the heyday of regulatory reformers pushing liberalized trading had passed. The primary issues facing the Ruckelshaus administration concerned how much to "tighten up" the proposed ETPS policies. After a long series of meetings, the administration settled upon a relatively moderate set of reforms. Before these could be finalized, however, Ruckelshaus and his chief administrator, Alvin Alm, having concluded that the worst damage done to the EPA during the Gorsuch administration had been repaired, both resigned.

When Lee Thomas took over as administrator, many issues that had previously been regarded as resolved were reconsidered. Following a series of meetings with representatives of environmental groups, industry, and state and local regulatory agencies, Thomas settled on a moderate policy generally following the lines worked out in the Ruckelshaus administration.[22] Rules applicable to trading in attainment areas remain relatively liberal on the whole. Rules for nonattainment areas are tightened somewhat from the Ruckelshaus formulation and considerably from the ETPS. For example, baselines from which ERCs are calculated are relatively strict; bubbles must achieve 20 percent net emissions reductions (rather than mere equivalence); bubbles in all areas must make relatively stringent showings of ambient equivalence; and generic rules are subject to somewhat increased EPA scrutiny.

On the whole, developments during the Reagan administration have left the rules significantly more complicated and the emissions trading process more heavily policed. But the basic system, and its underlying conception, are quite intact. Indeed, as the debate is now structured, it is almost impossible to call the basic concept into question. The problem is not whether to have a pollution market, but simply how to police it.

Use of Emissions Trading.   To be sure, the fact that the EPA has authorized emissions trading does not mean that it is in fact widely used. One potential limitation is that states have the option of whether or not to allow such transactions and to place them under a variety of restrictions. In fact, although the time it has taken to hammer out a federal framework has inhibited state use of emissions trading, by late 1983, my analysis of data compiled then (see Ritts, 1983) reveals the following: (1) forty-one states allowed some form of bubbling; (2) forty-three states allowed some form of offsetting; (3) twenty-six states allowed some form of banking; and (4) sixteen states allowed some form of netting. By early 1986, nine states had EPA-approved generic bubble rules, and at least as many were expecting to seek approval for such rules. Thus the states have generally exercised their statutory discretion in favor of the EPA initiatives and have created a regulatory environment in which emissions trading may occur.

A second potential limitation on the practical significance of emissions trading is that polluters may not be doing much of it. In fact, although there was little trading in the early years of the emissions trading initiatives, there has been a considerable amount in the last few years. The best available estimates through 1986 are as follows: (1) approximately 130 significant bubbles; (2) approximately 2,000 offset transactions, 200 of them between different firms; (3) somewhat less than 120 banking transactions; (4) between 5,000 and 12,000 netting transactions (Hahn and Hester, 1986). The authors of the study estimate that the transactions involved have saved firms several billion dollars and that the potential savings will be vastly greater once a stable, clear program is in place. Whatever the ultimate magnitude of emissions trading, it is clear that the program has signifi- cantly influenced polluters' emissions control strategies. Despite the growing use of emissions trading by regulatees recently, however, they did not conceive it and were far from unanimous in supporting its development. I will now consider why it developed at all.

Why Emissions Trading?

Why have the EPA and the state agencies undertaken the considerable task of transforming their legal mandates and past regulatory practices to facilitate emissions trading? To address this question, I carried out an in-depth study of the policy process in the federal government and in four states with different political traditions and pollution problems in different parts of the country. The study is based on approximately forty in-depth interviews of knowledgeable individuals as well as extensive analysis of documentary records and contemporary reports of policy developments. About two-thirds of the individuals interviewed were federal, state, and local government officials. The remainder were equally divided among industry and environmental representatives. I found two of the most obvious explanations for the rise of emissions trading to be completely unsatisfactory in their ordinary forms (for a more thorough report, see Meidinger, forthcoming).

TWO INADEQUATE EXPLANATIONS

Efficiency It has become common not only to evaluate legal and policy changes in terms of economic efficiency but also to try to explain them in these terms. This framework attempts to understand such changes as natural attempts to achieve equal or greater social benefits for lower or equal social costs (for example, Posner, 1977).[23] The development of emissions trading, however, is not well explained as an efficiency move. Not only is the efficiency criterion indetermi-

nate regarding the choice between alternative regulatory techniques
at the abstract level (see Pearce, 1984), the EPA had no empirical
data on possible cost savings available through market mechanisms
compared with those available through other regulatory strategies
until well after the basic bubble and offsets initiatives had been taken.
Moreover, the very transformation of the system to allow trading
created much uncertainty which could have been avoided by using
"fine-tuning" or "generic" regulation to reduce control costs. Finally,
as I will show in greater detail below, there was virtually no "demand"
for the emissions trading system by its ostensible beneficiaries, polluting industries, who would presumably have been in the best position to assess potential cost savings.[24]

At its most abstract level, the efficiency thesis is neither verifiable nor refutable. Demsetz (1967), for example, argues that property rights emerge in response to "new benefit-cost possibilities" and
that they "internalize externalities when the gains of internalization
become larger than the cost of internalization." But internalization
can occur through either "private" or "state" ownership (here regulation), the choice being dependent on "community tastes." Thus one
could quite reasonably argue that the external costs of pollution
were already being internalized by traditional regulation, and that
the internalization could have been made increasingly precise by fine-
tuning the existing system. On the other hand, one could also argue
that the system change reflected the relative inefficiency of public
ownership compared with private ownership, and that the switch-
over was a response to "new benefit-cost possibilities." Unfortunately,
we have no meaningful way of measuring those benefit-cost possibilities (and the EPA had none when making its policy decisions).
Demsetz eschews any position on whether the cost-benefit decision
is conscious. He retreats to the evolutionary high ground that, when
property rights are created, the reason is that they were worth the
costs. Conversely, if they are not created (or not preserved), the reason is that they were not worth the costs. Because his perspective
thus becomes tautological and incapable of discriminating among
different kinds of choices in other than a conclusory way, it can play
no further role in this analysis.

Pressure Groups   A second conventional explanation for the development of emissions trading is that it was a response to the pressure groups in the EPA's regulatory domain. The explanation has

a certain amount of truth in this case, but the situation is more complex and contradictory than might be expected.

Although netting and bubbling have generally been pursued and embraced by polluting industries, their response to programmatic emissions trading, starting with the early offsets program and continuing to the present, has varied between indifference and hostility. Indeed, although environmentalists have been among the strongest and most effective opponents of the EPA's regulatory innovations, Kelman's early research (published in 1981 but carried out in 1978–79) found them more receptive to and more knowledgeable about market mechanisms (in that case emissions charges) than industry lobbyists. Given the vaunted cost reduction possibilities, as well as the transfer of much pollution control decisionmaking from regulatory agencies to industry, why was industry so cool to the project? My research suggests several reasons. Not least of them is the sheer conceptual complexity of the enterprise. A significant amount of industry opposition, especially in the late 1970s, was based on the premise that the scheme was so complicated and hard to understand that it would not be very workable. This concern was bolstered by the long time periods involved in development of the program and the frequent changes in agency policy. While complexity, delay, and uncertainty contribute most to understanding the hesitancy of firms to transfer emission reductions to other users, they also suggest why many of the policy proposals were viewed with such skepticism by many industry representatives.

Other considerations, however, seem more telling in understanding industry's opposition. First, market mechanisms were perceived as an initiative of the Carter administration, which had irritated many industry interests by placing seasoned environmentalists in important policy positions. There seems to have been a sense, thus far expressed only in veiled or oblique ways by industrial representatives whom I have interviewed, that the move to emissions trading might have been a Trojan horse of sorts. Industrial interests were suspicious that they might welcome it into their midst, only to find in it the sources of more burdensome regulation and expanded bureaucratic power. More concretely, as one especially articulate executive director of an industry association suggested, marketable permits could give regulators greatly increased knowledge of industrial practices, leading to the ability to track them too closely. Indeed, it might embolden them to tighten standards upon finding that particular polluters could afford it.[25]

Second, some sectors, or firms within sectors, probably benefited from the uniform rule system because of the costs and barriers to entry it imposed on competitors and were loath to change it for that reason. Although none of my interviewees acknowledged that their companies were such beneficiaries, a number of them found quite plausible the Maloney and Yandle (1981) thesis that some firms use pollution control requirements to garner economic rents. This thesis, however, falls well short of explaining the phenomenon. The primary advantage is held by existing firms over new entrants. Not only would existing firms be able to keep their advantage under the emissions trading system, but they would also have the profit-maximizing choice of keeping or selling it. No one has explained in a remotely plausible way how existing firms might collude to give up individual profits from pollution sales in order to benefit existing industry as a whole.

Perhaps the most significant factor in explaining industry opposition is a strategic one. The market mechanism proposals evolved in a period widely perceived by industry as one of declining support for environmental protection. The stagnant, then recessionary economy was expected to contribute to that trend. By the last two years of the Carter presidency, many analysts thought it quite possible that a Republican president more sympathetic to business interests could be elected in 1980. Industry interests had little incentive to embrace the new proposals, and therefore get committed to them, when the next election might bring significant relief from overall regulatory requirements.

Environmentalists, in contrast, have generally been both more informed and more divided about the use of market mechanisms than industry. My data suggest that the divisions follow two axes. The first is ideological and runs between types that we might label the moralist and pragmatist points of view. The moralist position holds essentially that pollution is bad and wrong, and that it would be a serious moral distortion to treat it simply as a commodity to be paid for. The pragmatist position sees pollution as essentially a social problem that can be solved only through application of the most effective available means.

Not all pragmatists favor market mechanisms. If anything, the strongest opposition to market mechanisms has come from environmentalists stating the problem in pragmatic terms. Several arguments are commonly raised. Perhaps most basic is opposition to giving polluters any form of entitlement either to continue polluting at current levels or to increase emissions simply by buying permits or paying taxes. In its strongest form, this is the fear of giving a "property right" to pollute (it thus carries some of the overtones of the moralist position as well). In weaker form it is expressed as an administrative concern: once emissions credits are given (or charges set), it will be significantly harder to require any further reductions than it would be using traditional emissions limits, which are taken to imply that emissions are allowed at the pleasure of the agency. A second argument is that market mechanisms will be harder to administer because they require exact emissions data over which polluters exercise a virtual monopoly and which they are under incentives to manipulate. Thus existing sources will be prone to overstate past or present emissions to receive the largest possible credits for reductions. Conversely, new sources will be prone to understate their true emissions to minimize the total number of credits they must obtain. Since accurate emissions data are difficult and expensive to obtain in the best of circumstances, regulatory agencies will be increasingly at the mercy of polluters who propose innovative control technologies, measurement methods, and so on. The ultimate result, it is argued, will be "innovations in evasion" rather than in pollution control. Finally, some assert that a move toward market mechanisms signals polluters that there will be a let-up in environmental regulation, which encourages both further political attacks on regulation and practical efforts to evade it. Overall it is my impression that environmentalists' analysis and discussions have been growing increasingly pragmatic over time, but this preliminary hypothesis cannot be asserted with any conviction in the absence of more data.

The second axis on which environmentalists' positions seem to vary is governmental level. Quite simply, a lower proportion of the local and state-level environmentalists I have interviewed show hostility to market mechanisms as a concept than do those working primarily at the national level. Since the numbers are very small and do not seem to comport with conventional wisdom, this sample could well be unrepresentative. Nonetheless, the difference in attitudes poses some intriguing questions. The explanation offered by several state and local interviewees was that national environmental leaders know little about everyday local issues, whereas local environmentalists must be more concerned about making regulation work and conserving their limited political resources for truly serious pollution threats. Their typical attitude is that the way to deal with market mechanisms is to ensure that they have "adequate safeguards."

It is thus clear that the environmental agencies' embrace of emissions trading cannot be explained in terms of the demands of their client groups. There was neither political nor significant economic demand for emissions trading when the major initiatives were taken. Moreover, as noted above, the EPA's move (and the state agencies' willingness to follow along) is all the more intriguing because it is quite inconsistent with the structure of the CAA and because, by creating quantitative, entitlementlike interests, it poses the possibility of a further narrowing of the agencies' discretion and flexibility to respond to changed circumstances.[26] Why, then, did it happen?

A MORE ADEQUATE FORMULATION

Practical Considerations   First, the move makes some practical sense on its own terms. As noted above, the Clean Air Act is sufficiently complicated and unwieldy to invite efforts at revision. Moreover, emissions trading may indeed offer some cost savings to polluters – although they may also prove more expensive for the agencies to administer. But it must be remembered that the EPA had no actual estimates of those savings until 1979, well after the fundamental policy initiatives had been taken.

A second class of reasons for moving to market mechanisms can be found in the political exigencies confronting the EPA and the state environmental agencies. While the movement to emissions trading cannot be understood as simply responding to the direct demands of interest groups, the agencies were under considerable pressure by the mid-1970s not to define environmental protection as inconsistent with economic efficiency or, in particular, growth. Although the offsets policy was the clearest response to the problem, its logic was much broader. But here again, other responses would seem to have been equally plausible. The most obvious, based on the traditional model of regulation, would have been more fine-tuning of existing standards, more ready allowance of variances, and the like. However, the conservative swing in the United States during the late 1970s (as I show in somewhat greater detail below) was not simply a return to the demand for economic prosperity. It also had a very substantial, antigovernment, antibureaucracy component. It seems to have been that element of public opinion which the Carter administration was responding to (and perhaps fostering) with its regulatory reform efforts.

Regulatory Entrepreneurs and the New Regulatory Culture
Nonetheless, the political interest thesis also falls short in light of the early development and somewhat crusading tenor of the market mechanisms movement. The movement was an *initiative,* not just a response. That initiative had several bases. An obvious one lay in the career aspirations of new staff members. Pollution regulation was a booming business in the early and mid-1970s, and it attracted numerous bright, ambitious people. As commonly happens in such situations, many of them cast about for new initiatives to which they could hook their stars and by which they could separate themselves from the crowd. As it happened, a number chose emissions trading, and, to a significant degree, the strategy succeeded. But this finding just pushes our question back one step: why did they choose it, and why did it work? I suspect part of the answer to the latter question lies in the sheer energy and entrepreneurial ability of the program's early promoters. A number of them were unusually capable and persuasive individuals by any standard.

The larger reason, however, seems to lie in a revised understanding of regulation which was emergent in the early part of the decade and regnant at the end. I have already outlined the general disenchantment with traditional regulation which had emerged by the time the CAA was enacted. It seems to have gained a significant purchase on the agencies through the graduate schools: public policy, economics, and law. Each of these disciplines had been involved for varying periods of time in debunking the myth of the benign public interest state. Economics departments had long taught that the agglomeration of individual self-interested decisions is more likely to contribute to public welfare than is the imposition of uniform, politically determined policies. Public administration programs had somewhat more recently come to the view that public planning is "politics," not science. And the law schools had since the legal realist movement of the 1930s been involved in thrashing to death the idea that law simply reflects and implements the logic of justice or the public interest. Each discipline's perspective is, of course, more complicated and more qualified than this portrayal suggests. But students who go into practical affairs tend to be interested in "the basics" and have little time for niceties. Here the basics are simple: you better not put much faith in politics or bureaucracy; they are very unreliable.

My hypothesis is that infusion of this perspective into the on-going regulatory process had combined with it to yield what we may usefully regard as a new strain of regulatory culture and a new basis for choosing regulatory strategies.[27] Before discussing how this culture became decisive, I will sketch what appear to be its central elements. There appear to be four core premises and three notable secondary ones. All of them can be seen in significant part as responses to the acceptance of interest-group liberalism as the dominant and essentially unchangeable model of contemporary politics.[28] And all appear to take the form of stable compromises rather than deep structures.

Science does not provide a basis from which emissions *standards* or other regulatory requirements can simply *be deduced.* Science can be deployed in the interest of contending parties. It is quite useful for documenting the effects of various decisions on affected parties and, given sufficient resources, can do so accurately. But only in an unusually naive political environment can it be deployed as the determinant or the legitimating basis of a regulatory decision.

Regulatory decisions are *inherently compromises* among contending interests rather than applications of correct principles. There are almost never "best" solutions (based on either science or shared morality). Therefore, the only role that the regulatory official can play and still survive involves maintaining a posture of neutrality and seeking compromises which minimize social conflict and the vulnerability of the agency. If both goals cannot be achieved, the latter will naturally predominate.

The goal of the regulatory agency is to create a *stable framework* in which the pull and haul of interests can take place and through which compromises can be implemented. Any such stable framework must be capable of including all significant interests (both active and latent). Moreover, it should be able to legitimate current decisions on the basis of past compromises. This arrangement should minimize future conflict by piggybacking future policies on current solutions. It is worth noting that (but for its explicitly pragmatic basis) this view bears a striking resemblance to the rule-of-law imagery that has been a recurrent element in American political thought. It is also worth noting that marketable permits might be acceptable to both environmental and industrial interests because they reflect a stable compromise which will be less subject to the vagaries of politics than would more traditional mechanisms. Recent efforts to reauthorize and amend the CAA give neither interest any reason to place great confidence in its ability to bend the legislative process to its purposes. Emissions trading essentially institutionalizes rights to air of a certain level of cleanliness and a certain level of pollution simultaneously, and lets polluters work out who will pollute it.

Regulatory decisions should be pinioned insofar as possible on the *interests and compromises of private parties*. Broad participation can thus be used to remove sole responsibility for the legitimacy of a decision from the regulatory agency, and public regulations can be portrayed as "natural" outcomes of private relationships.

The framework also seems to assume a set of more conventional axioms: (5) the superiority of decentralized decisionmaking over centralized decisionmaking by hierarchically situated, "disinterested" experts; (6) the superiority of the market over political authority for resource allocation, and (7) the superiority of incremental and experimental social change over comprehensively planned social change.

The Regulatory Arena   To understand the emergence of this new regulatory culture further, we must consider the social arena in which it emerged.[29] Two features seem important.

Access.   The first is the exceedingly technical and complicated nature of air pollution regulation. No discussion of appropriate regulation can proceed for long without delving into the scientific and practical aspects of the problem. What, for example, are the comparative health and macroeconomic implications of the alternatives? What are the costs, the technical possibilities, the practical problems? These questions arise as soon as it is accepted that some pollution must be allowed if industrial society is to continue, that regulatory discourse does not allow calling the existence of industrial society into question, and that agents producing permitted pollution will therefore not necessarily be committing wrongs. This recognition inherently limits access to the discussion to parties willing to commit substantial time and resources to becoming "experts." Conversely, those who show themselves "nonexpert" by making significant "mistakes" in the discussion are relatively easy to exclude from effective participation.[30]

Overall, the group of effective participants in air pollution policy discussions is quite small. The emission trading discussions in the four case study states, for example, were carried on among knowledgeable participants numbering fewer than twenty. (Typically, perhaps a dozen others would become involved at some point in the process, but they would have had no effect on the outcome unless they were especially knowledgeable or had power over the decision as a result of legal position.) The small number of participants seems typical in complex regulatory problems of this sort. Moreover, most of the participants have a substantial history of involvement with air pollution problems. Only about 10 percent, for example, have worked in the area less than four years (although perhaps half of the environmental group representatives also work in other environmental problem areas).

Thus despite the partially conflicting interests of the parties involved, they have been able to develop a relatively large shared understanding of the problem. Moreover, this is not just "factual" or "scientific" understanding. The dominant element in our constructed understanding of air pollution problems is uncertainty. The policy domain for which confident predictions can be made is far smaller than that for which they cannot. Nonetheless, it is necessary to manipulate problems lodged in the domain of uncertainty, and for these purposes conventional understandings, or working assumptions, are developed. Their exact nature varies greatly with the area. One generic form is that a smaller number of significant mistakes are likely to be made when all affected interests are part of the policymaking discussion than when some are excluded. (Thus interest-group liberalism becomes technically as well as politically functional.) An example that has emerged in the discussion of emissions trading is the belief that it will probably not lead to any "major problems" as long as the agencies implement it carefully and "keep close tabs" on it. Of course, we do not really know that, since the system has never been tried. Moreover, that is to say not that market mechanisms are good but only that they are not inherently bad. Still, consensus on the last point allows the discussion to proceed to the particulars of defining a market mechanism policy and its implementation. This process, because of its significant movement along the ideological spectrum, might be much more difficult or impossible if the number of discussants were much larger.

Organizational Location. Another factor that has contributed significantly to the rise of the new regulatory culture, and to the development of the market mechanism concept, is functional specialization within organizations. Like Western legal institutions generally, regulation is typically conceived in terms of two functions: rule formulation and rule application. The organization of most environmental agencies reflects a rough division according to these two functions. Policy is to be formulated by one group of typically centralized, upper-level staff and applied by another group of typically field-based, lower-level staff. Regulatory practice is of course more complicated. It is widely understood that field (or often enforcement) staff do a substantial amount of policymaking in their everyday work (for example, Hawkins, 1984). Similarly, members of policy staffs frequently participate in particular rule applications (especially at the state level), for example, in drafting important pollution permits.

Perhaps more important, until recently air pollution rule makers and rule appliers were more similar to each other than they were different. The technical complexity of air pollution problems meant in practice that they had similar science-based backgrounds, most often in engineering. Moreover, their interests generally converged in the same legal forms: categorically uniform emissions standards. For policymakers, categorical rules both allowed simple (formulaic) determinations of allowable emissions for particular sources and legitimated particular applications by their very uniformity. For enforcement staff they accomplished the same purposes but also allowed a certain amount of discretion, since it was equally well understood that uniform rules will be inappropriate for certain individual sources. In those cases, special dispensations (variances and decisions not to enforce) are appropriate. That dispensations might be given formally (and by implication legitimately) or informally (and by implication illegitimately) gave rise to a major debate on the appropriate structure and use of discretion which need not be rehearsed here. The important point is that air pollution officials commonly saw their interests in terms of categorically uniform rules applied with discretion.

Until perhaps the mid-1970s, pollution control agencies as wholes saw their interests in the same way. However, in addition to the external factors already noted, several internal developments opened them to revised views. First, the agencies were increasingly undertaking major new program responsibilities (for example, toxic substances and hazardous wastes). Typically they responded by creating separate subdivisions to handle these programs. They thus became significantly more internally differentiated. While this response made sense in terms of the detailed, technically quite different problems posed by each type of pollution, it simultaneously raised the possibilities of program autonomy and interprogram inconsistency. The latter was almost certain to be raised because any given polluter is likely to be regulated under more than one program and is equally likely to point out any major inconsistencies among them.

Accordingly, the EPA was organized with several cross-program offices – one on the policy level (currently titled the Office of Policy, Planning, and Evaluation, or OPPE) and one on the enforcement level (currently the Office of Enforcement and Compliance Monitoring).[31] The OPPE's interests were not synonymous with those of the individual program offices. Its role was to evaluate the performance of the program offices and to propose ways of improving them. It therefore had an incentive to be especially amenable to approaches not currently followed in the program offices. Moreover, its efforts to minimize the costs of individual programs and eventually to achieve cross-program comparability suggested the need to limit the discretion of the individual programs. Not surprisingly, the OPPE became the natural base for the new policy types described above, and its Regulatory Reform section (recently renamed "Regulatory Innovations") became a hothouse for the development and advocacy of market mechanism proposals. With direct access to top administrators and relative autonomy from the Air Program Office, OPPE staff members had substantially more policy leverage than they would have enjoyed within the Air Office. In the state agencies (at least the larger ones) there were parallel but structurally less pronounced changes. The key development was the emergence of regulatory entrepreneurs in state policy offices. Typically young (under forty years old), policy oriented rather than technically oriented, ambitious, and often initially funded by federal money,[32] these entrepreneurs effectively forced discussion of market mechanisms at the state level.

Initially, the federal Air Office and most of the state offices vigorously opposed the emissions trading initiatives. For a while during the early 1980s, most of them seemed to go along with emissions trading to varying degrees. From about 1984 to the present, they became more resistant, drawing attention to various "abuses," actual and potential. But whatever their real desires might have been, they generally did not feel able to oppose the fundamental concept of emissions trading; their discussions were framed entirely in terms of imposing adequate safeguards. As I noted in the preceding section, they succeeded to a limited degree, but emissions trading appears to be growing institutionalized in a relatively strong form.

Given the substantial opposition from the program office and from many regional and state offices, the question to be answered is why the regulatory entrepreneurs have nonetheless prevailed. Their organizational position is not by itself enough to explain this outcome. Indeed, the implementing offices probably have the organizational edge, since they have direct program responsibility, real world experience, and the ability to accuse the policy offices of backing away from the legal mandate of the CAA. But when the capacity of regulatory entrepreneurs to force their proposals to the forefront of the agency agenda by virtue of their organizational location is combined with the factors already discussed, a structured explanation emerges. It has four basic elements, three of which have been elaborated above:

1. The practical attractiveness of emissions trading due to the relative unwieldiness of the original CAA structure and the potential cost savings available to polluters;

2. The growth of a new regulatory culture of sufficient breadth, coherence, and attractiveness to provide a strong analytic rationale and basis of moral authority for new proposals such as emissions trading;

3. The rise of talented regulatory entrepreneurs promoting emissions trading proposals (1) within relatively high-level, autonomous, and crosscutting organizational subdivisions and (2) affecting program areas to which there is relatively limited access.

SOCIAL ENVIRONMENT

While the first three elements are largely internal to the environmental agencies in their focus, the fourth element stresses the broader social environment in which the agencies operate. It has two salient aspects, which correspond roughly to elements 1 and 2 above. First, as already noted, emissions trading has been attractive to environmental agencies in part because it allows them to argue that they are adopting the most efficient available means to preserve environmental quality and that they are therefore not significantly or unduly hindering economic growth. Preventing a serious conflict between environmental regulations and economic growth was a major impetus behind the original offset policy. Similarly, the Carter EPA was especially amenable to expanded use of bubbling because of its desire to preempt possible political challenges. Those challenges were based on the twin arguments that (1) environmental regulations were a significant drag on the economy and (2) there were much more efficient ways to regulate. By defusing the second argument, EPA and the state agencies hoped to blunt the overall challenge.

The existence of the larger challenge is not self-explanatory, however. During the first half of the 1970s, there was little concern with either the costs of environmental regulation or the possibility that it might slow economic growth. Public opinion focused on the costs of environmental degradation and the benefits of environmental regulation. By 1978, the focus had shifted considerably to the costs of environmental regulation (although relatively few ventured further to argue the benefits of environmental degradation! See Schnaiberg, 1980). In part, this change of focus seems attributable to a large-scale, relatively well funded movement to research and critique regulation. Conservative think-tanks and business associations supported a spate of studies that examined the costs and benefits of regulation — especially the costs, since it was assumed that the agencies would take care of the benefits.[33] However, while these studies are important, they do not seem to explain the change in attitude either.

The changing public opinion to which the environmental agencies have sought to respond is also tied to a continuing evolution in the public understanding of the capacities and most desirable role of government. Certain broad-scale tendencies in public attitudes present at the passage of the CAA have continued to the present, and the new regulatory culture appears closely connected to those larger trends. While a thorough analysis is out of the question here, I can offer a brief outline. First, the distrust of government (or, perhaps more precisely, of the welfare state) has continued and, if anything, has grown. To a significant degree, however, it has been uncoupled from distrust of big business (originally the other major member of "the system"), and business has undergone substantial rehabilitation. Witness, for example, the framing of issues and the outcome of the 1984 and 1988 U.S. presidential elections.

No doubt this process is in part the purposive achievement of discrete social interests pursuing deliberate, rational strategies. But just as clearly its success draws on long-standing, deep-seated, and widely shared social images. Perhaps the core ones show the market as the natural organizing framework for society and individual freedom as exercised within the market framework. Market imagery, of course, has been central to the rise of interest-group liberalism since the Second World War. Indeed, as suggested above, the new regulatory culture may be seen as the more or less natural working out of the premises of interest-group liberalism. It had to overcome two significant obstacles: (1) the early twentieth-century faith in rational scientific solutions to social problems and (2) the long-standing belief that all "political" compromises should be achieved in elected legislatures (the nondelegation doctrine and so forth).[34] In the very process of overcoming them, however, the theory of regulation was also fundamentally transformed, because it had lost its scientific and democratic terms.

Evaluation and Conclusions

The development and wide-scale use of emissions trading poses at least two kinds of potentially fundamental problems. The first concerns the nature of politics and the ability of the citizenry to define the nature of desirable behavior. The second is distributional and concerns the pattern of costs and benefits of the new policy.

Emissions trading strongly implies that pollution decisionmaking is an economic problem to be worked out by business firms rather than a moral or political problem to be worked out by political institutions. In this regard, it may be simply a logical extension of interest-group liberalism, which treats politics as merely a surrogate market for the expression of political preferences. When interest-group liberalism's image of politics as a market prevails, the role of the state recedes. Similarly, acceptance of the affiliated image of market freedom reduces political actors to choosing among and bargaining for options, on the basis, of course, of their individual interests and preferences. No longer is freedom the right to participate in defining a larger collective good. "Market-derived terms like interest and incentive dominate the contemporary policy-making vocabulary, depriving it of the very language needed to think about public purposes. Market imagery transforms the public's view of itself from one of an active, deliberate citizenry to one of a gaggle of consumers shopping for policies from shelves stocked by governmental experts" (Landy and Plotkin, 1982:8). Gradually, then, the "private," nonstate sphere becomes the sole source of legitimate policy; the correct policy is that chosen by the affected parties through an aggregation of their interests. The role of government is merely to enforce the rules of the game and the terms of particular outcomes. There is no other image of collective action, decisionmaking, or value creation available in this model.

While offering efficient means of implementing existing well-defined objectives, and while putting the problem of governmental discretion in a convenient box, emissions trading could in fact make it more difficult to discuss and create guiding values. In the process of defanging the technocratic state, emissions trading may make its operations more inaccessible and irreversible. Indeed, social policy seems likely to become increasingly invisible as it recedes into the organizational apparatus of the private world and becomes defined as part of the natural state of affairs. Thus in the name of making the regulatory machine work better, we may well make it even more difficult to redesign.

The second potential problem is that by defining pollution control decisions as allocational rather than distributional issues, emissions trading may make it more difficult to adjust the distributional impacts of pollution control policies. The problem can easily be illustrated using a basic question: what should be done if some social groups suffer greater impacts from pollution than others? The answer, on the basis of market logic, would be that they should buy some emissions permits away from the responsible polluters (assuming again that to be inhibited such pollution should pose greater costs to pollutees than benefits to polluters). And indeed, the emissions trading framework allows for this possibility. However, if the affected group happens to be poor rather than wealthy, chances of its buying away permits are correspondingly lower. To be sure, efficiency-based arguments could be deployed to argue for state intervention regardless of the wealth of the affected group. Thus the high transactions costs of organizing the almost inevitably diffuse affected groups may justify regulatory action where it could achieve the same adjustment at lower cost. But by the terms of its rationale, such an adjustment should seek to achieve only as much reduction as the pollutees would pay for if they could organize themselves to do so.

More important, any distributional adjustment would have to confront the increasingly private sphere of pollution entitlements and intrude in that sphere. The expert agency, after all, has already set a uniform baseline with the NAAQS (to protect all citizens to the same level) and has developed a system by which trades should maintain that baseline. Claiming reliance on that baseline and system, threatened polluters would point to significant investments not only in emission rights, but in related factors of production which, they would argue, should also be protected. They may be able to draw relatively wide support for their arguments by drawing an analogy between their interests and other private property which must be protected, according to the conventional imagery, both to provide a bulwark against a potentially capricious state and to provide an arena for the exercise of economic liberty and independence. By drawing an analogy between pollution rights and other forms of property, polluters would attempt to draw upon the more general cluster of beliefs holding that it is necessary to respect property and that undermining one kind of property interest might facilitate the subsequent undermining of other kinds.[35]

It is true that environmental agencies have taken great care legally to state that polluters will not have formal claims to permanent protected property rights in emissions reduction credits. But of course, to stretch the analogy less than it might seem, William the Conqueror did the same thing when he distributed the lands of England after 1066. Yet those landholdings gradually grew inheritable, then alienable, increasingly free from sovereign interference. At the same time the sovereign's legal ownership of all land came to have little more than theoretical significance. The twin cultural beliefs in private property and market organization that developed during that period are now, of course, much stronger and more fully articulated. They become all the more available to polluters as pollution is defined as an economic activity rather than a moral one and as the appropriate forum for pollution decisionmaking becomes the firm rather than the regulatory agency.

In sum, the rise of emissions trading seems to have a built-in tendency against redistributive policymaking because: (1) the ability to obtain any given commodity is differentially distributed according to the existing distribution of wealth and (2) the important conceptual apparatus which grew up to protect private property is available to polluters seeking to protect their emissions interests. At the same time, the key counterarguments – the possibility of scientific (nonmarket) rationality and the possibility of creating a public (nonprivate) definition of the good – are on the decline.

Whether the constriction of public decisionmaking and cost redistribution in fact occur remains an open question. We are still a considerable distance from the time when property rights in pollution constitute a powerful bulwark against regulatory adjustment. One of the most important reasons lies in the posture of pollution control agencies toward polluters' rights. In implementing emissions trading, it seems unlikely that agencies will ever define their interests as becoming identical to those of registries of land deeds (which play purely record-keeping functions). There are a variety of reasons. First, of course, modern regulatory agencies simply do not act in such a way. Much like other complex organizations, they seem to define their interests in terms of survival and, often, expansion (for example, Michels, 1949; Nonet, 1969; Wilensky, 1969). Furthermore, they tend to pursue power, at least where doing so will not threaten survival (for example, McCullough and Shannon, 1977). Second, unlike land registries, environmental agencies face substantial uncertainties in accounting for their resources. Estimating the actual effect of any given pollution entitlement on the total stock of air quality is a very complicated matter that requires sophisticated scientific modeling, monitoring, and so on. Third, and perhaps most important, there is an enormous constituency with organized representatives whose interests may be defined as inconsistent with strong pollution entitlements. The environmental agencies' ability to define themselves as the protectors of public health allows them to reclaim much latitude that the emissions trading framework might otherwise concede. Organized environmental groups have the ability and the developed relationships to maintain pressure in that direction. Finally, there is an alternative legal imagery, that of the "privilege" rather than the "entitlement," which pulls in the other direction. Reformist efforts to define interests in the largess of the welfare state, such as Aid to Families with Dependent Children or Social Security payments, as propertylike interests have not been very successful.[36]

The final emissions trading policy statement promulgated by the Reagan EPA fits with this model of agency behavior. It is considerably more careful in granting ERCs than strong emissions trading proponents would have liked. In it EPA has retained substantial oversight authority and has limited the conditions in which ERCs will be allowed in many other detailed ways. If anything like a protected property right (and a complete fencing out of regulatory agencies from pollution control decisionmaking) is to emerge, that time is still relatively far in the future. Whether it will arrive depends heavily on the process and politics of implementation. Two issues, the use of discretion and the effectiveness of enforcement, seem likely to be particularly important.

As I indicated in the first section, a major focus of the critique of traditional regulation was the use and abuse of administrative discretion. The primary criticism of discretion was that it often meant that like cases were not treated alike, typically because the agency had been "captured" by an interested party. A major purpose in the design of the CAA was the reduction of administrative discretion. Similarly, a major rationale for emissions trading was that it would further reduce discretion, because emissions control decisions would be made primarily by polluters operating within clear, propertylike parameters. However, the complexity of emissions trading rules and the numerous points of explicit oversight and administrative judgment, from the setting of baselines to the meaning of "enforceability," make it increasingly unlikely that the reduced discretion envisioned for emissions trading will become reality anytime soon. In fact, the net effect might simply be to hide expanded administrative discretion behind a veneer of private entitlements.

The second issue is the potential difficulty of administration and enforcement. Many of the state and local officials interviewed for this study expressed the view that an emissions trading system will probably be harder to administer than a uniform rule system. They often doubted whether they would be able to garner the resources necessary to do so effectively. If environmental agencies fail to obtain the necessary resources over the long term, emissions trading may eventually come to be seen as a cause of environmental degradation rather than a solution. A key aspect of this problem will be enforcement. Economists Baumol and Batey Blackman stated these problems starkly in a 1979 report to the EPA.

> Where emissions are of a sort that are difficult to observe and monitor, neither effluent charges nor emission permits will be practical. It is, after all, useless to offer for sale a permit authorizing no more than x units of emission per day if no one knows whether the emitter is producing half or twice this amount on any given day. In that case, direct controls which require the installation of specified control devices, or which prohibit certain particularly polluting processes, or which limit or prohibit the use of particularly polluting inputs may be the only effective option available.

Some environmentalists are betting that emissions trading will suffer from serious enforcement failures. If it does, the politics of emissions trading may become much more adverse.

It is conceivable that polluters themselves will conclude that they have a sufficient stake in the system to find solutions to these problems. They could, for example, invest significant resources in developing innovative monitoring and enforcement technologies. Similarly, they could foster the growth of accountability systems to police themselves, perhaps along the lines of financial accounting systems. But without strong agency and environmental group involvement in the details of pollution control, there is little reason for optimism in this regard. The situation seems equally likely to degenerate in the same way that many other "prisoner's dilemma" situations do.

We will have to wait and see what happens in the day-to-day politics of emissions trading. Perhaps the pessimistic view of some industry representatives will turn out to be accurate, and pollution control agencies will actually use emissions trading to gain increased control of emissions processes. Conversely, the pessimistic view of some environmental group representatives may prove to be correct, and the agencies will lose some of the tenuous control that they now exert over pollution activities. Ironically, it is quite possible that whichever interest wins in the short run will lose in the long run.

Notes

1. The primary advantages conventionally attributed to emissions charges are that the revenues they generate go to public (rather than private) coffers, that they do not require the creation of a new market, and that the cost of emissions becomes relatively predictable. The primary disadvantages of emissions charges are that total emissions are relatively unpredictable (because of unknown cost functions of individual polluters), that they require extensive monitoring and enforcement efforts, and that local adjustments may be necessary every time a major new source starts up (thus undercutting the predictability of emissions charges). The case for marketable permits is essentially the reverse. Because total emissions are set by the total number of permits available, emissions are more predictable and adjustments are less likely to be necessary. Less intensive monitoring and enforcement are necessary because of the possibility of implementing permit limits in terms of control technologies. Conversely, the costs of emissions to polluters using marketable permits are less predictable, the revenues generated go to private coffers, and to make the system work it is necessary to create a wholly new market. See, for example, Hahn and Noll (1982). See also Stewart (1981).

2. It should be noted that the jurisdictional domains of the traditional

agencies were both fluid and arbitrary. The jurisdiction of the ICC, for example, was originally limited to railroads and was later expanded to include water carriage and trucking. The Federal Power Commission (now the Federal Energy Regulatory Commission) gradually had its jurisdiction extended from federal hydropower to interstate natural gas, interstate electricity, and oil transported in interstate pipelines. Similar examples could be given for many other agencies. Moreover, there is no inherent reason why jurisdictional domains should have been defined exactly as they were; in most cases they might well have been larger or smaller. Nonetheless, the general logic was to apply regulatory expertise to a particular type of business, often one in which significant tendencies toward monopoly were argued to exist. See Weidenbaum (1980).

3. To fill in the picture, it should also be noted that the rise of traditional economic regulation occurred in tandem with another form of broad economic regulation aimed at *creating a national market*. The major elements in this development were the use of the "dormant commerce clause" to constrain state regulation of interstate commercial activity and the antitrust laws to constrain the development of oligopolies and monopolies outside the spheres of economic regulation in which they were purposefully permitted and encouraged. For an interesting European perspective on this form of regulation, see Reich (1983).

4. Expanded participation rights are not unique to social regulation; they have also been grafted onto economic regulatory systems. But they became popular as solutions to regulatory failure with the surge of social regulation in the late 1960s and early 1970s, and they therefore serve to typify it.

5. See, for example, *Lead Industries Association* v. *Environmental Protection Agency*, 545 F.2d 320 (CA2, 1976), upholding EPA's lead NAAQS.

6. See *Lead Industries Assoc.* v. *Environmental Protection Agency*, id.

7. It should also be noted, however, that the CAA sets specific deadlines for review and possible revisions of the NAAQs and that such review processes are currently under way at EPA (see 42 U.S.C. sec. 7409[d]).

8. In those areas in attainment with the NAAQS, significant deterioration must be prevented by keeping ambient pollution levels from rising by more than a set increment during any given year.

9. The 1977 amendments to the act subjected states which failed to meet the deferred deadlines (1982 for most pollutants) to cutoffs of significant federal funds.

10. I am indebted to David Pearce for correcting my earlier characterization of this literature, in which I overstated the popularity of marketable permits and understated the popularity of private bargaining in the discussion (personal correspondence, June 5, 1984).

11. For more detailed discussions, see Liroff (1980, 1986), Levin (1982), and Meidinger (1988).

12. *ASARCO* v. *EPA,* 578 F.2d 319 (1978).

13. *Alabama Power* v. *Costle,* 606 F.2d 1068 (1979); *modified* 636 F.2d 323 (1979).

14. LAER standards were to be at least as strict as NSPS and possibly stricter, since costs were to be given less weight in LAER than in NSPS determinations. In practice the two standards seem generally to have been similar. See 41 Fed. Reg. 55525 (December 21, 1976). See also Liroff (1980); National Commission on Air Quality (1981).

15. For the record it should be noted that a parallel proposal had been discussed in the Senate Subcommittee on Environmental Pollution during the same period. The so-called steel amendment would have met the expansion needs of American steel plants (most of which were located in nonattainment areas and traditionally expanded at existing sites rather than developing new ones) by allowing them to open new facilities using "best available control technology" and emitting less pollution than concurrently shut-down facilities. The amendment stirred up much controversy for failing to provide means for new companies to move into nonattainment areas and apparently benefiting previously recalcitrant companies (which would have more emissions available to reduce) more than cooperative ones. See Liroff (1980).

16. It should be noted that technically bubbles may be allowed *between* (and not just within) plants as long as both qualify as existing sources. The key distinction – and major issue in litigation – is what emissions will be treated as coming from existing sources as opposed to new ones.

17. 43 Fed. Reg. 26383, 26394 (1978) (upheld in Alabama Power).

18. 44 Fed. Red. 3274 (1979).

19. 46 Fed. Reg. 50766 (1981).

20. 46 Fed. Reg. 20551 (1981).

21. The internal documents were generally not made public. The final policy is "Emissions Trading Policy Statement," 47 Fed. Reg. 15076 (7 April 1982) and 48 Fed. Reg. 39580 (31 August 1983).

22. 51 Fed. Reg. 43814 (1986).

23. Note, however, that, for reasons he has not persuasively stated, Posner (1981) asserts that regulatory and legislative changes generally will not be efficient, whereas judge-made common law changes will.

24. Polluting industries frequently did support the bubble but not the idea of a larger emissions trading system, to which the bubble was allied.

25. See Levin (1985) for a discussion of the "stopping point" problem in implementing the emissions trading system. Compare Pedersen, 1984.

26. I take it as axiomatic that social organizations prefer to retain maximal flexibility to alter their relationships to their social environments.

27. I use "culture" in the limited but important sociological sense to connote a *set of shared understandings that make it possible for people to act in concert with each other.* Although I will argue below that the new regulatory culture has derived part of its potency from connections to ideologi-

cal currents in the larger society, this localized form is neither logically deducible from nor determined by the larger system. Moreover, culture need not be fundamental or enduring in any major way. All that I imply by using the term is a set of mutual understandings which help define and evaluate options for regulatory action. For a much more thorough elaboration of its use in the context of regulation, see Meidinger (1987).

28. The classic analysis of interest-group liberalism is Lowi (1969); for a careful tracing of the phenomenon in administrative law, see Stewart (1975).

29. My use of the term "regulatory entrepreneurs" may also invite reference to the work of James Q. Wilson (1980). His typology categorizes as entrepreneurial those regulatory situations in which the benefits of regulation are widely dispersed while the costs are concentrated. The type of regulation discussed here fits this categorization. But my use of the term "entrepreneur" was inspired by my interviews with the individuals involved; the connection to the typology only came to mind as I revised this paper. More important, though, it does not seem to me that Wilson's analysis is of any particular aid in predicting or understanding the developments here. The reason is in part that the move to emissions trading reflects a tendency also present in other types of regulation.

30. I will note but not develop the point that ease of exclusion may be somewhat asymmetrical: those with more immediate interests – for example, money – to lose may be permitted more mistakes than those with more abstract interests. But I have found sufficient counterexamples to make me skeptical of any simple formulation at this stage of the research.

31. It should be noted that a major part of the original Gorsuch effort to change EPA policy involved breaking up the enforcement office and reassigning staff to program offices (Lash, Gillman, and Sheridan, 1984). This move was later partly reversed in a series of incremental steps, but the enforcement program still suffers from incomplete restaffing and the lack of clear lines of authority.

32. The most important of these was the Air Quality Technical Assistance Demonstration program, through which the OPPE helped fund six state-level studies, none of which was particularly successful on its own terms but all of which brought emissions trading advocates into state and local program offices. See, for example, Palen et al. (1982).

33. See, for example, Business Roundtable (1980a, b) and Crandall (1983).

34. Expanded participation rights, discussed above as one of the structural features of social regulation, can also be seen as a response to this problem.

35. Gordon (1982) offers an illuminating analysis of this sort of conceptual interrelationship:

Law, like religion and television images, is one of these clusters of belief – and it ties in with a lot of other nonlegal but similar clusters – that convince people that all the many hierarchical relations in which they live and work are natural and necessary. A small business is staffed with people who carry around in their heads mixed clusters of this kind: "I can tell these people what to do and fire them if they're not *very* polite to me and quick to do it, because (a) I own the business; (b) they have no right to anything but the minimum wage; (c) I went to college and they didn't; (d) they would not work as hard or as efficiently if I didn't keep after them; a business can't run efficiently without a strong top-down command structure; (e) if they don't like it they can leave," etc. – and the employees, though with less smugness and enthusiasm, believe it as well. Take the ownership claim: the employees are not likely to think they can challenge that because to do so would jeopardize their sense of the rights of ownership, which they themselves exercise in other aspects of life ("I own this house, so I can tell my brother-in-law to get the hell out of it"); they are locked into a belief-cluster that abstracts and generalizes the ownership claim. [At 287]

36. See Reich (1964) for an optimistic argument for treating state-conferred privileges like property rights. The argument seemed to gain some credence in the 1970 Supreme Court decision of *Goldberg* v. *Kelly* (397 U.S. 254), but by 1976 it had eroded into an inconclusive form of procedural balancing [*Matthews* v. *Eldridge,* 424 U.S. 319 (1976)].

References

Baumol, W. J., and S. A. Batey Blackman. 1979. "Emissions Permits vs. Effluent Charges." Draft paper for the U.S. Environmental Protection Agency, in author's files.

Becker, H. S. 1982. "Culture: A Sociological View." *Yale Review* 71:513–27.

Bernstein, M. H. 1955. *Regulating Business by Independent Commission.* Princeton, N.J.: Princeton University Press.

Boyer, B. B., and E. Meidinger. 1986. "Privatizing Regulatory Enforcement: A Preliminary Assessment of Citizen Suits under Federal Environmental Laws." *Buffalo Law Review* 34:833–964.

Buchanan, J., and G. Tullock. 1975. "Polluters' Profits and Political Response: Direct Controls versus Taxes." *American Economic Review* 65:139–47.

Business Roundtable. 1980a. "Cost Effectiveness and Cost-Benefit Analysis of Air Quality Regulation." In *Air Quality Project,* vol. 4. Prepared by National Economic Research Associates, Inc.

————. 1980b. "The Effects of Prevention of Significant Deterioration on Industrial Development." In *Air Quality Project,* vol. 3. Prepared by Arthur D. Little, Inc.

Coase, R. H. 1960. "The Problem of Social Cost." *Journal of Law and Economics* 3:1–44.

Crandall, R. 1983. *Controlling Industrial Pollution: The Economics and Politics of Clean Air.* Washington, D.C.: Brookings Institution.

Dales, J. H. 1968. *Pollution, Property, and Prices.* Toronto: University of Toronto Press.

Demsetz, H. 1967. "Toward a Theory of Property Rights." *American Economic Review: Papers and Proceedings* 57:347–57.

Eads, G., and M. Fix. 1984. *Relief or Reform? Reagan's Regulatory Dilemma.* Washington, D.C.: Brookings Institution.

Gordon, H. D. 1964. "The Economic Theory of a Common Property Resource: The Fishery." *Journal of Political Economy* 62:135.

Gordon, R. W. 1982. "New Developments in Legal Theory." In *The Politics of Law: A Progressive Critique,* ed. D. Kairys. New York: Pantheon.

Hahn, R. W., and G. L. Hester. 1986. "Where Did All the Markets Go? An Analysis of EPA's Emission Trading Program." Unpublished, School of Urban and Public Affairs, Carnegie Mellon University, Pittsburgh, Pa. 15213.

Hahn, R. W., and R. G. Noll. 1982. "Implementing Tradable Emissions Permits." In *Reforming Social Regulation: Alternative Public Policy Strategies,* ed. L. Graymer and F. Thompson. Beverly Hills, Calif.: Sage.

Hawkins, K. O. 1984. *Environment and Enforcement: Regulation and the Social Definition of Pollution.* Oxford: Clarendon Press.

Hughes, J.R.T. 1977. *The Government Habit: Economic Controls from Colonial Times to the Present.* New York: Basic Books.

Huntington, S. P. 1952. "The Marasmus of the I.C.C.: The Commission, the Railroads, and the Public Interest." *Yale Law Journal* 61:467–509.

Kamerschen, D. R. 1966. "An Estimation of the Welfare Losses from Monopoly in the American Economy." *Western Economic Journal* 4:221–36.

Kelman, S. 1981. *What Price Incentives? Economists and the Environment.* Boston: Auburn.

Landy, M. K., and H. A. Plotkin. 1982. "Limits of the Market Metaphor." *Society* 19, no. 4:8.

Lash, J., K. Gillman, and D. Sheridan. 1984. *A Season of Spoils: The Story of the Reagan Administration's Attack on the Environment.* New York: Pantheon Books.

Levin, M. 1982. "Getting There: Implementing the 'Bubble' Policy." In *Social Regulation: Strategies for Reform.* San Francisco: San Francisco Institute for Contemporary Studies.

———. 1985. "Statutes and Stopping Points: Building a Better Bubble at E.P.A." *Regulation* 9, no. 3:33–42.

Liroff, R. A. 1980. *Air Pollution Offsets: Trading, Selling, and Banking.* Washington, D.C.: Conservation Foundation.

———. Forthcoming. *Reforming Air Pollution Regulation: The Toil and*

Trouble of Regulatory Reform. Washington, D.C.: Conservation Foundation.

Lowi, T. 1969. *The End of Liberalism: Ideology and the Crisis of Public Authority*. New York: Norton.

———. 1984. "The Welfare State, the New Regulation, and the Rule of Law." Prepared for the Conference on Distributional Conflicts in Environmental Resource Policy, Science Center, Berlin, 26–27 March.

Macavoy, P. 1962. *Price Formation in Natural Gas Fields: A Study of Monopoly, Monopsyny, and Regulation*. New Haven, Conn.: Yale University Press.

McConnell, G. 1966. *Private Power and American Democracy*. New York: Knopf.

McCullough, A., and M. Shannon. 1977. "Organization and Protection." In *Critical Issues on Organizations*, ed. S. Clegg and D. Dunkerly. Boston: Routledge and Kegan Paul.

Maloney, M. T., and B. Yandle. 1981. "Rent Seeking and the Evolution of Property Rights in Air Quality." Unpublished, Department of Economics, Clemson University, Clemson, S.C.

Meidinger, E. 1987. "Regulatory Culture: A Theoretical Outline." *Law and Policy* 9, no. 4:355–86.

———. 1988. *Politics, Markets, and Power: The Social Construction of Property Rights in Air Pollution*. Buffalo: State University of New York at Buffalo Law School.

Michels, R. 1949. *Political Parties*. Glencoe, Ill.: Free Press.

Mill, J. S. 1862. *Principles of Political Economy*. New York: J.A. Hill.

National Commission on Air Quality. 1981. *Breathe Clean Air*. Washington, D.C.: NCAQ.

Nonet, P. 1969. *Administrative Justice: Advocacy and Change in Government Agencies*. New York: Russell Sage Foundation.

Palen, F. S., W. Katkin, and J. M. Thomas. 1982. "Local Government and National Regulatory Reform: A Case Study of the Air Quality Technical Assistance Project in Buffalo, New York, 1978 to 1982." Unpublished, Baldy Center for Law and Social Policy, State University of New York, Buffalo, N.Y.

Pearce, D. 1984. "Efficiency and Distribution in Corrective Mechanisms for Environmental Externality." Presented at the Conference on Distributional Conflicts in Environmental Resource Policy, Science Center, Berlin, 26–27 March.

Pedersen, W. F., Jr. 1984. "Pollution Accounting Under the Clean Air Act." *Environmental Forum* 3, no. 1:36–39.

Pigou, A. 1932. *The Economics of Welfare*. 4th ed. London: Macmillan.

Posner, R. 1977. *Economics Analysis of Law*. 2d ed. Boston: Little, Brown.

———. 1981. *The Economics of Justice*. Cambridge, Mass.: Harvard University Press.

Reich, C.   1964.   "The New Property." *Yale Law Journal* 74:733–87.

Reich, N.   1983.   "The Regulatory Crisis: American Approaches in the Light of European Experiences." *American Bar Foundation Research Journal* 1983:693–704.

Reiter, S., and J. Hughes.   1981.   "A Preface on Modelling the Regulated United States Economy." *Hofstra Law Review* 9:1381–1421.

Ritts, L. S.   1983.   *State Emissions Trading: Analysis and Compendium of State Regulations.* Washington, D.C.: Environmental Law Institute.

Schnaiberg, A.   1980.   *The Environment: From Surplus to Scarcity.* New York: Oxford University Press.

Stewart, R.   1975.   "The Reformation of American Administrative Law." *Harvard Law Review* 88:1667.

———   1981.   "Regulation, Innovation, and Administrative Law: A Conceptual Framework." *California Law Review* 69:1256.

Stigler, G.   1956.   "The Statistics of Monopoly and Merger." *Journal of Political Economy* 64:33–40.

Weidenbaum, M. L.   1980.   "The Changing Nature of Government Regulation of Business." *Journal of Post-Keynesian Economics* 2:345–57.

Wilensky, H. L.   1969.   *Organizational Intelligence: Knowledge and Policy in Government and Industry.* New York: Basic Books.

Wilson, J. Q.   1980.   *The Politics of Regulation.* New York: Basic Books.

III

The Design of Policy Rules and
the Management of Discretion

The three essays in part III analyze issues of regulatory policy for-mation which are basic to administrative law and procedure: the de-sign of rules and the delegation of discretion to regulatory officials. Rule making and the management of discretion are viewed as highly interdependent factors which influence the way regulated firms per-ceive enforcement methods and choose to comply or not to comply. The analysis of compliance effects illustrates the utility of consider-ing these policy decisions in terms of the concepts of bounded ration-ality and social construction.

Colin Diver observes that the capacity of agency policymakers to design rules rationally is limited or bounded by compliance effects such as the expected level of rule violation by the regulated popula-tion. From a social constructionist perspective, however, the notion of "expected levels of rule violations" itself is not necessarily an ob-jective and measurable property of the process. Rather it is based upon both sides' interpretations of the nature of interaction between agency actors and the regulated.

Daniel Gifford emphasizes the importance of understanding the way in which the nature of regulatory cases can influence policy gov-erning the delegation of discretion. Using the normative framework developed by Davis, which advocates the importance of "structur-ing" discretion, Gifford argues that the decision should reflect prior assessments of the importance of types of cases for agency goals and whether the factual pattern in cases is unique or recurring. Gifford concludes his essay with a discussion of the implications of his analy-sis for the agency decision to disclose to the regulated public the stan-dards governing regulatory decisions.

In the concluding essay, the editors analyze the relevance of the frameworks of bounded rationality and social construction for the design of rules and the management of discretion. The discussion is based on a review of the central themes and issues in the essays by Diver and Gifford.

7

Regulatory Precision

Colin S. Diver

I F , A S Oliver Wendell Holmes once said, "a word is . . . the skin of a living thought,"[1] then a "rule" is the skin of a living "policy." A rule is the verbal manifestation of policy that is typically – but not necessarily – encased within a written text and issued with the formality suited to a solemn occasion. As the skin of a policy, a rule hardens an inchoate normative judgment into the (temporarily) frozen form of words. Its issuance marks the transformation of policy from private wish to public expectation.

If one is to take at face value much recurrent criticism of government regulation, that act of transformation is often badly performed. The pens of regulatory drafters, so one would gather, leave in their wake a maze of confusing, ambiguous, obscure, misguided, and Byzantine rules. Part of the blame for the situation rests, presumably, on the unwisdom or downright perversity of the underlying policy. But much of the blame, one senses, is attributable to a failure to choose the most appropriate linguistic vehicle in which to embody that policy.

My objective in this chapter is to examine the implicit assumption underlying these criticisms, that one can articulate standards for evaluating the work product of regulatory rule writers. Rules may, like skin, be the visible manifestation of an unseen reality, but unlike skin, they are the product of conscious choice. The framing of a rule is, indeed, the climactic act of the policymaking process. Any system of advice calculated to improving that process must, then, include criteria for making the choice. In the following pages I develop an efficiency criterion for selecting the optimal "precision" of a regulation. I then apply it to three distinct types of regulatory policies: a rule of conduct (the Security and Exchange Commission's "Rule 144," governing the resale of unregistered securities); a rule governing the imposition of sanctions (the Transportation Department's policies for punishing violators of the Hazardous Materials Transportation Act); and a licensing policy (the Federal Communications Commission's broadcast licensing criteria). In the concluding section, I extract lessons from these case studies for the drafters of regulatory policies generally.[2]

Three Critiques of Legal Rules

Criticisms of legal rules tend to cluster in three discernible camps: the vagueness critique, the overinclusiveness critique, and the complexity critique. The evil on which the vagueness critique focuses is indeterminacy.[3] Vague rules leave persons whom they affect (or whom they may affect) to guess at their meaning in particular circumstances. They confer large areas of largely uncontrollable discretion on those entrusted with their enforcement. Vagueness is a common affliction of regulatory standards, especially those that rely on such open-ended terms as "in the public interest," "feasible," or "reasonable."

Recent criticism of specification standards in health and safety regulation illustrates the overinclusiveness critique.[4] The problem with overinclusive rules is not that they are vague — their meaning is usually commendably clear — but that they command (or forbid) many actions that are not beneficial (or are harmful) to society. The fit between the outcomes demanded by literal adherence to the rule and those desired by the policymaker is poor. The complexity critique focuses on the sheer length and intricacy of a rule's verbal formula. Complex rules, like the tax code or many environmental regulations, make the determination of legal consequences turn on a maze of considerations, conditions, and exceptions.[5] The consequence is to drive the cost of applying the rule to excessive levels.

These three critiques suggest three corresponding qualities that should characterize well-drafted legal rules: transparency, congruence, and simplicity. A transparent rule, like a transparent window, allows each observer to see the same image — to reach the same conclusion about legal consequences when confronted with the same evidence. Transparency thus increases the likelihood that the rule maker's intention will be communicated without distortion to the rule's audience. A congruent rule identifies as proscribed (or mandatory or permitted) only those actions that ought – under the policymaker's governing normative system – to be proscribed (or mandated or permitted). Congruence, in this sense, essentially determines the efficacy of a rule's verbal formulation in achieving its intended outcome. Simplicity, finally, is a function of the number of steps required by the regulation's decision rule and the quantity and accessibility of the evidentiary inputs that it demands. The simpler the rule, the more likely that its audience will remember it and the less costly its application to concrete situations.

Determination of the appropriate verbal form in which to cast regulatory policy decisions, then, could be understood as a problem of simultaneously maximizing a rule's transparency, congruence, and simplicity. Unfortunately, these values frequently conflict. Consider, for example, a rule setting a highway speed limit. A uniform speed limit like "maximum speed 55 m.p.h." has the virtues of transparency and simplicity. Virtually everyone understands the meaning of "55 m.p.h." (it is interpreted as "any speed at which the needle on my speedometer lies to the right of '55'"). The differences of interpretation that arise (resulting mostly from variations in the calibration of speed-measuring equipment) will be modest in all but the rarest of cases. The rule is also simple: the legal test relies on a single variable (speed), and the evidentiary input (speedometer reading) is easily accessible and relatively objective.

The problem with the rule is its incongruity. Under any plausible assumption about the purpose of highway speed regulation, a uniform speed limit will overinclude or underinclude. If the objective were absolute safety (zero accidents), a uniform speed limit (of zero) might be defensible. But more realistically, one must assume a policy objective that combines concerns about safety with other values such as the facilitation of movement and efficient consumption of motor fuel. However one might combine these values into a single objective function, it is inconceivable that a uniform speed would maximize that function. An "efficient speed" criterion (minimize the sum of the costs of accidents, delays, fuel consumption, and so forth), for example, would surely require a speed limit that varied with weather conditions, time of day, type of vehicle, purpose of travel, and the like. A variable speed limit of this sort might significantly enhance the rule's congruence but with an unavoidable loss of simplicity (since the decision rule would contain multiple criteria and perhaps require less objective and accessible evidentiary inputs, such as "time value of vehicle's occupants"). Transparency might also suffer if the new variables (such as "icy conditions") are less susceptible to uniform interpretation than a simple speed limit.

One could restore at least the appearance of simplicity with a rule such as "do not exceed a reasonable speed." But transparency suffers badly in such a formulation. And one has little basis for confidence that such a congruent-sounding rule will in fact produce congruent outcomes, since it effectively confers a broad, unlimited discretion upon drivers and enforcers.

An Efficiency Criterion

One possible way to make choices among such competing verbal formulations is to invoke some a priori moral value such as fairness or equity. Unfortunately these principles frequently conflict. The principle of "fair notice" may require the interpretive clarity of a highly transparent rule, while the principles of "participation" and "individualized treatment" may require the flexibility of a more opaque formulation. Even taken singly, moreover, few plausible moral principles point in an unambiguous direction. "Equity," for example, may be interpreted to require all three qualities: transparency, to assure equivalent interpretation by those subject to the rule; congruence, to assure equivalent treatment of those similarly situated in relation to the ultimate policy objective; and simplicity, to minimize differences in treatment resulting from cognitive or litigative advantages.

Constructing a metric for evaluating the work product of regulatory drafters, then, requires us, however crudely, to measure and compare the competing interests at work, in an effort to locate the appropriate mix of transparency, congruence, and simplicity. Adoption of this approach may convert the argument from the elevated rhetoric of moral principle to the crasser language of costs and benefits. But it provides a more promising basis for making the unavoidable tradeoffs entailed in decisions about the form of rules.[6]

In order to adopt such an approach, we need some intelligible criterion for characterizing the form of various rules. For ease of exposition, I will rely primarily on the "transparency" dimension. Of the three dimensions described earlier, transparency is probably the easiest to understand and to apply, at least in a rough qualitative sense, to different verbal formulations. We commonly make impressionistic judgments about the relative vagueness or clarity of rules. One could, moreover, construct a more objective and quantitative measure of rule transparency: namely, the ratio of agreement among a sample of a rule's audience confronted with a set of hypothetical questions regarding its application to concrete situations.[7] Finally, much of the debate about regulatory form has been conducted in the language of transparency (or in such near-synonyms as "specificity," "objectivity," "precision," and the like).

The next step in constructing an efficiency criterion for rule formality is to identify the principal consequences likely to flow from variations in regulatory transparency. Rules may be viewed as an intermediate good – the product of a process (which I call "rule making") and an input into other processes ("compliance" activities by private persons whose primary behavior is addressed by the rule and "enforcement" activities by private persons and government officials engaged in enforcing the rules). Variations in the transparency of a rule, then, can have consequences for all of these processes.

Rule Making. The writing of a transparent rule may require a larger initial investment of resources in obtaining and evaluating information. This cost is at least a partial substitute for the costs of overinclusiveness. Careful initial analysis reduces the scope of misspecification and its attendant costs. Rule making also typically requires the accommodation of conflicting views. This statement is especially true of collegial bodies but also holds for most hierarchical agencies as well. The more precise a rule, the larger the range of agreement necessary and consequently the higher the costs of reaching agreement. A related cost, from the rule maker's perspective, is the risk that enhanced visibility of policy may increase political criticism (and thereby increase agency costs of blunting the criticism).

On the other hand, greater initial precision can reduce the need for future rule-making activity by leaving fewer policy questions open for later resolution. An investment in more precise draftsmanship can thus reduce the volume of resources that must be devoted either to "common-law" rule making (elaboration of reasoned justifications in individual cases having precedential value) or to subsequent generic "legislative" rule making. Enhanced initial rule transparency can also reduce the agency's subsequent investment in internal mechanisms for quality control, such as employee training or auditing to assure consistency and correctness of decisions made by individual enforcement personnel.

Compliance. Increased rule transparency may increase the rate of compliance with a rule (and decrease evasion or concealment costs) by reducing the cost, to the rule's addressee, of determining how the rule will apply to his intended conduct. It may also increase the rate of compliance by raising the estimated probability in the eyes of the addressee that undesirable conduct will be punished or desired conduct will be rewarded. If increasing a rule's transparency causes the rule to become more complex or less congruent, however, at some point further clarification may reduce the rate of compliance by driving up the cost of locating the applicable provision or by reducing the rule's moral acceptability.

Increasing the clarity of a rule also increases the risk of unintended overinclusiveness. This problem may result from the rule maker's inability to predict all of the consequences of applying the rule or to predict all of the circumstances to which it may apply. While presumably the rule maker can later change the rule upon learning of the misfit, social losses will be incurred in the interim. The cost of subsequently amending the rule is also an ingredient of the cost of overinclusiveness.

On the other hand, a relatively opaque rule may be overinclusive *in application,* because vagueness invites misinterpretation. Increasing a rule's transparency may therefore substitute errors of misspecification for errors of misapplication.

Enforcement. Greater transparency can reduce enforcement costs in several ways. First, it can simplify the task of monitoring the relevant environment for rule violations. Government inspectors or private persons enforcing a transparent rule can more readily detect violations and can prosecute them with greater confidence in the accuracy of their judgments. Indeed, to the extent that transparency enhances voluntary compliance, there will be fewer violations to prosecute. Second, greater transparency should reduce the number of disputes arising in the course of the enforcement process by causing the parties' prediction of the dispute's outcome to converge. Given the relatively higher cost of litigating than settling a dispute, convergent outcome assessments will produce more frequent settlements. By sharpening the contested issues, moreover, a transparent rule can reduce the cost of resolving those disputes that do arise.

To the extent that rule clarification sacrifices simplicity or congruence, some of these advantages may be lost. Even if its separate elements are transparent, a highly complicated rule may be costly to interpret and apply in particular instances. An extremely incongruent rule may invite frequent attempts at circumvention whose detection and prosecution will prove costly.

Having classified the various consequences flowing from a change in rule precision into these three categories, one must specify a decision rule for drawing an ultimate normative judgment about any particular rule formulation. The procedure implicit in the approach sketched above would be to aggregate the favorable and unfavorable impacts under the three headings into one overall "score." One could then evaluate any particular verbal formulation, taken in isolation, merely by looking at the sign of its score (positive = acceptable; negative = unacceptable), or compare two or more alternatives by selecting the one with the highest positive score.

This procedure is, of course, impossible to carry out with anything approaching mathematical precision. Aside from the usual problems of measuring and valuing consequences, it is often difficult to isolate the impact of formal variations in a rule from substantive shifts in the underlying "policy." Indeed, it is intrinsically difficult to identify the objectives of a rule, since the latter is usually the most reliable evidence of the former. Nonetheless, extrinsic evidence is usually available to enable the investigator to make educated estimates of the direction and magnitude of crucial variables. In the three sections that follow, I use this approach to illustrate how it can help us evaluate three widely divergent types of regulatory rules.

The SEC's "Safe Harbor" Rules for Resale of Unregistered Securities

The Securities Act of 1933 generally prohibits the public sale of securities that have not been "registered" with the Securities and Exchange Commission (SEC).[8] Registration requires the filing of a statement containing detailed financial, operating, and ownership information about the company issuing the securities (issuer).[9] The act exempts private securities offerings from the registration require-

ment.[10] Since purchasers at private offerings – often the issuer's in-
corporators, officers, directors, and their associates – are usually
knowledgeable and sophisticated investors, the act's public information requirements are considered unnecessary in that context. An
important question then arises as to whether and under what circumstances purchasers at a private sale may resell unregistered securities to the public. An absence of restrictions could permit easy
circumvention of the registration requirement, while a flat prohibition would impair the value of privately issued securites by seriously
restricting their alienability.

The statute is not particularly instructive in resolving this common problem. The area of greatest uncertainty involves the definition of "underwriter," since the act exempts transactions by persons
"other than an . . . underwriter."[11] The definition of "underwriter"
leaves considerable room for doubt about its application to resellers.
An "underwriter" is a person who purchases from an issuer "with a
view to . . . the distribution" of a security.[12] If the resale of an unregistered security to the public were considered part of its "distribution," the sale would expose the seller to civil and criminal liability. It has fallen to the SEC, as the act's principal interpreter and
enforcer, to resolve the uncertainty. With respect to the prohibition
against public sale of unregistered securities, the SEC has both a
prosecutorial and a legislative role. It may initiate a civil or criminal
enforcement action against an alleged violator, and it has explicit
authority to insulate transactions against collateral attack in a private suit.

For the first four decades of its existence, the SEC interpreted
the "underwriter" exemption primarily through the vehicle of "no-
action" letters.[13] Prospective resellers of unregistered securities could
seek formal clearance for the proposed transaction, in the form of
a letter from the SEC's staff announcing its binding commitment not
to take enforcement action based on the transaction. Most no-action
letters were issued by the Commission's Division of Corporation Finance, although a few were approved by the commission itself. Either
way, the commitment was treated as binding on the SEC, provided
that the facts were as stated in the request.

Although no-action letters contained justifications for the staff's
ultimate conclusions, they were not considered precedents. Until
1970, in fact, the SEC did not even make them publicly available.[14]
According to a 1969 SEC staff study (the "Wheat Report"), the staff

used a "subjective" test to determine whether the purchaser had taken the securities "with a view to distribution."[15] While the length of the holding period was considered probative of original intent, the commission emitted rather confused signals about the length of time necessary to demonstrate "investment intent" (the opposite of "distribution intent"). One commissioner publicly suggested a two-year period,[16] while staff said sometimes five years, sometimes three.[17] Whatever the holding period necessary to cleanse a transaction, an investor who alleged a sufficiently compelling "change of circumstances" could obtain permission to sell a security held for a shorter period. One could say with some assurance that a "change of circumstance" relating solely to the investment itself (such as one causing a decline in its market value) would not qualify. But it was more difficult to predict the sort of personal circumstances that might move the staff.

Pressure to clarify the SEC's policy mounted in the late 1960s and early 1970s. Private practitioners and commentators deplored the lack of "certainty" in the commission's policy, the apparent conflict between the staff's and commission's interpretations, and the resulting "unpredictable environment for investors."[18] After extensive discussion, the SEC decided to issue more transparent guidelines for the resale of unregistered securities. The resulting rule (known as "Rule 144") used the so-called safe harbor technique: transactions that met all of its conditions were "deemed" to be exempt from the act's registration requirement (and were therefore immunized from civil or criminal liability).[19] Transactions not fully satisfying the rule might also qualify for exemption, said the commission, but the burden of proof on the proponent of exemption would be "substantial."[20] Even this small window was effectively closed by a simultaneous announcement that the SEC staff would no longer issue no-action advice concerning resale of restricted securities acquired after the rule's effective date.

Anchorage in Rule 144's safe harbor, as originally dredged, required satisfaction of five conditions: (1) availability of "adequate current public information with respect to the issuer"; (2) a minimum holding period between purchase and proposed sale; (3) a quantity limitation on the amount sold; (4) sale in a "brokers' transaction"; and (5) notification of the sale to the SEC. The rule expressed each of the five conditions in highly objective terms. For example, the condition regarding the holding period required that the seller have owned the security for a period of two years prior to the resale and contained elaborate conditions for establishing the acquisition date for securities acquired by promissory note, option, stock dividend, conversion, gift, bequest, or other means.

In a series of amendments since its adoption, the SEC has steadily relaxed the original restrictions, at least as applied to sales by "non-affiliates" (persons not in a control relationship with the issuer). Non-affiliates who have held securities for a specified holding period (now three years) have gradually been excused from compliance with other conditions (volume limits, manner of sale, and notice). This development suggests a gradual movement toward a simple test based on the length of the holding period, although at the present time the rule is a complex amalgam of the original conditions overlaid with newer exemptions.

The SEC's official explanation for adopting Rule 144 in 1972 featured both substantive and formal arguments. The rule renounced the old "change of circumstances" test in favor of an approach more directly linked to the goal of assuring adequate protection of unsophisticated purchasers. "The circumstances of the seller," explained the commission, "are unrelated to the need of investors for the protections afforded by the registration and other provisions of the Act."[21] But Rule 144 sought to change more than the focus of commission policy. It sought to achieve greater "certainty" as well. It was a deliberate exercise in precision enhancement, and we are principally interested in the success of that exercise.

Contemporaneous justifications for Rule 144 invoke both enforcement and compliance arguments. Although the Wheat Report cited the "growing burden" of responding to no-action requests,[22] the magnitude of the burden on the SEC itself was not very impressive. The no-action process was extremely informal and efficient, involving essentially only an exchange of correspondence. Internal legal research was very limited, dialogue between the agency and the applicant rare, and internal review perfunctory. More than half of the requests were answered in a month, and more than 80 percent within two months. One study estimated that the total staff resources devoted to no-action letters in the division amounted to only 7.6 person-years.[23]

A proper accounting of the social cost of the SEC's policy before Rule 144, however, must also include the resources expended by potential resellers (or their brokers) to obtain private legal advice on the transaction's exempt status. Although this cost does not figure in official SEC justifications for Rule 144, and we lack direct evidence of its magnitude, it undoubtedly exceeded SEC staff costs by a wide margin.

The magnitude of the investment in private legal advice undoubtedly reflects the size of the seller's financial risk. The principal legal risk incurred by the reseller of unregistered securities is liability to the purchaser. Section 12 of the act gives the purchaser an absolute right to rescind a sale in violation of the registration requirement, effectively making the seller a guarantor against decline in the securities' value. The risk undertaken by a reseller, then, is a function of the sale price, the probability of a future decline in the securities' market value, and the probability that the resale will be judicially determined not to be exempt. The larger the first two variables, the more the reseller should be willing to invest in pretransactional legal advice to estimate or reduce the third variable. This calculus would undoubtedly often justify substantial investments in legal advice.

Although the SEC still entertains informal requests for "interpretive" advice, the volume of these requests is less than 10 percent of the previous volume of inquiries. Since Rule 144 is far more accessible and compact than the previous sprawling body of no-action letters, moreover, the cost of obtaining private legal advice must also have fallen markedly. These savings in the transaction costs involved in applying rules have been eroded, to be sure, by an increase in rule-making costs. The commission has revised Rule 144 repeatedly during its brief life and has also issued extensive "interpretive releases."[24] But it seems safe to conclude that overall Rule 144 has had a favorable impact on enforcement costs.

Another concern articulated by the Wheat Report is the "constant problem in providing reasonably consistent advice."[25] As applied to SEC staff interpretations, the concern with inconsistency seems overstated. The SEC's clearance function was highly centralized. Requests for no-action letters were handled by some forty lawyers in the division, organized in branches defined by class of corporate activity. Drafts of all responsive letters were in turn reviewed by one of two assistant chief counsels in the division's Office of Chief Counsel and were submitted to the chief counsel for signature. As the Wheat Report acknowledges, the difficulty of controlling consistency in so centralized a process is not particularly formidable. A more serious problem, the report claimed, was erroneous application of policy by private counsel. Undoubtedly, many errors (both excessively restrictive and excessively liberal interpretations) did in fact occur. But the ready availability of inexpensive official advice and the sophistication of the regulated population could be counted upon to hold the number and magnitude of such errors in check.

The rule was also designed to enhance the rate of compliance. The Wheat Report complained that the commission's "vague and imprecise" policies encouraged "unprincipled counsel" to endorse improper transactions. "The pressures are strong," says the report, "and the temptation to cut the statutory corner is magnified by uncertainty."[26] The incentive to evade registration was indeed powerful in many cases, but that incentive was also constrained by some rather powerful counterforces, such as the exposure to civil and criminal liability and the reputational interest of many "repeat players" involved in the securities business.

Set against these rather modest compliance and enforcement benefits are the incongruity costs of a bright-line exemption rule. While the preamble professed monolithic concern for protecting innocent purchasers, the SEC clearly recognizes a competing obligation not to discourage capital formation unduly. The history of Rule 144 suggests that its original restrictive conditions did have that effect. Fear of underinclusiveness drove the agency to the opposite excess and, in the process, undoubtedly discouraged venture capital investment in new enterprise. In its recent amendments to the rule, however, the SEC appears to be moving toward a better balance of transparency and congruity. The standard for sale of restricted securities by nonaffiliates is evolving toward a simple test of the holding period plus requirement of public information. This simplified test promises to reduce overinclusiveness losses to manageable proportions while greatly simplifying the task of interpreting and applying the rule. Thus, while the original Rule 144 was itself a questionably successful step in the quest for certainty, it has triggered an ongoing evolution that has brought the SEC closer to its goal.

DOT's Standards for Assessing Penalties for Hazardous Materials Transportation Violations

Federal regulation of hazardous material transportation has expanded steadily since 1871, culminating in the passage of the Hazardous Materials Transportation Act of 1975 (hereinafter called the HMTA).[27] The U.S. Department of Transportation (DOT) is charged with enforcing the HMTA. The act authorizes the secretary of transportation to designate materials whose transportation in commerce "may pose an unreasonable risk to health and safety or property" as a "hazardous material" and to promulgate regulations "for the safe transportation in commerce" of such materials.

The act's chief enforcement provision authorizes the secretary to impose, "after notice and an opportunity for a hearing," a civil money penalty of not more than $10,000 per violation on anyone who "knowingly commit(s) an act which is a violation" of the act or a rule issued thereunder. Each day of violation of a rule relating to shipper or carrier obligations constitutes a separate violation. The statutory standard for computing the appropriate penalty reads:

> In determining the amount of such penalty, the Secretary shall take into account the nature, circumstances, extent, and gravity of the violation committed and, with respect to the person found to have committed such violation, the degree of culpability, any history of prior offenses, ability to pay, effect on ability to continue to do business, and such other matters as justice may require.[28]

Once a penalty has been administratively determined, it may be recovered by civil action in a federal district court by the attorney general. Before referring a case to the attorney general, the secretary may compromise the claim.

Pursuant to the statutory authority to promulgate safety standards, the secretary designated some 1,800 substances as "hazardous materials," ranging in apparent danger from bombs and chlorine gas to oil paint and straw. The secretary then proceeded to adopt some 1,200 pages of rules specifying in exquisite detail how these various substances must be labeled, documented, handled, loaded, and stored.[29] Most of these rules were based on preexisting consensus standards issued by private standard-setting organizations.[30] As is the case in much contemporary health and safety regulation, these rules consist overwhelmingly of specifications standards rather than performance standards.

The secretary delegated responsibility for enforcing these standards against carriers and shippers by air, highway, rail, and water to the Transportation Department's four "modal" units (the Federal Aviation Administration, Federal Highway Administration, Federal Railroad Administration, and Coast Guard, respectively). The Research and Special Programs Administration, also responsible for writing the standards, received authority to enforce the container specifications against container manufacturers. In marked contrast to the excruciating detail of the substantive standards, this delegation of enforcement authority was accompanied by virtually no guidance on enforcement priorities or sanctioning policy.

In four of these five administrative units (all but the Coast Guard), prosecution of HMTA violations is the responsibility of a small group of attorneys in the Washington office. For almost all of these attorneys, HMTA enforcement is only one of several areas of responsibility. In the Coast Guard, in contrast, the prosecutorial function is exercised by nonlawyer "hearing officers" in the district offices.

The discretion of the department's prosecutors, like that of criminal prosecutors, has two dimensions: charging and sentencing. The charging decision involves the nature and the number of offenses to cite in the notice of violation. Even though the governing regulations prescribe highly objective and readily verifiable standards of conduct, agency prosecutors exercise considerable discretion over the selection of detected violations to cite, the aggregation or disaggregation of related offenses, and the appropriate unit for defining the violation (by separate package or entire shipment, per day or per incident). The prosecutor's sentencing discretion consists of selecting the amount of the fine to propose and accept in compromise within the statutory ceiling of $10,000 per violation.

Neither the secretary nor the administrators of the agencies that enforce the HMTA have made much effort to constrain the exercise of their prosecutors' sentencing discretion by explicit instructions. Yet this low degree of verbal precision is not surprising. None of the factors customarily impelling policymakers toward a high degree of regulatory transparency operates with much force here. The caseloads, first of all, are modest. In the twelve-month period ending on June 30, 1979, for example, the department processed fewer than 350 penalty cases to completion. No single enforcement unit handled more than 130 cases. And while the statute requires the department to offer respondents an "opportunity for hearing," the procedure followed in most cases is highly informal. Although respondents contest initial notices of violations in about four of every five cases, rarely does the challenge involve more than an exchange of correspondence or informal conference.[31] The relatively modest penalties demanded in most cases—the median penalty assessed by the five units ranged from $650 to $8,000—discourage heavy investment in defensive tactics by respondents.

It is true that the nominal penalty assessment rarely measures the accused's stakes in a case fully. Nonpenalty costs associated with a determination of liability – such as the cost of correcting a violation or preventing its recurrence – can dwarf direct penalty costs.[32] But liability is rarely an issue in HMTA cases. The substantive regulations rely very heavily on specification standards, compliance with which can be verified objectively by observation or testing. The multilevel screening process from inspection to prosecution, moreover, tends to filter out cases of doubtful liability. Since most nonpenalty costs flow from the determination of liability rather than from computation of the penalty, the nominal penalty amount does in fact define a reasonable outer bound on the potential payoff from challenging a violation notice.

Quality control costs do not loom especially large in HMTA enforcement, either. In four of the five enforcement units, the prosecution function is concentrated in the hands of a few attorneys located at the agency's headquarters. Frequent interaction among these attorneys probably maintains decisional consistency at a fairly high level. Nor do clearer rules promise to save rule-making costs. The agency's current investment in penalty-severity rule making is virtually zero, since it is under no legal obligation to explain the basis of its initial assessments or final settlements. An increase in the number of fines imposed after a contested hearing would undoubtedly magnify the explanatory burden but only modestly in view of the extreme judicial deference customarily extended to administrative sanctioning decisions.[33]

Penalty standards might plausibly enhance compliance with the substantive rules by more clearly communicating the consequences of their violation. This hypothesis is debatable even in principle, since the deterrent effect of uncertainty depends on whether the regulated population is risk averse or risk preferring.[34] If, as some assert,[35] modern business leaders are inherently risk averse, uncertainty could enhance deterrent impact. The pursuit of general deterrence in this context, moreover, is itself controversial. Agency officials believe that most violations result from ignorance or carelessness, especially by low-level employees of carriers and shippers. The cost of effectively monitoring and controlling their conduct may often exceed any plausible estimate of the expected cost of a first-time violation.

Even if one accepts the premise that greater certainty would enhance compliance, the incremental contribution made by penalty standards would be small. The probability of detection and punishment is, for most regulated firms, very small and highly uncertain.[36] Similarly, the potential nonpenalty costs of committing an HMTA violation – such as potential tort liability for a resulting mishap – are subject to highly unpredictable odds and magnitudes. Estimating the total predicted cost (magnitude times probability for each adverse consequence) of a potential violation is thus enveloped in a fog of uncertainty that even a perfectly transparent penalty formula would barely penetrate.

The greatest source of resistance to policy clarification here, however, seems to be concern for incongruity. Agency prosecutorial personnel have steadfastly maintained that bright-line rules would impair their ability to tailor the sanction to the precise circumstances of the offense and the offender. This position has much force. Discretion at the remedial stage is often a safety valve for the over-inclusiveness of substantive rules.[37] It manifestly serves that function in this instance. In their single-minded pursuit of objectivity, the department's primary rules inevitably sweep large categories of harmless or beneficial conduct into the prohibited zone. Enforcement discretion enables the department to respond to legitimate contextual considerations – such as the location, size, and other contents of the shipment, the degree of personal culpability or corporate neglect, and the numbers of people exposed – that determine the hazard presented by an individual violation.

Articulated penalty standards could also undermine the corrective function of enforcement by impeding adjustment to peculiarities of the offender's situation. Sometimes a heavy hand is necessary to attract the attention of remote or recalcitrant upper-level management; at other times, securing a firm commitment to correct violation-breeding practices diminishes the utility of added punishment. This is to say not that more transparent penalty standards must necessarily ignore these contextual concerns but rather that any sensible body of standards would necessarily preserve a generously open texture.

Cries of incongruity have a hollow ring, of course, if the current regime produces wildly incongruent outcomes. The evidence suggests otherwise, however. On an aggregative basis, at least, the agency's behavior seems consistent with an "efficient deterrence" model. That is, most penalty collections relate to activities – bulk shipment of highly explosive, flammable, or toxic materials by rail or highway – that generate most of the social losses from hazardous materials transportation.[38] Similarly, the quite low reported rate of recidivism suggests that the agency's "correctional" policy is successful. Against that backdrop, the benefits from anything more than a modest elaboration of penalty criteria are unlikely to be great enough to justify the rule-making costs and enhanced incongruity risks.

The FCC's Broadcast Licensing Standards

The standards employed by the Federal Communications Commission (FCC) to select among competing applicants for a broadcast license, especially if one of them is an incumbent licensee seeking renewal, have long been criticized as a paragon of administrative opacity.[39] Despite countless proposals and several major efforts at reform, this body of standards has stubbornly resisted significant clarification.

The Federal Communications Act, embellished by FCC rules, articulates relatively transparent threshold criteria that specify minimal citizenship, financial, and technical qualifications for a broadcast license.[40] These include, for example, bright-line regulatory restrictions on joint ownership of other broadcast licenses or colocated newspapers[41] that have been judicially sustained against fierce attacks on their alleged incongruity.[42]

In the area of selecting among competing applicants who satisfy these threshold criteria, the FCC has been beset by particularly celebrated inarticulateness. A 1965 policy statement identified seven factors to be considered in choosing among competitors for an unoccupied frequency – "diversification of control of the media of mass communications, full-time participation in station operation by owners, proposed program service, past broadcast record, efficient use of frequency, character, and other factors."[43] Although the policy statement did describe diversification as "a factor of primary significance" and full-time participation as a factor "of substantial importance," it provided little guidance on the meaning or relative weight of these factors.

Once most of the desirable broadcast frequencies had been assigned, the major avenue for entry into broadcasting became challenges to the renewal of incumbents' licenses. This fact, plus the enormous financial stakes in major market broadcasting, focused great attention on the comparative renewal process. Since the 1965 policy statement was expressly inapplicable to license renewal cases, the

FCC adopted a policy statement on that subject in 1970.[44] The new statement, which purported to codify existing practice, identified the incumbent's "past record" in the "last license term" as the critical factor. If the incumbent's broadcast service had been "substantially attuned to meeting the needs and interests of its area" and free of "serious deficiencies," renewal would be granted without regard to the quality of the challenger's application. If not, the agency would weigh the comparative merits of the competing proposals, favoring a promising challenger.

Displaying its inexhaustible capacity for understatement, the FCC conceded that its standards "lack mathematical precision." Nonetheless, they would have simplified matters to a degree by focusing attention – at the initial stage at least – on only the one factor of the incumbent's past record. The heavy weight placed on this factor, however, highlighted its hopeless vagueness, and shortly after issuing the policy statement, the FCC opened Docket 19,154 to develop criteria for "substantial service."[45] In its notice of inquiry, the FCC specifically requested comments on a proposed set of mathematical guidelines for the minimal amount of broadcast time (expressed as percentages of total on-air time and of prime time) to be devoted to "local programming," "news," and "public affairs."

The ink was scarcely dry on the notice of inquiry when a federal court invalidated the 1970 policy statement because it effectively denied challengers the "full comparative hearing" guaranteed by the Communications Act.[46] Seizing on the court's dictum that "*superior* performance should be a plus of major significance," the FCC redoubled its effort to "clarify in both quantitative and qualitative terms what constitutes superior service." Yet despite the receipt of numerous comments and the issuance of two further notices of inquiry, in March 1977 the commission finally abandoned the effort to establish quantitative program standards.[47] To the extent that its order contains any affirmative statement of its renewal standard, it is the following:

> The renewal applicant must . . . continue to run on its record, and we believe that that record should be measured by the degree to which the licensee's program performance was sound, favorable, and substantially above a level of mediocre service which might just minimally warrant renewal. Where the renewal applicant has served the public interest in such a substantial fashion, it will be entitled to the "legitimate renewal expentancy" clearly "implicit in the structure of the [Communications] Act". . . . Thereafter, we will di-

rect our attention to the comparative factors set forth in the 1965 Policy Statement. . . . While that policy statement will otherwise govern the introduction of evidence in the comparative renewal proceeding, the weight to be accorded the legitimate renewal expectancy of the incumbent licensee and the significance of other comparative considerations will depend on the facts of the particular case.[48]

This "standard" is, to say the least, opaque. Its application in the celebrated *Central Florida* case[49] demonstrates its almost infinite elasticity. There, the FCC managed to renew the incumbent's television station license by finding its "superior" past performance sufficiently weighty to overcome its opponent's apparent advantage in the character, diversification, and integration categories. The commission made these apparent advantages disappear with a series of rapid gestures that a professional magician would envy. But the beauty of its performance was apparently lost on the Federal Court of Appeals, which rejected the FCC's reasoning as "completely opaque to judicial review, fall[ing] somewhere on the distant side of arbitrary."[50]

Undaunted, the FCC returned to the drafting table and concocted a new rationale for the same result. This opinion more candidly conceded to the challenger advantages on the standard comparative criteria and devalued the incumbent's past broadcast record from "superior" to "substantial." Nevertheless, the commission's magical scoreboard once again declared the incumbent the winner. A weary Court of Appeals finally threw in the towel, and another renewal challenge had been successfully beaten back.[51]

What accounts for this steadfast adherence to extreme opacity, in the face of recurrent external criticism and internal calls for reform? Our cost-benefit framework suggests the lines of an argument in the FCC's defense. One might begin by noting, for example, that the investment in developing more precise licensing criteria would not pay off in substantially enhanced voluntary compliance. In the first place, licensing standards are not really rules of conduct but rather criteria for selecting among competing applications. Even to the extent that they are designed to influence behavior, moreover, the fear of nonrenewal gives licensees ample incentive to "comply" with renewal standards, no matter how inscrutable. Since the regulated activity is highly visible, broadcasters cannot realistically expect to conceal noncompliant behavior.

Nor, the FCC's defenders might add, is transparency needed to reduce future rule making or enforcement. Despite the publicity received by such celebrated cases as *WHDH*[52] and *RKO*,[53] license renewal proceedings are relatively rare. From 1961 through 1978, there were only seventeen hearings on contested television license renewals and thirty hearings on contested radio license renewals.[54] Some of these proceedings have been obscenely expensive, it is true. But the principal reason for that fact is probably the huge financial interests at stake, a factor not affected by increasing the transparency of the underlying standards.

A critic of the FCC's policy might answer that the relative infrequency of renewal contests is itself a result of the very regulatory opacity whose justifiability is at issue here. An important conduct-regulating function of renewal standards is to "spur" potential competitors to challenge mediocre incumbents. The spur of competition may well depend for its operation on the clarity of the selection criteria articulated. Few potential entrants will risk the substantial investment in mounting a renewal challenge without some reliable basis for estimating the odds of success. Obscure rules can thus defeat public service goals by insulating incumbents from challenge. The infrequency of renewal challenges, despite the consistently high rates of return in the broadcasting industry, suggests that opacity may have had precisely this effect. An even better explanation, however, is the content of the FCC's de facto renewal policy: namely, the incumbent (almost) always wins.

To the commission, the decisive argument against more transparent standards has been the risk of incongruity. In its report and order terminating Docket 19,154, for example, the commission asserted: "Increasing the amount of [favored] programming would not necessarily improve the service a station provides its audience."[55] Licensees might simply "spread their resources thinner" or focus on trivial issues (the commission's illustration is "canoe safety"). The FCC found, in short, no necessary congruence between a quantitative programming criterion and the underlying goal of responsiveness to "community problems, needs, and interests." Given the enormous variety of "community needs" that a licensee is expected to serve during its three-year license term, moreover, *any* objective criterion carries with it a high risk of overemphasizing or slighting important values. And the First Amendment exhorts us to attach a very high social value to increments of broadcast speech discouraged or necessitated by overinclusive licensing standards.

The task of evaluating the incongruity argument, never easy, is rendered virtually impossible here, I believe, by the problem of goal ambiguity. The political system in this country has been unable to achieve anything resembling consensus on the meaning of "good" performance in broadcasting. Views about what is wrong with broadcasting and what the government should do about it remain irreconcilably fragmented and divergent. One major reason may be a powerful cultural resistance to government censorship that discourages explicit public debate about how the government should go about assessing the quality of broadcast performance.[56] The result is chronic inability to reduce value conflict to manageable dimensions.

One of the more visible manifestations of this general state of goal ambiguity is the protracted conflict between the FCC and the District of Columbia Circuit Court of Appeals on the subject of "renewal expectancies." A majority of the commission, responding in large part to the hopeless intractability of the performance criterion, proposed in 1970 and again in 1977 that comparative evaluation be abandoned altogether.[57] Renewal would be automatic, at least in the absence of egregious misconduct warranting license revocation. This solution would, in effect, reconcile conflicting conceptions of the public interest by adopting a free-market (advertiser-sovereignty) model. The District of Columbia Circuit Court, however, has staunchly resisted this model as inconsistent with the Communications Act. What the commission is doing, then, can be explained as either (1) avoiding policy choice or (2) trying to conceal a distinct but improper policy choice from the prying eyes of reviewing courts. Either way, opacity is the predicted – if not wholly honorable – tactical response. The commission's existing "standard" avoids any explicit elevation or subordination of politically contending values. It also provides a particularly dense smokescreen behind which it could seek to pursue a deliberate strategy of consistently favoring incumbents. One can assuredly criticize the commission's inarticulateness, then, but only if one is sanguine about the prospects that the Congress or the commission can first narrow the range of underlying value conflict.

The Rewards of Regulatory Precision

Stated most abstractly, the prescription to be extracted from the foregoing analysis is this: regulators should think consciously about rule precision as one dimension of their "output." When confronting a choice among possiblé verbal formulations, rule drafters should consider explicitly the tradeoffs among the three dimensions that I have called transparency, congruence, and simplicity. Advice expressed at so high a level of generality is probably no more useful than it is controversial. Administrative policymakers face many competing demands on scarce analytic and creative resources. Rigorous estimation of the costs and benefits associated with alternative rule formulations would be an extraordinarily demanding task. Most of us would be surprised to discover policymakers seriously attempting it in any but the rarest of circumstances.

Rather we would expect to find policymakers making these judgments intuitively and piecemeal, successively comparing a few alternatives according to a few simple qualitative criteria, relying heavily on guesswork and on trial and error. Given the high cost of more rigorously analytic methods, this sort of qualitative incremental approach can be expected to yield satisfactory results in a wide range of circumstances. On occasion, however, the magnitude of the interests at stake will justify a heavier investment in more systematic analysis. Whatever the decisionmaking model appropriate for a particular context, though, the analysis presented here provides useful clues about the circumstances in which a particularly heavy investment in generic policy articulation is likely to be justified. Agencies should use these clues as an aid to the allocation of their scarce analytic and drafting resources, as should their potential critics in focusing their attention.

RULE-MAKING COSTS

An impediment to precision enhancement is the cost of developing transparent rules that are sufficiently congruent to withstand future attack or circumvention. As indicated earlier, this cost has two components – the cost of conducting research and analysis so as to anticipate the rule's impact and the cost of securing agreement among participants in the rule-making process.

It is interesting that agencies rarely invoke rule-making costs *explicitly* as a justification for resisting precision-enhancing rule amendment. They tend, instead, to speak in the language of possibility: "It is impossible to formulate any general standard" with respect to diversification of ownership, the FCC once said.[58] Taken literally, such an assertion is obviously false. Rather, it must be interpreted as a statement about the costs and benefits of analysis. In effect, "it is too expensive to attempt to formulate any more precise general standard."

The weight to be attributed to the "rule-making cost" element of such an argument depends on the extent to which initial rule clarification reduces the demand for subsequent policy specification. As discussed earlier, the administration of a program creates pressures — usually, but not always, irresistible — for elaboration of "policy" into intelligible principles. To the extent that an investment in initial rule making can mitigate these pressures and displace later rule making, the "rule-making costs" argument loses force as a defense for opacity.

Comparing the cost of initial rule making with the present value of future rule-making activities thereby avoided is never easy. The outcome of such a comparison will depend on two variables: (1) the procedural formalities actually employed in administering the program, and (2) the degree of centralization of the decisionmaking process. At one extreme is a program such as the SEC's resale policy, vintage 1970, centrally administered through an extravagantly informal process involving only an exchange of correspondence. At the other extreme is a program like the Social Security disability insurance program. Not only does the statute provide for an elaborate, sequential process of decisionmaking, requiring the agency to provide intelligible explanations to disappointed claimants, but the program is administered by an extremely decentralized apparatus.[59]

For cases falling in between these two extremes, estimating the net rule-making cost is more difficult. Where — as in administering the HMTA penalty policy — the degrees of procedural formality and decentralization are relatively low, the net rule-making cost of precision enhancement is likely to be positive. Intermediate cases such as broadcast licensing (high procedural formality, low decentralization), present the hardest case. Since rule-making costs rarely loom very large relative to the other two factors, an assumption of zero net rule-making costs will usually be justified unless one factor seems clearly to predominate.

RULE APPLICATION COSTS

Increasing a rule's verbal clarity should reduce the costs, incurred by both the regulated population and the government, of applying a policy to specific circumstances. The magnitude of this saving, and the consequent relative payoff from investments in enhancing the clarity of different rules, will depend on the magnitude of the underlying transaction costs involved in applying the rule. For our purposes, it is useful to distinguish between "planning" costs and "enforcement" costs. Planning costs include resources expended on rule interpretation by private persons interested in determining the legal consequences of contemplated behavior or the legal status of a current or anticipated condition. Enforcement costs include the resources expended by the government (or a private enforcer) and the regulated party in the course of authoritatively determining whether a violation has occurred and, if so, what should be done about it.

The relative magnitude of planning and enforcement cost depends, of course, on the type of rule. Conduct-regulating rules typically generate larger planning costs than enforcement costs, whereas status-recognition rules involve little or no planning costs. Thus the planning costs incurred by potential resellers of unregistered securities (and probably their brokers as well) undoubtedly dwarfed the cost of administering the SEC's clearance system. The only planning cost incurred by an applicant for an initial broadcast license, in contrast, relates to the decision of whether to file an application.

The magnitude of planning costs presumably depends on both the volume and the value of the potential transactions to which the rule plausibly applies. Each potential transaction presents an occasion for an exercise in rule interpretation that could be simplified by clearer drafting. So, for example, DOT's substantive standards for transporting hazardous materials come into play each time a shipper makes a shipment or a carrier handles one. Yet because the incremental value of compliant behavior in individual cases is usually small, employers will rarely invest heavily in rule interpretation. Potential resellers of unregistered securities, on the other hand, often face a much higher exposure to loss from an incorrect interpretation. As a group, then, they can be counted upon to invest heavily in legal advice.

Enforcement costs are more easily estimated. The number of enforcement actions and the agency's share of enforcement costs are directly observable. Where the agency lacks relevant enforcement experience, it can make predictions based on plausible assumptions. Once again, the volume and value of regulated transactions will strongly influence the result. The larger the number of persons or events governed by the rule, the larger the number of times that the agency is called upon to make an authoritative determination. This is especially true of rules that govern the dispensation of benefits or privileges, since private applicants control the volume of cases. Agencies exercise far more control over the volume of formal proceedings for enforcing regulatory commands. But even here, there is probably a rough correlation between enforcement activity and regulated activity.

The resources expended by participants in enforcement proceedings will generally depend on the value, to each party, of the desired outcome. Thus a shipper or carrier will typically expend far less to resist an HMTA penalty assessment than an applicant for a broadcast license will spend on preparing and defending an application. For the same reason, the government will usually allocate more resources to the latter. The formality of the procedure afforded to a private applicant or respondent for contesting an adverse decision also influences the magnitude of enforcement costs. Before Rule 144, the SEC's no-action process handled thousands of cases at a fraction of the cost of some comparative broadcast licensing cases. The availability of formal procedures is, of course, no guarantee of their use. HMTA violators have considerable procedural rights yet rarely use them. Only when the value of a favorable decision is held constant, then, does procedural formality make a significant difference.

COMPLIANCE EFFECTS

Compliance Rate A major affirmative argument for regulatory precision is the promotion of voluntary compliance by the rule's addressees. Consequently, situations in which compliance problems loom especially large are good candidates for enhancing rule precision. The three case studies reported earlier suggest that these situations will have the following characteristics.

First, they will involve rules that attach legal significance to conduct rather than status. It is not always simple to distinguish between conduct-regulating and status-evaluating rules, since virtually all rules seek to influence behavior in some ultimate sense. The form of the rule will, however, usually serve as a helpful guide to the intensity of its compliance function. Rules that explicitly forbid (or command) particular actions are most clearly conduct regulating. Also in this category are safe harbor rules, such as the SEC's Rule 144, that define the boundary line between conduct exempt from legal attack and conduct exposed to legal attack.

Standards for the grant of a permission or privilege, on the other hand, often fall into the status-evaluating category. This statement is especially true of initial licensing standards, such as the FCC's 1965 policy statement, that predicate eligibility to enter a business on the presence or absence of certain durable characteristics (such as broadcast experience) or short-range conditions beyond the applicant's immediate control (such as community "need").

Standards for *renewal* of a scarce privilege, on the other hand, often serve quite important and explicit behavioral objectives. The threat of nonrenewal of a broadcast license is a powerful inducement for the broadcaster to comply with the FCC's wishes during the three-year license term. Renewal standards double as conduct-regulating and merit-rewarding standards. By encouraging periodic contests for the licensed franchise, moreover, renewal standards can indirectly replicate the benefits of a competitive market in a regulated industry.[60]

The regulatory function of standards for imposing sanctions also varies with context. Severity of penalty occupies a central place in the theory of general deterrence.[61] Consequently, criteria for determining penalty severity would seem to serve an important compliance-related function. But general deterrence is only one of several functions performed by regulatory sanctions,[62] and — as in the HMTA example — sometimes a relatively unimportant one.

The second variable on which the magnitude of the compliance factor depends is the size and sophistication of the rule's audience. An investment in verbal clarification promises to yield the largest compliance payoffs when the rule's audience is large, diverse, and remote. DOT's substantive rules for handling hazardous materials, for example, attempt to influence the conduct of thousands of truck drivers, shipping clerks, railroad workers, dockworkers, package manufacturers, and the like. Verbally transparent rules usually provide the most efficient method of communicating administrative policy to large audiences. An administrative policy — such as the FCC's broadcasting rules or the SEC's resale rules — aimed at a smaller, more stable, and more sophisticated audience can rely on alternative methods of communication, such as response to informal inquiries, public statements, and the grapevine.

The incremental payoff in enhanced rule compliance from clarifying a rule also depends on the expected level of rule violation by the regulated population. Rule clarification discourages noncompliance by reducing the perceived probability of its success. The expected level of noncompliant behavior (before the effect of enforcement is considered) is a function of the cost of compliance and the difficulty of concealment. Where compliance with a regulatory policy requires the rule's addressees to incur substantial incremental costs or to forgo substantial benefits, the predicted rate of evasion is high. Those who own large blocks of unregistered stock in especially shaky companies would have the greatest incentive to evade registration requirements, whereas few carriers benefit greatly from failing to label or placard hazardous material shipments properly.

The likelihood and magnitude of noncompliance also depends on the ease or difficulty of concealing prohibited conduct. Where concealment is relatively easy, as in the case of dumping toxic wastes or overharvesting fisheries, bright-line rules are needed to facilitate detection by investigative personnel and reporting by victims or observers. This justification applies with less force to any conduct, such as broadcasting or the sale of securities, that is highly visible or easily traced. Private enforcement, through the tort system (as in transportation of hazardous materials) or industrial self-policing (as in the securities market), may also reduce the need for a priori rule clarification.

Incongruity Effects   The most powerful argument against adopting highly specific rules is their unavoidable overinclusiveness or underinclusiveness. Transparent rules often "trap the unwary" (overinclude) or enable evaders to exploit "loopholes" (underinclude). A strategy for achieving the optimal degree of rule precision must concentrate on minimizing these unintended consequences. To begin with, it is impossible even to incorporate this factor into the analysis without some reasonable degree of agreement on the underlying policy objective. "Incongruity" measures deviations of rule-dictated results from desired outcomes. As the broadcast regulation case study illustrates, identifying the class of "desired outcomes" in some regulatory programs is very difficult. Fortunately, most modern regulatory statutes furnish much clearer direction to policymakers than the 1934 Communication Act. Most agencies, moreover, have internalized generations of advice that they articulate their goals more concretely.

In the search for areas where the incongruity losses are likely to be small, it is essential to remember that incongruent outcomes can result from excessively opaque rules as well as from excessively precise ones. Opaque rules characteristically produce errors of misapplication, whereas precise rules produce more errors of misspecification. But there is no a priori reason to believe that, as between competing rule formulations, the more precise will necessarily yield more numerous errors or socially more costly ones.

Consequently, in searching for candidates for precision enhancement, the agency should first look for programs that involve a high inherent risk of application errors. Programs administered on a highly decentralized basis tend to have this characteristic. The physical, organizational, and professional isolation of decisionmakers in a program such as Social Security disability insurance virtually assures that, in the absence of relatively concrete guidelines, individual decisions will deviate from the outcome desired by the agency in a high percentage of cases. While a centralized review of decisions can reduce the rate of application errors, the corrective is itself costly.

The other variable in measuring net incongruity losses is the cost of the misspecification errors likely to be produced by a bright-line rule. Agencies should favor precise formulations whenever this quantity is small. Identifying contexts a priori in which that will be the case is no mean feat. In principle, misspecification is most likely when the conduct regulated is especially heterogeneous. But this idea is extremely difficult to operationalize, since "heterogeneity" is not a self-defining or intrinsic concept but derives meaning only from the regulatory context.

The "scope" of a rule is one possible proxy for heterogeneity. We would expect to encounter greater difficulty, for example, in defining the conduct expected from a broadcast licensee over a three-year term than the conditions under which to immunize a particular sale of restricted securities. In this sense, the FCC's license renewal standards illustrate the "lumpiness" of business licensing decisions. They typically involve an all-or-nothing judgment about conduct potentially affecting a large number of market transactions. Although continuing supervision can reduce the risk of untoward consequences, their detection may come too late to prevent significant social losses. At the other extreme are decisions like the HMTA penalty computations. In addition to involving relatively small sums of money, these decisions involve a continuous range of possible outcomes. The penalty determination (as opposed to the liability determination) is not an all-or-nothing choice. In a system of continuous possible outcomes, the consequence of errors is not likely to be as great as in a system of binary choice.

Another proxy for heterogeneity is rate of change over time. The more rapid the rate of change in either the regulated behavior or human knowledge about that behavior, the greater the risk that bright-line rules will freeze policy into undesirable patterns. This argument was made to justify the open-ended delegation of policy-making authority to the FCC in 1934 and has been periodically revived ever since as broadcast technology undergoes wave after wave of change.

In measuring incongruity losses, one must look at the consequences as well as the rate of "misspecification errors." A single error by the FDA in incorrectly licensing a harmful new drug (or, for that matter, excluding a life-saving new drug) should trouble us a great deal more than a thousand citations for harmless parking violations. The response to this condition will depend, of course, on the perceived distribution of high-cost errors. If they cluster on one side of the equation, regulators will often prescribe a highly transparent rule that leans heavily against the feared consequence. Inadequate precaution is the type of error most feared in the application of rules regulating transportation of hazardous materials. Therefore, the rules will be structured to provide transparent assurance against underinclusion, at a high resulting cost in overinclusion.

A policymaker equally troubled by errors of overinclusion and underinclusion is more likely to adopt an opaque formulation that permits flexible adaptation and adjustment. This may help explain the FCC's behavior. Whatever one's personal taste in broadcasting, there is little a priori reason to prefer errors of overregulation or underregulation. Each can produce unwanted speech, none of it terribly harmful. In the face of evenly balanced risks, the rational response is frequently a platitudinous opacity such as the FCC's renewal standard.

Conclusions

In assessing the various arguments for further clarification of administrative rules, then, several contextual variables emerge as particularly useful indicators. These include: the volume of transactions governed by the rule; the value of the interests typically at stake in those transactions; the sophistication and resourcefulness of the rule's audience; the formality of procedures provided for authoritative application of the rule; and the degree of decentralization in the enforcement process. The virtue of these indicators is that they can be fairly readily observed and qualitatively "measured" while at the same time serving as a reliable proxy for several categories of costs or benefits in our "precision calculus." Thus, for example, the volume of transactions governed by a rule is a good predictor of the payoff from rule clarification because it correlates well with: (1) the social cost of noncompliance, (2) the number of misapplication errors, (3) the level of future demand for case-by-case policy elaboration, and (4) the level of social investment in rule application. Similarly, the greater the degree of administrative decentralization, the greater the potential for achieving savings by reducing the volume of quality control activities and misapplication errors. Clarifying rules that govern transactions affecting very large individual or social stakes, moreover, can significantly reduce evasion costs, litigation costs, and future (ex post) rule-making costs.

While these parameters can thus serve as useful signposts in the search for optimal precision, they do not, and cannot, substitute for morally sensitive judgment. An empirical analysis that focuses on measurable costs and benefits admittedly depreciates "soft" values that cannot readily be quantified. Most of us would maintain, I suppose, that such basic values as fairness, dignity, or equity demand some threshold degree of verbal precision from any legal regime, irrespective of its measurable impact on error rates or transaction costs.

There may well be occasions when the results produced by a more explicitly deontological approach would diverge from those generated by the utilitarian approach offered here. But I suspect that those occasions will be rare. Mercenary as my approach may seem to some, such variables as compliance rate and enforcement cost usually do a pretty good job of mirroring the intensity of participants' feelings (if not those of observers) about relative fairness or equity. Moreover, the empiricism used here – and likely to be used by any practitioner of the method – is sufficiently casual to accommodate a healthy dose of nonquantifiable values.

Notes

1. Towne v. Eisner, 245 U.S. 418, 425 (1918).
2. For an application of this thesis to the judicial review of regulatory

policy, see C. Diver, "The Optimal Precision of Administrative Rules," *Yale Law Journal* 93 (1983): 65.

3. Classic examples of the vagueness critique include K. C. Davis, *Discretionary Justice: A Preliminary Inquiry* (Baton Rouge: Louisiana State University Press, 1969), and T. Lowi, *The End of Liberalism*, 2d ed. (New York: Norton, 1979).

4. See, for example, E. Bardach and R. Kagan, *Going by the Book: The Problem of Regulatory Unreasonableness* (Philadelphia: Temple University Press, 1975); A. Kneese and E. Schultze, *Pollution, Prices, and Public Policy* (Washington, D.C.: Brookings Institution, 1975).

5. The tax code is the favorite target of complexity critics. See, for example, Bittker, "Tax Reform and Tax Simplification," *University of Miami Law Review* 29 (1974): 1; Brannon, "Simplification and Other Tax Objectives," in *Federal Income Tax Simplification*, ed. C. Gustafson (Philadelphia: American Law Institute–American Bar Association Commission on Continuing Professional Education, 1979.

6. For an earlier attempt to use this approach to evaluate legal rule making generally, see I. Ehrlich and R. Posner, "An Economic Analysis of Legal Rulemaking," *Journal of Legal Studies* 3 (1974): 254.

7. See Ross, "On Legalities and Linguistics: Plain Language Legislation," *Buffalo Law Review* 30 (1981): 317, 334–35.

8. Securities and Exchange Act of 1933, sec. 5, *codified at* 15 U.S.C. sec. 77e (1981).

9. 15 U.S.C. sec. 77f (1981). For an analysis of the act's disclosure requirements, see Anderson, "The Disclosure Process in Federal Securities Regulation: A Brief Review," *Hastings Law Journal* 25 (1974): 311.

10. 15 U.S.C. sec. 77d(2) (1981) (exempting "transactions by an issuer not involving any public offering").

11. 15 U.S.C. sec. 77d (1981).

12. 25 U.S.C. sec. 77b(11) (1981).

13. For descriptions of the no-action process, see Lockhart, "SEC No-Action Letters: Informal Advice as a Discretionary Administrative Clearance," *Law and Contemporary Problems*, 1972:95, and Lowenfels, "SEC No-Action Letters; Some Problems and Suggested Approaches," *Columbia Law Review* 72 (1971): 1256.

14. SEC Securities Act Rel. No. 5098, 29 October 1970, *CCH Federal Securities Law Reporter*, para. 77921.

15. SEC, Disclosure to Investors – A Reappraisal of Federal Administrative Policies Under the '33 and '34 Acts 163 (1969), (*reprinted at* CCH Fed. Securities L. Rep. No. 5213) [hereinafter cited as Wheat Report, named after Commissioner Francis M. Wheat, who directed the SEC staff].

16. See ibid., p. 165.

17. See Levenson, "Rule 144 and Other Current SEC Developments," *PLI Second Annual Institute on Securities Regulation*, ed. R. Mundheim

and A. Fleischer, Jr. (New York: Practicing Law Institute, 1971:60, 69, 70).

18. See Leiman, "Registration Provisions in Venture Capital and Similar Financing Agreements," ibid., p. 101.

19. Securities Act Rel. No. 5223, 37 Fed. Reg. 596 (1972), *codified as amended at* 17 C.F.R. sec. 230.144 (1981).

20. 37 Fed. Reg. 596 (1972).

21. Ibid.

22. Wheat Report, p. 175.

23. Lockhart, "SEC No-Action Letters," p. 109.

24. See SEC Interp. Rel. No. 5306, 37 Fed. Reg. 23180 (1972); SEC Interp. Rel. No. 6099 (2 August 1979).

25. Wheat Report, p. 176.

26. Ibid., p. 177.

27. Pub. L. 93-633, Title I, 88 Stat. 2156, *codified at* 49 U.S.C. secs. 1801–12 (1980).

28. 49 U.S.C. sec. 1809(a)(1) (1980).

29. 49 C.F.R. pts. 171–79 (1986).

30. For a general description of this process, see Hamilton, "The Role of Non-Governmental Standards in the Development of Mandatory Federal Standards Relating to Safety or Health," *Texas Law Review* 56 (1978): 1329.

31. C. Diver, "A Study of the Effectiveness and Fairness of DOT Hazardous Materials Enforcement Penalties," Final Report to the General Counsel, U.S. Dept. of Transportation, June 1980, p. 30.

32. See C. Diver, "A Theory of Regulatory Enforcement," *Public Policy* 28 (1980): 257, 266.

33. For example, Butz v. Glover Lovestock Comm'n. Co., 411 U.S. 182, *reh. denied,* 412 U.S. 933 (1973); Nowicki v. United States 536 F.2d 1171 (7th Cir. 1976), *cert. denied,* 429 U.S. 1092 (1977).

34. See C. Diver, "The Assessment and Mitigation of Civil Money Penalties by Federal Administrative Agencies," *Columbia Law Review* 79 (1979): 1435, 1472-73.

35. For example, Breit and Elzinga, "Antitrust Penalties and Attitudes Toward Risk: An Economic Analysis," *Harvard Law Review* 86 (1973): 693, 704-06.

36. In 1979, DOT conducted 103,246 inspections, or about 1 for every 884 estimated shipments. Comptroller General of the United States, *Programs for Ensuring the Safe Transportation of Hazardous Materials Need Improvement,* 4 November 1980, pp. 7, 39, 57. Only 2,587 enforcement cases were actually commenced that year, and approximately 350 cases were closed with imposition of a fine.

37. See Veljanovski, "Regulatory Enforcement: An Economic Study of the British Factory Inspectorate," *Law and Policy Quarterly* 5 (1983): 75.

38. See C. Diver, "Regulatory Plea-Bargaining: A Case Study of the Enforcement of the Hazardous Materials Transportation Act," presented at the

Annual Meeting of the American Political Science Association, New York, 3–6 September 1981, pp. 9–11.

39. See, for example, Jaffe, "The Scandal in TV Licensing," *Harper's*, September 1957, pp. 77, 79; Schwartz, "Comparative Television and the Chancellor's Foot," *Georgetown Law Journal* 47 (1959): 655; H. Friendly, *The Federal Administrative Agencies* (Cambridge, Mass.: Harvard University Press, 1962), pp. 70–73; Jaffe, "*WHDH:* The FCC and Broadcasting License Renewals," *Harvard Law Review* 82 (1969): 1693; Anthony, "Toward Simplicity and Rationality in Comparative Broadcast Licensing Proceedings," *Stanford Law Review* 24 (1971): 1; Botein, "Comparative Broadcast Licensing Procedures and the Rule of Law: A Fuller Investigation," *Georgia Law Review* 6 (1972): 743; Geller, "The Comparative Renewal Process in Television: Problems and Suggested Solutions," *Virginia Law Review* 61 (1975), 471; Brinkmann, "The Policy Paralysis in *WESH:* A Conflict Between Structure and Operations in the FCC Comparative Renewal Process," *Federal Communications Law Journal* 32 (1980): 55.

40. See 47 U.S.C. sec. 310 (1986); 47 C.F.R. pt. 73 (1986). The statutory standard for determining whether to grant an application to an applicant meeting these threshold criteria – unchanged since passage of the Communications Act in 1934 – is "public interest, convenience, and necessity." 47 U.S.C. sec. 309(a) (1986).

41. 47 C.F.R. sec. 73.3555 (1986).

42. See, for example, FCC v. National Citizens Comm. for Broadcasting, 436 U.S. 775 (1978); United States v. Storer Broadcasting Co., 351 U.S. 192 (1956); National Broadcasting Co. v. United States, 319 U.S. 190 (1943).

43. Public Statement on Comparative Broadcast Hearings, 1 F.C.C. 2d 393, 393 (1965).

44. Policy Statement concerning Comparative Hearings Involving Regular Renewal Applicants, 22 F.C.C. 2d 424, 424 (1970).

45. Notice of Inquiry, In the Matter of Formulation of Policies Relating to the Broadcast Renewal Applicant, Stemming from the Comparative Hearing Process, 27 F.C.C. 2d 580, 580 (1971).

46. Citizens Communication Center v. FCC, 447 F.2d 1201 (D.C. Cir. 1971).

47. Report and Order, 66 F.C.C. 2d 419 (1977), *aff'd sub nom.* National Black Media Coalition v. FCC, 589 F.2d 578 (D.C. Cir. 1978).

48. 66 F.C.C. 2d at 430, *citing* Greater Boston Television Corp. v. FCC, 444 F.2d 841, 854 (D.C. Cir. 1970), *cert. denied,* 403 U.S. 923 (1971).

49. Cowles Florida Broadcasting, Inc. (WESH-TV), 60 F.C.C. 2d 372 (1976), *rev'd sub nom.* Central Florida Enterprises, Inc. v. FCC, 598 F.2d 37, 50 (D.C. Cir. 1978), *petition for cert. dismissed,* 441 U.S. 959 (1979), *reinstated,* 86 F.C.C.2d 993 (1981); *aff'd,* 683 F.2d 503 (D.C. Cir. 1982), *cert. denied,* 460 U.S. 1084 (1983).

50. 598 F.2d at 50.

51. 683 F.2d 503 (D.C. Cir. 1982).

52. Greater Boston Television Corp. v. FCC, 444 F.2d 841 (D.C. Cir. 1970), *cert. denied,* 403 U.S. 923 (1971).

53. Fidelity Television, Inc. v. FCC, 515 F.2d 684 (D.C. Cir. 1975), *cert. denied,* 423 U.S. 926 (1975).

54. See Central Florida Enterprises, Inc. v. FCC, 598 F.2d 58, 61 (D.C. Cir. 1978) (denying petition for rehearing per curiam).

55. 66 F.C.C. 2d at 427.

56. See Central Florida Enterprises, Inc. v. FCC, 598 F.2d 37, 54 (D.C. Cir. 1978) (citing "First Amendment questions" raised by "inquiry into the content of programming"). Compare Banzhaf v. FCC, 405 F.2d 1082, 1095 (D.C. Cir. 1968), *cert. denied,* 396 U.S. 842 (1969) (FCC must walk a "tightrope between saying too much and saying too little").

57. See Policy Statement, 22 F.C.C. 2d 424 (1970); Report and Order (Docket No. 19154), 66 F.C.C. 2d 419, 429 (1977).

58. Further Notice of Inquiry, 31 F.C.C. 2d 433, 445 (1971).

59. See J. Mashaw, *Bureaucratic Justice: Managing Social Security Disability Claims* (New Haven, Conn.: Yale University Press, 1983); Diver, "Optimal Precision," pp. 88–92.

60. This is the theory of "contestable markets." See W. Baumol, J. Panzar, and R. Willig, *Contestable Markets and the Theory of Industry Structure* (New York: Harcourt, Brace, Jovanovich, 1982).

61. See Becker, "Crime and Punishment: An Economic Approach," *Journal of Political Economy* 76 (1968): 169; Polinsky and Shavell, "The Optimal Tradeoff Between the Probability and Magnitude of Fines," *American Economic Review* 69 (1979): 880.

62. See Diver, "A Theory of Regulatory Enforcement," p. 257.

8

Discretionary Decisionmaking in Regulatory Agencies: A Conceptual Framework

Daniel J. Gifford

THIS CHAPTER SEEKS to help lawyers understand, and therefore cope in appropriate ways with, the varying degrees of unconfined and unstructured administration in regulatory agencies of different types. It also seeks to suggest ways of thinking about discretionary power exercised by government officials. My present effort is a modest one: my primary objective is to further the understanding of discretion as a phenomenon in the hope that greater insight will increase the manageability of the problem.

I will therefore (1) address the problem, posed by Kenneth Culp Davis, of how to determine the optimum allocation of rules, standards, and discretionary power in a regulatory agency (Davis, 1969) and (2) provide some preliminary guides for making such determinations. I will examine the varying contexts in which agency regulatory decisions are made and consider how context affects the feasibility of limiting or structuring discretion and the kinds of structuring appropriate to several differing contexts. I will then draw some conclusions as to where efforts could most profitably be directed toward narrowing and structuring discretion, with attention to the nature of those efforts. My approach takes as its premise that the guiding, structuring, or confining of discretionary decisionmaking is ultimately a function of the process of information collection and evaluation, because the widely held view that authoritative rules or guides ought to be employed by superior officials to guide or constrain the behavior of their subordinates rests, to a large extent, upon the unstated premise that those rules or guides are themselves predicated upon information superior to that available to their subordinates.

Areas in Which Discretion Can and Cannot Be Confined and Structured

Kenneth Culp Davis dramatized the problems associated with administrative discretion in his widely read book published in 1979. Davis has insisted that these problems must be examined in an analytical framework which provides a basis for exploring the relationships between discretion and its exercise, on the one hand, and devices, such as standards and rules, for structuring or confining it, on the other (Davis, vol. 2, 1979:167–69). It is apparent – and Davis agrees – that official behavior can be visualized as occurring on a spectrum where precisely drawn rules confine or eliminate the choices of officials at one end and at the other end the choices and hence discretion of officials are at a maximum (see ibid.: 168). This spectrum, Davis has observed, in conjunction with the inherent flexibility of the language, means that rules can be tailored to embody the exact amount of precision or vagueness desired and hence can confer as much or as little discretion upon the officials administering them as a rule maker might wish (ibid.: 183–92). Rules can also, as Davis has reminded us, structure and guide choice by embodying standards or by setting forth factors which a decisionmaking official must take into account in reaching his own decisions (ibid.: 169, 189–90).

While Davis has performed the invaluable service of heightening public and professional awareness of the prevalence and extent of uncontrolled discretion permeating governmental administrations and bureaucracies and has provided the legal community with a refined collection of tools for controlling discretion, still Davis himself has continually noted that a major problem remains unresolved: the development of criteria for optimizing the extent of official conduct which is, in various ways, confined or structured, and the extent of official conduct which is properly made discretionary (see ibid.: 191).

Davis's main recommendation for remedying the problem of uncontrolled administrative discretion contains within it the seeds of a promising approach for resolving the larger problem of working out the criteria for optimizing the use of rules, standards, and discretion within governmental administration. Davis has long acknowledged that in many circumstances legislative bodies will find it impractical themselves to formulate precise standards to be employed by administrative officials. Still, he has urged the administrative bodies themselves to shoulder this task and, as a result of their experience over time, to create their own standards. Much of Davis's language suggests that the experience of administration will itself aid agencies in narrowing over time the extent of their own discretionary powers. Indeed, Davis sees a process through which initially wide discretion is narrowed into guidance, first by principles and then by standards; finally that discretion is constrained by rules (see Davis, 1970:57–58). Thus Davis has urged: "When legislative bodies delegate discretionary power without meaningful standards, administrators should develop standards at the earliest feasible time, and then, as circumstances permit, should further confine their own discretion through principles and rules" (ibid.: 213).

Davis, of course, is not the only commentator to have advocated such a process. Even before Davis was urging that administrators gradually structure and confine the discretionary decisionmaking power that the legislature had bestowed upon them, the late Judge Henry Friendly recommended a similar course:

> Where the initial standard [provided by Congress] is thus general, it is imperative that steps be taken over the years to define and clarify it – to canalize the broad stream into a number of narrower ones. I do not suggest this process can be so carried out that all cases can be determined by computers; I do suggest it ought to be carried to the point of affording a fair degree of predictability of decision in the great majority of cases and of intelligibility in all. [Friendly, 1962:14]

Inherent in Davis's and Friendly's positions is the assumption that the administration of a statute is a learning process for the agency; that the process of repeatedly applying the statute to differing situations forces the agency to focus upon and to evaluate the various problems faced by regulated subjects and otherwise affecting the administration of the act; that this repeated contact with the subjects and subject matter of the regulation in a variety of circumstances helps the agency to develop an overview of the problems which it faces and to develop insights into methods for solving them. The Davis and Friendly positions, in short, assume that the needed narrowing of discretion will come from rules, standards, and precedents which gradually emerge as the agency acquires more information about its tasks and that this needed information will come, in part, from the repetition of the decisional process itself.

Before pursuing the connection between the acquisition of needed information and the narrowing of an administrator's discretion, I should note an approach to administrative decisionmaking which appears strikingly different from that process of continual narrowing and channeling of discretion described and advocated by Davis and Friendly. This other approach is taken by those apologists for agency behavior who emphasize the "factual" component of agency decisions and typically deemphasize the extent to which agency decisionmaking depends upon rules or precedents. Usually these commentators describe agency work as resolving numerous cases in which the particular factual mixes rarely repeat themselves. Because of this continuing variety in the facts, the agencies find that precedents or rules play a smaller role in the decision of their own cases than they do in judicial decisions. Sharfman, the historian of the Interstate Commerce Commission, spoke in this way:

> Perhaps the most comprehensive evidence of the pragmatic character of the Commission's regulative processes is to be found in the relatively minor role played by precedent in the flow of administrative determinations. The special facts of each controversy constitute the dominant factor in its disposition, as a result of which very few new complaints are foreclosed by prior determinations and even proceedings which have already been adjudicated are reopened with striking frequency. The adjustments enforced by the Commission come to manifest themselves in a continual process of change and modification, induced by the dynamic forces constantly at work and reflected in the adoption of trial-and-error methods tested by their practical consequences. Not only do concrete findings change repeatedly, but the applicable rules, in terms of the guiding statutory standards, are also modified from time to time as occasion seems to require. The doctrines of res adjudicata and stare decisis, which exert an important influence upon the course of proceedings in the courts and upon the substantive character of judicial determinations, are not permitted to impose limitations upon the exercise of administrative discretion. Neither specific determinations nor principles of decision are clothed with any controlling degree of finality. While the advantages of establishing certainty in rules of conduct is not without recognition, and while the goal of maintaining stability and consistency in regulatory policy is constantly in the foreground, these considerations have not precluded the primary stress upon the need for flexibility of performance. Such need arises from the very nature of the administra-

tive method. Even quasi-judicial determinations are made in the enforcement of standards which have not crystallized into specific rules of law, and hence must depend, in predominant measure, upon the special facts and circumstances in each particular proceeding; and the affirmative adjustments prescribed, which are essentially legislative in character, must necessarily be unrestricted by prior determinations. Under these circumstances the certainty and stability that might flow from rigid rules and unvarying principles are appropriately subordinated to the demands of just and reasonable performance, as molded by enlightened experience and informed judgment. [Sharfman, 1931:367–68]

Sharfman's different approach to administrative discretion results not from a rejection of positions like those of Davis and Friendly about the value of decisional consistency but from his different perception of the kinds of cases which form the bulk of the workload of the agency he is writing about. The nonrepetitious nature of these cases accounts for his emphasis upon the importance of "the special facts of each controversy" and of his belief in the relative unimportance of precedent in that agency's work (see Gifford, 1971: 460–61).

These differing assumptions about the composition of administrative workloads lend themselves to greater articulation. Sharfman studied decisionmaking in an agency where the factual patterns relevant to official disposition recurred infrequently. Hence the agency found it impractical to develop rules for handling cases in advance. Even actual case dispositions lacked much significance as precedents because of the fluidity in the factual composition of the cases.

In an agency whose workload resembles that of the Interstate Commerce Commission studied by Sharfman, these assumptions destroy the efficiencies normally associated with rule making (see Gifford, 1967:762–63). Ordinarily, rule making enables an agency at one time to formulate criteria for the resolution of a whole class of cases, and thus an investment in rule making will tend to pay off in lessening the decisional burden which the agency would otherwise incur in deciding each of the cases to which the rule applies. Moreover, the agency may be able to improve the quality of its decisions by concentrating decisional resources in a rule-making proceeding. By such an effort, it may be able to explore the underlying regulatory problem more deeply and to develop a set of more effective solutions than would be feasible in a series of cases each of which involved only one or a few parties. Finally, if the decisional criteria developed in the rule-making proceeding are made known to persons whose behavior is subject to agency evaluation, those persons may shape their own course of action to avoid behavior which would fare poorly under the decisional criteria developed in the rule-making proceeding.

The assumptions underlying Davis's and Friendly's prescriptions – in contrast to Sharfman's assumptions – are that relevant factual patterns repeat themselves with some regularity. For the sake of greater clarity I point out the limitations of the Davis-Friendly assumptions: not that the factual patterns which repeat themselves constitute all of the facts of the cases in which they are present – only that those aspects of factual configurations which the agency deems relevant repeat themselves in the same or similar patterns. This is another way of saying that the relevance for deciding of those factual patterns that do recur tends to outweigh the relevance of other, nonrecurring, factual aspects of the agency's cases.

These two conceptions which I have associated with Sharfman, on the one hand, and with Davis and Friendly, on the other, stand at opposite ends of a continuum representing the way various classes of an agency's cases might occur. Between the ends of that continuum in which factual patterns frequently recur and in which factual patterns infrequently recur lie the middle areas in which core factual patterns tend to recur but in association with nonrecurring sets of relevant facts, some of which rise to a level of decisional relevance which affects the decision and other sets which do not. In the circumstances represented by these middle areas of the continuum, an agency may establish standards or principles or lists of factors that must be employed in decisionmaking but do not always govern the outcome.

A second factor affecting decisionmaking is the "importance" of the agency's decision to the achievement of overall regulatory goals. It is necessary to a proper exposition to explore the nature of this variable. First, an agency decision in a particular case may be important solely for the impact of that decision on the agency's regulatory goals apart from any significance which the case may or may not have as precedent. Thus, for example, the decision of the Department of Justice in the late 1940s to institute proceedings against E. I. du Pont de Nemours and Company to require the divestiture of the stock held by that company in the General Motors Corporation was important in itself. At least in the view of the department, the extremely large size of the two companies whose ownership connection was challenged meant that the governmental action affected a significant part of the national economy; this particular challenge, therefore, rose to a level of importance rivaling or exceeding that of much of the department's other work. It would not matter that the peculiar features of the du Pont–General Motors affiliation which led the agency to consider the question of divestiture were so unique that the case would have virtually no effect as precedent for the decision of other cases.

Second, an agency decision in a particular case may be important for its development of one or more standards or guides to be used in the resolution of subsequent cases. Here the regularity with which the relevant factual patterns recur would contribute to the importance of the decision developing the standard.

If the standard provides substantial guidance for the decision of future cases, even if it does not resolve all of the issues that may arise in them, then the importance of the standard will be a function of the number of times the issue would be likely to arise and the degree to which the resolution of the issue would aid in disposing of those cases. Thus, for example, had the National Labor Relations Board in the years before the Taft-Hartley Act adopted standards under which workers were not automatically excluded from the protection of the National Labor Relations Act because the common law would have treated them as independent contractors or because they performed supervisory roles, those standards would have assisted the board in disposing of many future cases by eliminating two potentially recurring issues.

Third, an agency decision may be important because it itself provides for the resolution of a class of cases. Thus as a precedent a single decision may effectively dispose of numerous future cases. A decision by a workman's compensation board that hernia claims are not compensable in the absence of corroboration by immediate and sustained disablement at the time when the employee first claimed symptoms would eliminate a multitude of future cases at one stroke. Another example would consist in agency rule making in – say – the environmental area, where a determination of tolerable pollution levels effectively imposes quite rigid prohibitions upon a whole class of industrial firms.

The degree to which an agency decision attains a level of importance is, of course, a function of the aggregate impact of that decision on the attainment of regulatory goals. Thus the aggregate impact of an agency disposition of a particular case with little or no precedent effect is measured by that particular disposition alone. However, the external aggregate impact of an agency decision in an environmental rule-making proceeding is measured by the total behavioral change of all firms produced by the role. And from the perspective of the supervising regulatory agency, the aggregate impact of an agency decision which formulates a standard for addressing recurring issues seems to consist largely in (1) the effect of the standard in avoiding results in particular cases which would have been reached without it, (2) the saving in enforcement costs which the standard provides, and (3) the consistency in approach to the issue to which the standard is addressed. Such a statement of the matter tends to put standard formulation into perspective. If the standard is primarily useful in avoiding results which the agency might sometimes reach in ad hoc determinations of a series of cases, then the importance of the standard will be reduced when the avoided results in their aggregate would not have significantly detracted from the achievement of the agency's overall regulatory goals.

In summary, an overview of the different kinds of regulatory situations faced by agencies can be represented as a matrix in which the horizontal scale measures the degree to which patterns of relevant facts or factors tend to recur and the vertical scale measures the degree of importance which each decision bears to the achievement of the regulatory goals of the agency. Figure 1 is such a matrix.

In box 1 fall those cases whose individual disposition is of major importance to the achievement of the agency's regulatory responsibilities. An example might be a utility rate proceeding. Normally a public service commission will oversee only a few rate proceedings, and each proceeding will determine the utility rates which thousands of consumers must pay. The commission's decision in each such case will therefore constitute a significant part of the commission's overall responsibilities. These considerations indicate that the proceeding should fall in the upper half of the matrix. To the extent that the facts in each rate case are perceived by the commission as unique to the time, place, and identity of the particular utility, such a rate proceeding falls to the left side of the matrix's upper half.

In box 2 fall those cases in which the agency decision is significant to the achievement of the agency's regulatory goals because of the combination of the actual disposition of the case being decided and of the precedent effect of the agency's decision. These cases tend

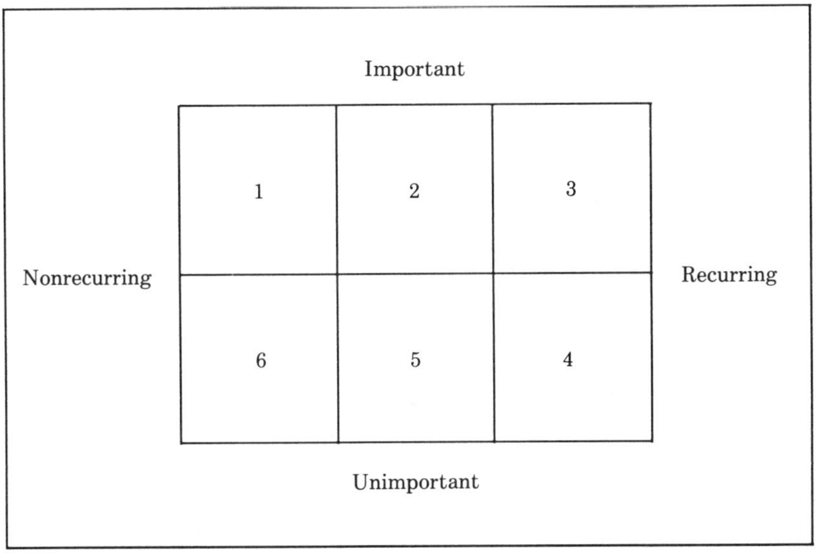

FIGURE 1

to involve recurring factual patterns but may also contain other sporadically occurring elements which sometimes offset, to a degree, the pull of the recurring factual elements toward a particular decision. In box 2, agency decisions tend to create and to apply standards rather than rules. Agency decisions are freer than in box 3 but are more constrained than in box 1. An example of such a case might be the determination as to whether a given corporate merger was banned by section 7 of the Clayton Act. The Antitrust Division of the Department of Justice would find many such determinations relatively important parts of its own overall responsibilities. Yet the merger standards used by the department are now well developed, largely as a result of the department's promulgation of "guidelines" in 1982 and 1984. Because of the individual importance of each case, however, and because the factual patterns may vary somewhat from case to case in ways not covered by the guidelines, the division's upper-echelon officials may not want to delegate merger clearances or prosecutorial determinations to lower-echelon staff but may wish to retain control over those determinations themselves.

In box 3 fall those agency determinations, such as precedent-setting and rule-making proceedings, which effectively determine the behavior of regulatory subjects in many instances where the relevant factual configurations are essentially repetitious. An example of such a decision by an agency might be the setting of pollution toleration limits affecting an entire industry.

Box 4 contains that class of cases whose facts tend to fall into recurring patterns and whose individual disposition does not significantly affect the attainment of the agency's overall regulatory goals. Because in this class of cases factual configurations tend to recur, it is possible for an agency to develop standards to govern their determination. Moreover, because the resolution of any particular case is not important to the agency, the agency can delegate decisional responsibility to lower-echelon personnel. For the reasons stated, this delegation can be accompanied by standards which the lower-echelon personnel are to employ in reaching their decisions. Note that, while the individual disposition of any particular case in this category is unimportant to the achievement of the agency's overall goals, the aggregate effects produced by all of the decisions in large classes of these cases may significantly further the agency's goals. A decision that set a precedent or established a rule for disposing of a large class of these cases would thus fall higher on the scale of importance than would the disposition of any individual case on individual grounds; indeed, such a decision could fall within box 3. Decisions applying the precedent or rule to individual cases would, of course, fall within box 4.

Box 6 contains that class of cases whose facts do not tend to fall into recurring patterns and whose individual disposition does not significantly affect the attainment of the agency's overall regulatory goals. Because the resolution of any individual case is not significant to the agency, the agency can delegate decisional responsibility to lower-echelon personnel. However, because the agency cannot develop standards for nonrecurring factual patterns, no standards will accompany this delegation.

The next step in developing a conceptual framework for viewing discretion is to assess the agency's workload in the light of the resources available to the agency and the methods which the agency employs to dispose of these cases. Sharfman describes a "managerial" mode of decisionmaking by an agency: because the agency perceives the factual patterns in the cases before it as largely nonrecurring, it can approach the decision of each case only as an ad hoc matter.

The result of this approach, of course, is that the agency is required to balance competing considerations in every case. It thus becomes more of a manager than a regulator. Figure 2 adds a managerial-nonmanagerial dimension to the grid of figure 1.

In effect the horizontal scale of figure 2 (in addition to measuring the degree to which particular regulatory problems contain recurring factual patterns) also measures the degree to which the agency decides in a managerial way, that is, decides on the particular facts of each case by balancing the pros and cons of that case, or, alternatively, decides on more of a rule-oriented regulatory basis by using criteria which apply to a class of cases, the criteria being formulated on the basis of the pros and cons affecting the entire class. This variable – a measure of the degree to which the agency decides in a managerial mode – ought largely to correspond to the degree of recurrence of relevant factual patterns in the activities of the regulatory subjects to which the agency directs its attention. Should the agency decisional mode (that is, managerial or rule-oriented) fail to correspond with this measure of relevant fact recurrence, an examination by the agency of its decisionmaking procedures would be urgently required. Such noncorrespondence would a priori suggest that the agency was (1) employing an inefficient means of decisionmaking and was thus increasing the costs of regulation unduly as well as (2) meriting the criticisms of advocates of narrowing and structuring discretion.

Employing the horizontal scale to measure the degree to which the agency decides in a managerial or nonmanagerial way raises a second point. In the perception of the agency, the degree of managerial decisionmaking and the degree to which factual patterns fail to recur may substantially correspond. The recurrence of "relevant" factual patterns is being measured, after all, and the agency determines relevance. The determination that relevant factual patterns recur or do not recur is essentially a determination of whether to proceed in a managerial way or in a rule- or precedent-oriented way. But managerial decisionmaking may correspond to the agency's perception of its caseload as involving nonrecurring factual patterns and yet simultaneously mask a failure of the agency to uncover actual underlying recurring patterns in that caseload.

Critics of administrative behavior such as Davis and Friendly have urged agencies to develop standards and rules in order to reduce the amount of discretionary decisionmaking in their operations. These

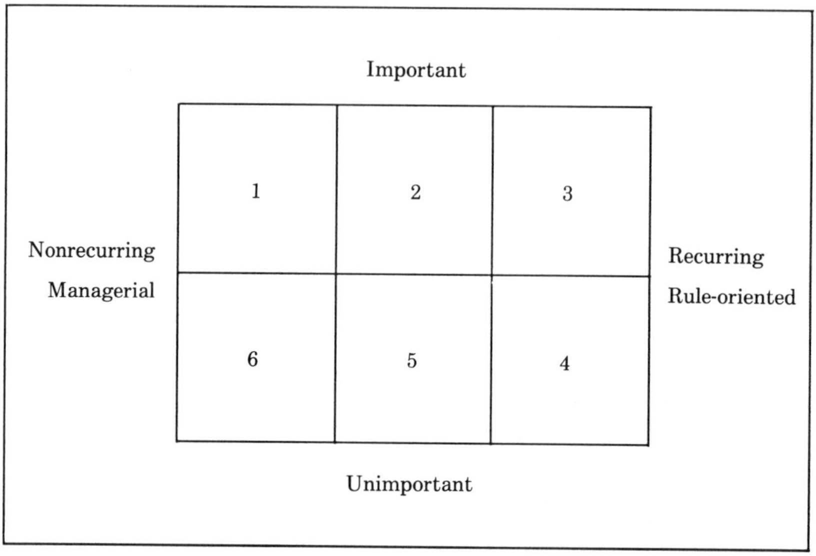

Important

1	2	3
6	5	4

Nonrecurring
Managerial

Recurring
Rule-oriented

Unimportant

FIGURE 2

criticisms seem to be limited to the cases falling within categories 3 and 4. Since categories 1 and 6 contain cases in which factual patterns tend not to recur, the development of standards or rules for those cases is not feasible. These critics, however, would probably contend that categories 3 and 4 are in fact larger than many agencies perceive; that factual regularities presently do recur within cases that agencies now treat as if they belong to categories 1 and 6. They would urge agencies to examine their cases more carefully; if agencies did so they would uncover as yet unobserved factual regularities. In a manner of speaking, these critics are urging the expansion of categories 3 and 4, respectively, into categories 2 and 5, and the expansion of categories 2 and 5 into categories 1 and 6.

Some critics, such as Landis (1960:65) and again Davis (1978:218–19), contend that agencies have failed to delegate sufficient decisional authority to subordinate personnel. These critics argue the policy-making echelons of many agencies dissipate their resources by spending too much of their time in the decision of particular cases. These critics thus again seem to fault agencies for overuse of a managerial mode of decisionmaking, because the delegation which they urge on agencies seems to require the concomitant formulation of decisional standards which the delegating agency would impose upon the subordinate personnel to whom the delegation would be made. An increase in delegation which would be accompanied by a set of decisional standards accompanying the delegation would affect the cases that fall into category 4. Thus a contention that the agency has insufficiently delegated appears here to be a claim (1) that the agency has improperly reserved to itself the decision of many cases that properly fall into the fourth category, or (2) that the agency has improperly perceived many cases as falling within category 3, whereas the limited individual significance of these cases actually places them in category 4.

However, the agency may have inadequately delegated even though it is unable to supply in advance a detailed decisional code to accompany the delegation. Indeed, the agency may be unable at any time – even after the delegation has been in effect for a substantial period – to supply such a detailed code. Yet the inability of the agency to supply detailed criteria for deciding does not mean that the agency ought not to delegate and hence that those criticisms directed at agencies which have refused to delegate are invalid. Indeed, category 6 consists of cases whose individual significance is minimal and which, therefore, ought not to be decided by the agency members themselves or other high-echelon personnel whose time can better be devoted to more significant matters. Yet the cases falling into that category tend to lack recurring factual patterns and hence are not susceptible to governance by precisely drawn rules. For cases falling into this category, the agency can do little but delegate without meaningful standards. For caseloads of this type, the agency must employ subordinate personnel whose judgments are mature and considered. Agency responsibility here consists largely in exercising with care its selection of personnel entrusted with decision-making power.

The police may be an agency whose basic workload is heavily weighted with category 6 cases. Many situations requiring decisions by police officers may not fall into recurring factual patterns and so are not susceptible to governance by rules; and the decisions which are made in each of these situations are individually of minimal societal significance. The police organization recognizes these characteristics of its workload by delegating decisionmaking to officers on patrol without attempting to circumscribe that delegation with rules or standards other than ones phrased in broad and conclusory language.

The Lack of Standards and the Process of "Muddling Through"

Despite the myth of agency "expertise," agencies sometimes exercise regulatory control over subjects about which they possess only limited and inadequate information. In such circumstances agencies tend to behave in the way that Lindblom in a brilliant essay has described as "muddling through" (Lindblom 1959). Such an agency accepts the basic patterns of past events and imposes changes only incrementally. If a change produces undesirable results, then the agency slightly enlarges the scope of its search for an alternative. If the change produces desirable results, then the agency continues in this incremental mode. The significant premise of this approach to decisionmaking lies in the safety attached to successful past experience: if everything has worked satisfactorily in the past, then future catastrophe can be avoided by staying close to what has already proven reasonably satisfactory.

Lindblom's conception of muddling through was intended as a substitute for more "rational" models of decisionmaking in which officials select the best decision from an exhaustive inventory of possible solutions. Lindblom quite correctly points out that fully rational decisionmaking models are unrealistic as either descriptions of, or norms for, actual regulatory decisionmaking because decisionmakers never have complete information. Most of the time, they have little information beyond the past history of the subject and their own dealings with it. Muddling through, then, is intended to be both a descriptive model of how actual decisions are made and a normative model indicating how an agency could make good decisions with incomplete information.

Difficulties with a muddling-through approach arise in a number of circumstances. First, when industry circumstances change drastically, past regulatory experience is rendered obsolete. The premise of the muddling-through approach, in such cases, is undermined. Second, when the cases coming before an agency do not manifest recurring factual patterns, the agency cannot use information acquired from past cases for the disposition of subsequent ones. In these situations, an agency is ill equipped to experiment, introducing gradual and incremental changes in the process visualized by the muddling-through theory, because its prior experience fails to provide a guide for future decisionmaking.

The deficiencies of the muddling-through mode of decisionmaking are dramatically illustrated by the failure of the Civil Aeronautics Board (CAB) during forty years of airline regulation to understand and replicate by regulation the impact of a competitive market. In a study of its decisions from 1938 through 1961, Friendly faulted the CAB for its inconsistent analyses of the role of competition in route and certification decisions (Friendly, 1962). During that period the CAB shifted course a number of times and never developed a thorough understanding of the workings of airline competition. The CAB muddled through in its regulation of air transportation. It never followed for a prolonged period a set of consistent standards about how much competition was desirable. Friendly faulted the CAB for failing to develop adequate information about the benefits and costs of competition, especially in the light of technological developments in the industry. His criticisms ultimately suggest that the CAB's failure to develop standards was due to the CAB's failure to search for and find adequate information about the industry which it was regulating.

When the airline industry was deregulated in the late 1970s, Congress became convinced that by permitting airlines to limit the number of flights, the airlines would strive to reduce the number of unfilled seats on each flight. As airlines competed for passengers to fill the seats on large airliners, prices would decrease. Patrons enticed by the low fares would fill the planes to capacity, and unit costs per passenger would fall. Airlines would incur lower costs, and passengers would pay lower fares. Yet despite its continued waffling on the competition issue, the CAB seems never to have attempted to employ a competitive model as a standard by which to assess the effects of its regulatory decisions. Indeed, its experience shows that it did not, until the eve of deregulation, appreciate the role that competition could play in the airline industry. This failure of the CAB directly resulted from the type of regulatory control which it exercised. Because it employed Lindblom's muddling-through method almost exclusively, it failed to garner the information it needed for an adequate understanding of the role that competition could play in the industry. As a result, its regulation failed to produce optimal air service for the public.

From what has just been said, it is apparent that the muddling-through model of decisionmaking is inappropriately employed in situations where (1) because of the variety of factual configurations in the cases coming before an agency for decision, or (2) because the facts that are most relevant to achieving an agency's regulatory goals are not disclosed even in a series of cases, or (3) because of significant changes in the industry, the agency cannot obtain the information it needs for deciding future cases from its experience with past cases. In these circumstances, adequate regulation requires an agency to collect and to evaluate significant amounts of information about the regulatory setting in which it must act beyond the particular facts of any one case before it. Indeed, in the situations described, the agency must collect information extensively, in the manner in which it would proceed were it to engage in rule making.

March and Simon have directed a general criticism at the managers of many organizations: when the managers become deeply involved in day-to-day (routine) decisionmaking, they frequently lose the time and the perspective which they need to take a long view of the organization's operations and hence are unable to plan, especially for major contingencies (March and Simon, 1958:185). Indeed, planning for major contingencies may be vital because incremental decisionmaking may be unable to cope with major contingencies. The phenomenon identified by March and Simon seems to have produced the inconsistent behavior of the CAB described by Friendly. The CAB's inconsistencies were due to a lack of in-depth information, and this informational lack resulted from inadequate information collection and evaluation devices in the CAB.

From the discussion in part 1, it may be concluded that several objectives might be served by developing standards and rules and thereby confining the extent of unguided administrative discretion. That discussion, however, also provides some insight into the various circumstances in which the development of standards appears most feasible, where it seems least feasible, the kind of standards which would be most likely to be forthcoming, the impediments to the development of standards, and the organizational tools which may be necessary to overcome those impediments.

First, decisions by regulatory agencies which apply previously developed standards may gradually supplant decisionmaking which does not apply previously developed standards. This is the model perceived by Friendly and Davis. It assumes that regularities in the factual patterns of the cases will gradually be perceived by the agencies and that, as those patterns are perceived, the agencies will react to them in a progressively consistent way.

For case-by-case agency decisionmaking to constitute a process through which, over time, standards gradually emerge, not only must the cases contain significant regularities, but those regularities must be perceived by the agencies as a result of handling a number of cases. Furthermore, these regularities must not be offset by the occurrence of one or more other factors which significantly affect the agency's ultimate evaluations. Finally, the regularities in the factual patterns must not be offset by underlying and overriding changes in the industry which render obsolete the standards that would otherwise emerge.

In the absence of (or apart from) factual regularities of whose existence an agency gradually learns over time in the process of deciding cases, an agency may devise standards as a result of collecting and evaluating information coming from sources beyond those which are normally drawn upon in the record of an adjudication. Agencies should make special efforts to collect information about developing technologies in the industry and its potential implications for the industry operations, including changes in the industry unit cost structure. Information of this kind may assist the agency in understanding and evaluating the industry's problems in ways which provide a deeper understanding than emerges from a narrow focus upon particular cases. Collecting information extensively in this way may also sensitize the agency to the dynamics of industry operation and development (as opposed to the static snapshot perception that an adjudicative record may produce). From this enlarged understanding, agency approaches may be structured in ways which are geared to industry changes and which properly anticipate those changes rather than in ways which produce a surprised post hoc reaction to structural changes in the industry.

The Justification of Decisions: Where It Occurs and How Much to Expect

I now wish to address the influences upon officials and agencies toward developing and disclosing decisional standards in the mode visualized by Davis and Friendly. Their model contemplates, it will be recalled, that standards will gradually grow out of an agency's justifications for each decision. I begin with an inquiry into the extent and types of justifications which can be expected from administrative bodies and officials in varying circumstances.

Justifications proffered for decisions might consist of an assertion, perhaps accompanied by an explanation, that the agency decision is authorized by an existing statute or regulation or by a prior precedent or body of precedents. To the extent that a decision involves a set of facts which tends to recur with some regularity, the easiest way for the deciding agency to justify its decision may often be by a reference to a governing precedent or rule. Conversely, to the extent that a decision involves a more or less unique set of facts, the agency, lacking precedents or governing rules, may be forced to justify its decision directly under the governing statute, joining its decision to the statute – when pressed – by a bridge of logical argumentation.

I propose to classify agency decisions by the degree to which they rely on precedent or a rule on one hand and by the degree to which they are justified on their individual merits as authorized by the enabling statute on the other. Second, I propose to classify agency justifications by the elaborateness of their logical structure. It need not be a surprise – nor need it detract from the usefulness of the classification – that the logical structure of agency justifications is likely to be more elaborate in those instances in which an agency is acting in a procedural context in which it is legally obligated to provide a justification for its action (see Gifford, 1980:590–91) nor, indeed, in those contexts in which the official deciding body is less overworked with a large caseload responsibility than in contexts where it is more overworked. In measuring this dimension I am initially more concerned with the elaborateness of the structure than with the reasons for that elaborateness.

In figure 3, the matrix from figure 2 is modified by adding these two measures to the horizontal and vertical axes. This superimposition embodies two suggestions whose accuracy must, of course, be assessed: first, that in "important" particular cases, an agency is likely to justify its action, often in an adjudicatory opinion accompanying its decision; second, that the justification for agency action in cases in which factual patterns tend to recur will be found in rules or precedents or prior practice. The reasons why an elaborate justification can be expected even in some cases where, perhaps because of the nonrecurring nature of the factual mix which is before the agency, the opinion will not have a significant precedential effect, are partly procedural: the agency is obligated under the law to provide a justification, partly because the agency will have assembled its workload in such a way as to make such a justification feasible, and partly because opposition from an adversely affected person presses the agency procedurally to respond to various objections which it makes.

When an agency approaches an area in which (1) it believes that relevant factual configurations are likely to recur frequently and (2) the settings in which regulatory policy are to be brought to bear are, in their aggregate effects, "important" to the implementation of the goals of the governing statute, then the agency will tend to announce its policy either in a "rule" or in an opinion which through its effect as precedent performs a function similar to a rule. Because the rule-making or precedent-setting decision will effectively set the standards or criteria for the treatment of many instances of regulated-subject behavior, the agency decision announcing the rule or precedent is itself likely to attain a degree of importance which the agency's later decisions applying the rule or precedent to particular situations do not attain. In these situations, the decision adopting the rule or

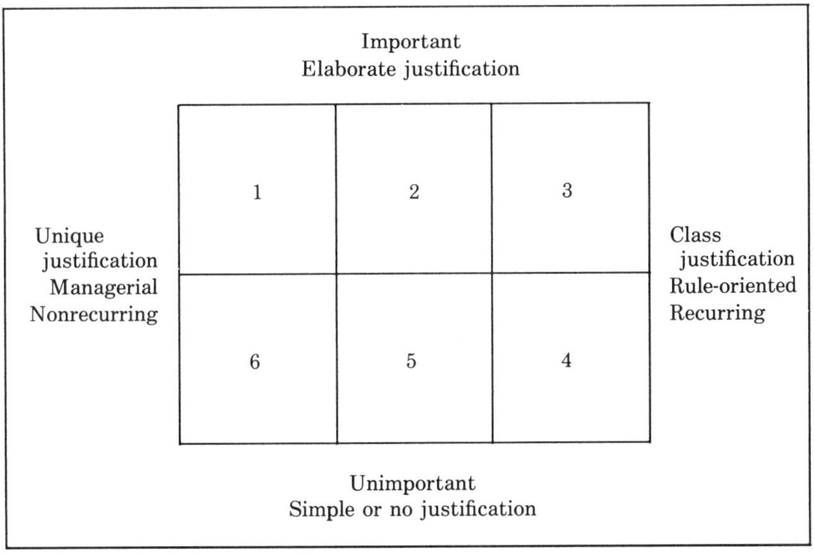

FIGURE 3

precedent will tend to fall higher on the vertical scale than the later decisions applying the criteria embodied within it. Both the initial rule-making or precedent-setting decisions and their subsequent applications would, of course, tend to fall to the right on the horizontal scale. Where the agency decision is designed to provide a standard for future cases, the decision will normally be accompanied by an opinion outlining the agency's conclusions and the factors which the agency considered in reaching those conclusions. Where the agency decision adopts a rule governing the disposition of a class of cases, such as a rule governing pollution toleration standards for a specific industry, as in the example above, the justification proffered by the agency will tend to take the form of a set of factual findings accompanied by scientific studies analyzing sets of data and supporting factual conclusions based upon the data.

On the lower part of the matrix – where the decisions of lesser importance fall – decisions will tend to be made by low-echelon officials. In those areas in which factual patterns tend not to recur with frequency, there will be little opportunity to justify a present decision by its conformity to a rule or precedent. Moreover, partly because of the relative unimportance of particular decisions, the frequency with which these cases are likely to arise (and hence the workload of the deciding official), the limited avenues of formal recourse and the often limited means of adversely affected persons to pursue available procedural routes of redress, officials charged with dealing with them will not feel compelled to provide any elaborate justification for their actions in individual cases. When necessary, an official may use one of a small number of stock justifications without further explanation, even though the applicability of the justification to the case at hand is not obvious. Such may be the normal practice, for example, with the police reports which an arresting officer is required to file, adverse decisions by welfare administrators, and such decisions by immigration officials pertaining to the eligibility of persons to enter the United States. In other areas in which cases of slight importance tend to embody more recurring factual patterns, officials will be more inclined to justify their decisions by rules or prior practice. In such areas officials will attribute significantly greater importance to rules or prior practice as justifications for their decisions than they will to the defensibility of a particular decision on its individual merits or to a bridge of logical argumentation purporting to bring the decision under the language of the governing statute.

The matrix suggests that, in the case of decisions in areas in which factual patterns tend significantly to recur, the primary justifications for decisions will tend to be rules or precedents or prior practice. The exception – in the upper right of the matrix – is the class of initial rule-making decisions and leading precedents which provide guides for future decisions; since these decisions create the governing rules and precedents, they cannot be justified by rules or precedents which were not previously in existence. As previously noted, this class of cases must be justified by a bridge of logical argumentation to the governing statute.

The matrix also suggests that as decisions are deemed "important" by an agency in terms of their relative contribution to the achievement of regulatory goals, the justifications accompanying such decisions will tend to become more elaborate. The complex reasons for this increasing complexity have already been mentioned. Such decisions will tend to be of a kind which must be made in a formal procedural setting, and they frequently tend to provoke resistance which, in turn, employs that set of formal procedures to impel the deciding agency to justify its decision in a relatively elaborate way. As previously noted, the matrix should be read as indicating directions and tendencies. The prior dissection of the matrix into six component areas or boxes was for convenience of presentation only and is not meant to suggest, for example, any correlation between regulatory importance and elaborateness of the decisional justification other than that the two often tend to increase in the same direction.

Informal Standards

I would add here a word about the work of police officers whose activities and decisions I have used as examples above. Much police work involves making large numbers of individual decisions, each of minimal social importance, many of which involve nonrecurring factual patterns, and almost all of which are made outside of the constraints of formal procedures. For these reasons I have used police decisions as illustrative of "unimportant" official decisions which are not governed by rules and which tend not to be elaborately justified, namely the kind of decisions which fall in the lower left of the matrix. However, while many police decisions are ungoverned by rules because (1) no formal rules exist and (2) they involve nonrecurring factual contexts, many other decisions do fall into recurring factual patterns. In such instances, it would be incorrect to assume that, because formal rules do not exist, these decisions are totally unguided. Their own experiences and the advice which they have received from fellow officers tend to provide guides for the conduct of police officers on patrol (see Gifford, 1972:3, 13, 22–26). In some identifiable areas, researchers such as LaFave have found that a set of descriptive criteria can be formulated and applied to police behavior and can, indeed, be employed to predict behavior (LaFave, 1965:83–152). The areas in which officers draw upon their experience or absorb advice of their colleagues are or may be areas in which (1) relevant factual patterns do recur but (2) the combination of experience and advice tapped could not be reduced to a set of written rules or guides because of the complexity of the factors, the difficulties of ascribing weights to those factors, and the variety of ways in which the presence of sporadic and unpredictable other factors alter the course of conduct actually pursued. It is further important to observe that, when police officers shape their conduct upon the basis of their own experiences and the advice which they have absorbed from their colleagues, they are in possession of information which their superiors may lack.

When superior officials lack the information possessed by their subordinates (compare Davis, 1975:13) or when their attempt to incorporate that information into a set of rules or standards would prove confusing to those subordinates, an attempt at rule making by the superiors seems misplaced. In such circumstances rules would tend to lower the quality of subordinate behavior.

In those areas in which cases tend to fall into recurring factual patterns, and where the low significance of the cases combined with their large volume indicates that they should be decided by low-level personnel, those personnel will probably be guided in their decision-making by rules which may in significant part have been prepared by officials on the middle or lower rungs of the agency hierarchy. Where low-level bureaucrats are charged with deciding large volumes of cases, issues of a recurring kind which are not governed by such rules will probably be decided on the basis of prior practice. And those low-echelon officials will probably tend not to manifest a great deal of flexibility in their approach to cases or be willing to provide an elaborate justification on the merits for their decisions. In short, decisions of this type will tend to be justified by precedent, rules, or prior practice; justifications on the merits will not be frequent; and deviations or flexible responses to novel questions will not be numerous.

The Disclosure and Nondisclosure of Decisionmaking

Agencies responsible for formulating and developing behavioral standards have incentives to publicize each new behavioral requirement, because people cannot follow such standards unless they know of their existence and content. To the extent that these behavioral standards are enforced by lower-echelon officials, superiors in the agency must make the standards known to both lower-ranking enforcement officials and the regulated public. Cases using standards designed to regulate future behavior tend to fall to the right on the two-dimensional grid because they necessarily apply to recurring sets of facts. Agency decisions that adopt the standards tend to fall in the upper portion of the grid, that is, category 3, while official actions taken in enforcing or applying those standards will tend to fall in category 4. Significant incentives exist, however, not to publicize certain types of decisionmaking that fall into categories 3 and 4. Figure 4, therefore, adds another dimension to the grid – an openness or secrecy dimension – that can be used, like earlier versions of the grid, as an aid in conceptualizing various types of agency decisionmaking.

Davis has discerned a pervasive reluctance on the part of low-level officials to disclose decisional standards that they themselves have developed. This reluctance to disclose internally developed decisional standards has affected parole board members (Davis, 1969: 129–30); officials examining applications regarding forfeitures of vehicles used in the narcotics trade (ibid.: 109–10); and other low-level administrators.

The reluctance of these officials to disclose their decisional standards derives from their belief that access to those standards by persons who have been or who will be affected by their decisions will subject the officials to more numerous challenges about how they apply the standards (Davis, 1969:126–31) and will substantially increase their workload. The officials will have to spend time justifying past decisions and countering objections rather than concentrating on making other decisions.

Officials who make decisions pursuant to a set of rules or stan-

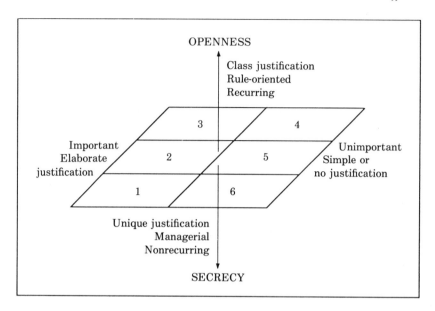

OPENNESS

Class justification
Rule-oriented
Recurring

Important
Elaborate
justification

Unimportant
Simple or
no justification

Unique justification
Managerial
Nonrecurring

SECRECY

FIGURE 4

dards not available to the public do not employ unconfined or unstructured discretionary power. Their decisions are confined and
structured by the set of rules and standards that they are in fact
using. The decisions of these officials would appear more confined
and structured, however, if the rules and standards which they employ in deciding cases were publicized or at least disclosed.

Disclosure will be more likely when the incentives to nondisclosure are reduced. Incentives to nondisclosure of rules or standards
could be reduced by allocating the task of applying them to persons
different from those who create them. In such circumstances the persons who formulate the rules or standards would not be faced with
the prospect of an increased workload as a result of the public disclosure of the rules and standards which they have formulated. The
difficulty in this suggestion, however, is that it is precisely the rules
and standards formulated by officials who make the day-to-day decisions that are at issue.

The incentives for officials engaged in routine decisionmaking not
to disclose the rules and standards which they have developed and
do in fact apply could be reduced by bifurcating the tasks of decid-

ing and justifying the decisions to external audiences. Thus once ways have been found to insulate deciding officials from the need to respond to contentions of dissatisfied or potentially affected persons, those officials would no longer perceive that disclosure of the rules and standards which they are applying will be likely to increase their workload, and their opposition to such disclosure will tend to diminish. This insulation might be provided by routing complaints to officials other than those who made the decisions. Moreover, the workload of this class of officials assigned to hear these complaints could itself be limited by requiring a threshold showing of substantial noncompliance with the guidelines before a complaint would officially be taken under advisement.

A decisionmaking official may occasionally conclude that the merits of an applicant in a particular case are unusually compelling and that a favorable decision will advance the goals of the statutory program. Yet the rules may make no provision for such a decision; indeed, they may literally require the opposite decision. A regulatory agency or upper-level official so confronted would probably decide in accordance with the statutory purpose, justifying its nonliteral approach to the statute in an accompanying opinion (Davis, 1969:110).

A lower-echelon official may not have the same opportunity to justify a nonliteral approach to the rules. Superiors may insist upon literal observance of the rules. The reason may in part be the recognition of their own inability to review such exceptions for coherence and general conformity with the statutory framework and goals. Such an attitude is not to be too quickly condemned; it exhibits a degree of sophistication about the extent of the resources that rational supervision over the administration of flexible rules would entail and a perhaps correct perception that those resources are lacking. Confronted with systemic inflexibility, a lower-echelon decisionmaker may occasionally decide as he believes the merits dictate, but in such cases he will tend not to explain the decision's nonconformity. To do so would merely call attention to the deviant act, possibly causing his superiors to reverse the decision and to issue a reprimand. It is sometimes true that the superiors of such an official may become aware of the subordinate's occasional flexible applications but may tolerate them on the ground that they trust the judgment of that particular official. Selective tolerance preserves the superiors' freedom to correct deviant decisions by other lower-echelon officials whose judgment they trust less. By being selectively tolerant in secret they also avoid subjecting themselves to the critical judgments of their own superiors as they would if they openly approved of their subordinate's flexible applications of the rules. These decisions fall at the lower portions of the social-and-regulatory-importance dimension of the grid, toward the midrange of the fact-recurrence dimension (because the unusual facts of the cases impel the decisionmaker to deviate from the assigned rules) and at the low end of the vertical (secrecy) dimension.

When an agency deals with large numbers of cases, most of which are individually insignificant apart from their impact as precedent or as behavioral guides for other persons, the agency may delegate decisionmaking authority to large numbers of low-echelon personnel. A problem then arises when a low-ranking official decides a case that falls into a potentially recurring pattern. The problem is exacerbated when the decision in question concerns the offical treatment of behavior that can be planned in advance, for example the taxation of various types of transactions. Public disclosure of the decision made by the low-ranking official may lead people to believe that his disposition of the single case manifests agency policy for similar cases. Of course, if the agency head knew that the case in question raised policy issues of broad import, then higher-ranking officials of the agency would consider the issues, and their decision would speak for the agency. But if the agency head is not aware that a particular decision has widespread ramifications, it may be too late for the superior officials to reconsider the disposition of that case. In the case of decisions delegated to low-level personnel, therefore, an agency may seek to limit disclosure to the actual parties and to deny information about that decision to the general public. For many years this was the approach taken by the Internal Revenue Service in rendering private tax rulings (Caplin, 1962:19–24). When the decisionmaking of lower-echelon officials is kept secret from the general public in order to avoid the creation of behavior-affecting precedent, their decisions fall to the right in the grid, in the lower half because of the trivial social or regulatory consequences of each decision taken individually, and on the secrecy end of the openness-secrecy scale.

The examples discussed in this section all involve decisionmaking falling into categories 3 and 4. In the examples, one reason why the agency or responsible officials would choose not to publicize the decisions would be to avoid the creation of a public precedent. In the last example, the agency sought to avoid a precedent which would have discouraged the regulated public from complying with the goals of the statutory program that the agency was administering. Disclosure of the decision would have encouraged private transactions designed to conform to standards which higher-echelon personnel had not approved. Here the agency or its officials would be seeking to avoid the creation of a public precedent that could be used to challenge its future regulatory actions. The maintenance of secrecy over lower-echelon decisionmaking can be understood as an attempt by an agency to prevent category 4 decisions from becoming category 3 decisions until the issues involved have been evaluated by higher-echelon agency personnel. Such secrecy is thus intimately connected with the agency's internal organization: delegation of decisionmaking to lower-echelon personnel is easier when secrecy prevents their decisions from becoming precedents to which substantial members of the public tailor their conduct and/or which impede future agency policy choices.

A second reason for the maintenance of decisional secrecy is also organizational: secrecy plays a role in overcoming organizational deficiencies such as rule inflexibility, caseloads which allow no time for decisional explanations or justifications, and delayed review by superiors. Thus, in one of the above examples, officials are not given adequate time to defend the validity of their decisions and there is no way for affected members of the public to complain without directly confronting the deciding officials. Secret standards enable these officials to minimize the time spent defending their decisions and disposing of their assigned caseloads. In another example, where officials decided in a context in which the inflexible rules failed to provide for exceptional situations such that rigid adherence to the rule caused injustice, decisional secrecy is an informal response by a perceptive lower-ranking official to oppressive bureaucratic constraint. In the last example, secrecy contains the impact of potentially precedential decisions prior to review by higher-ranking officials.

Conclusions

The matrix shown in figure 1 indicated the areas in which rules and standards might be expected to develop most easily and where they might be expected to develop with difficulty or not at all. As further developed, the matrix suggests that standard formulation in the manner visualized by Friendly and Davis will probably be further restricted to the more important cases and perhaps largely to those that are decided in the context of formal proceedings. To the extent that justifications either are not made or are not elaborate enough to distinguish and reconcile prior decisions, the process of gradual standard development as visualized by critics in the field of administrative law will not occur. As explained above, however, decisional standards may be developed by the practice of lower-echelon personnel, but these standards will often not be incorporated into formal rules because the lower-echelon personnel who have developed the practices on the bases of their own and their colleagues' experiences lack the authority and the mechanisms to formalize their behavioral practices, and their superiors lack the information essential to the formulation of standards which the lower-echelon personnel possess. The matrix calls attention to another administrative phenomenon: that rules which do govern decisionmaking by lower-echelon personnel will tend not to be as flexible as the merits of the cases would require. Finally, the matrix is helpful in identifying types of decisionmaking in which officials have significant incentives for secrecy.

References

Caplin, M. 1962. *Taxpayer Rulings Policy of the Internal Revenue Service: A Statement of Principles.* Institute on Federal Taxation. Vol. 20:1.

Davis, K. C. 1969. *Discretionary Justice.* Baton Rouge, La.: Louisiana State University Press.

———. 1970. *Administrative Law Treatise.* Vol. 2. *Supplement.* St. Paul, Minn.: West Publishing Co.

———. 1979. *Administrative Law Treatise.* Vol. 2. San Diego, Calif.:

———. 1975. *Police Discretion.* St. Paul, Minn.: West Publishing Co.

Friendly, H. 1962. *The Federal Administrative Agencies.* Cambridge, Mass.: Harvard University Press.

Gifford, D. J. 1971. "Communication of Legal Standards Policy Development and Effective Conduct Regulation." *Cornell Law Review* 56:409.

———. 1967. "Report on Administrative Law to the Tennessee Law Revision Commission." *Vanderbilt Law Review* 20:777.

———. 1972. "Decisions, Decisional Referents, and Administrative Justice." *Law and Contemporary Problems* 37:3.

———. 1980. "Rulemaking and Rulemaking Review: Struggling Toward a New Paradigm." *Administrative Law Review* 32:577.

Lafave, W. 1965. *Arrest: The Decision to Take a Suspect into Custody.* Boston: Little, Brown.

Landis, J. 1960. *Report on Regulatory Agencies to President-Elect, Staff of Subcommittee on Administrative Practice and Procedure,* 86th Cong., 2d sess. Washington, D.C.: GPO.

Lindblom, C. 1959. "The Science of 'Muddling Through.'" *Public Administration Review* 19:79.

March, J., and H. Simon. 1958. *Organizations.* New York: Wiley.

Sharfman, I. 1931. *The Interstate Commerce Commission.* New York: The Commonwealth Fund.

9

Rule Making and Discretion: Implications for Designing Regulatory Policy

Keith Hawkins AND *John M. Thomas*

A GENCY POLICY formation takes place in the context of the informal rule-making provisions of the Administrative Procedure Act (see Breyer, 1982:380). The procedures "involve discrete and deliberate exercises of agency power to make policy" (DeLong, 1979:261, n. 24). Policy also emerges, however, as agencies resolve controversies over existing rules. The ways in which disputes are adjudicated in individual cases allows for the creation of principle, thereby providing a basis for future decisionmaking. This form of policymaking, it has been argued, is preferred by regulatory administrators, since they are primarily motivated by a desire to control those whom they regulate. As Wilson has observed, "the greater the codification of substantive policy, the less the power the agency can wield over any client in a particular case" (Wilson, 1971:51). Consequently, agency administrators prefer case-by-case discretion to proactive, generalized formulation of policy by rule making. Some observers, however, may find Wilson's remarks too sanguine a view of regulatory policymaking. Indeed, according to a contrasting hypothesis, decisionmaking by agencies should lead to a preference for rule making. At the policy formation stage,

> One should expect agencies to prefer procedures that are least costly to them. The least-cost method is perhaps a single secret meeting, while the highest cost is evolution of precedent in a series of decisions after trial type proceedings. . . . What is to be noted is that the methods least costly to the agency are also those most likely to produce general policy rather than

limited decisions. The use of general rules both economizes on the resources an agency need commit to policy development . . . and maximizes the reach of any particular policy. [Mashaw, 1979:45–46]

Although these are competing hypotheses, both arguments emphasize the relationship between bureaucratic or economic incentives and the choice of policy formation methods.

Regulatory policymaking can be characterized as a decision-making process which, on the one hand, focuses on the formation of standards and regulations as a means of achieving goals and, on the other, reflects a problem-solving method – an approach to the selection of issues for attention, the evaluation of alternatives, and the interpretation of information. In addition, however, policymaking takes place in a political context which exerts a fundamental influence on the effectiveness of means-ends analysis and problem-solving methods. An understanding of the political context is important because this factor is central to the development of procedural rationality in policymaking – the design of a process which adequately reflects the dual concerns of efficiency and equity. Williamson, for example, has outlined a "decision process" method for regulatory problems involving considerable risk and uncertainty. This model specifically places equity before efficiency in the problem-solving sequence. The objective is to ensure that "efficiency should not serve special interest groups at the expense of people with less power" (Williamson 1981: 145; see also Tuohy, 1985).

An example of the role of political context is the way in which the problem of discretion is embedded in the traditional, ongoing debate over the delegation doctrine – that administrative and constitutional theory concerned with the statutory authority which should be granted to regulatory agencies (see Mashaw, 1985). There is little agreement as to the wisdom and efficiency of strategies to control discretion. (Compare, for example, Bardach and Kagan, 1982, and Abel, 1985.) Notwithstanding, however, the significant value questions at the heart of this controversy, it is clear that a particular political climate (which, in turn, affects legislation and judicial decisions) can subsequently influence agency policy toward the exercise of discretion by field-level officials.

Policymaking, however, is further complicated by the fact that the regulatory bureaucracy is, more often than not, preoccupied with a shifting and unpredictable political environment. The result may be a decisionmaking process which is at once designed to appease proregulation activist publics, by demonstrating agency activity, warding off blame and ensuring that a proper enforcement image is developed, while at the same time avoiding undue criticism of excessive activism from the regulated and other broadly antiregulation constituencies. One consequence may be that rule making fails to respond to the requirements of specific problems, as Gifford has shown in chapter 8. The result may be overregulation. The drive in this direction can be powerful. "No agency wishes to be accused of 'doing nothing' with respect to real or imagined problems," writes Wilson (1980:377), "hence every agency proliferates rules to cover all possible contingencies."

Rule Making

Rule making is a complex activity subject to a variety of legal, political, and bureaucratic constraints. The efficient design of rules, as Diver notes in chapter 7, requires an understanding of those circumstances in which it would be appropriate to depart from the incrementalist approach to rule making and invest in more systematic information gathering and analysis – in more "comprehensive rationality," to use Lindblom's terms. These issues arise because the policymaking process is such that rules will inevitably be subject to demands for further clarification. An effort to produce more systematic analysis in the design stage, however, can limit the costs of clarification incurred as rules are applied and enforced.

In addition to strategic analysis of the costs of rule clarification, it is important that the agency policymaker also assess application costs and compliance effects (see chapter 7). Application costs include calculations about the costs of enforcement proceedings. If these are high, it follows that more resources should be allocated to enhance the clarity of rule in the design stage. In a related analysis, McKean (1980:270) has observed that, while economic models have devoted attention to the problem of optimal enforcement, less attention has been devoted to "the implications that enforcement costs have for deciding whether or not to regulate and *what form of regulation to adopt*" (emphasis added). The allocation of resources for policy formation to reduce the incongruity which occurs when results deviate from intended objectives is arguably more effective in situations where the regulated perceive compliance as carrying a high cost.

Similarly, incongruity effects will be prominent in decentralized situations where, for example, senior officials have a considerable degree of discretion to apply rules on an individual basis (see chapter 7). Both of these principal compliance effects – the perception of the costs of compliance and the discretionary application of rules by enforcement officials – result from complex processes of interaction between the agency and the regulated affected by the meanings that people attach to rules, intentions, and goals. These compliance effects are outcomes of social processes of bargaining and negotiation which influence the way the costs of compliance are defined (see Hawkins, 1984). Thus compliance effects are constraints on the rationality of rule design, in part because they are socially constructed.

This is not to say, however, that policymakers are powerless to affect outcomes through greater efficiency in the design of rules. To look at matters from a social constructionist point of view would argue for greater understanding on the part of agency policymakers of the way compliance initiatives are interpreted and the way in which both enforcement officials and regulated firms respond to them. An important implication of Diver's analysis in chapter 7, however, is that if such knowledge is difficult to obtain and the process is not easily influenced, greater rationality in the way decisions about rule design are made can help mitigate the costs of compliance effects. Furthermore, some of these effects can be measured and used as inputs in the design of rules, for example the volume of transactions to be regulated, the formality of procedures mandated in applying a rule and the degree of centralization (or otherwise) in the organizational structure of enforcement. In essence, then, Diver's analysis of rule design calls attention to the importance of two types of policy choice in the regulatory process. The first is connected with substantive rule making, that is, the development of standards for regulatory conduct under constraints which limit rationality. The second is concerned with the organizational rules which define procedures for implementing such standards and the degree and kind of discretion available to enforcement officials.

The value of the perspectives of bounded rationality and social construction for thinking about rule making is also suggested by the fact that agency officials use a variety of both formal and informal analytic techniques in this process. This is so for basically two reasons. In the first place, statutes – the legislative basis for agency policy – rarely provide a clear guide to the development of rules. Second, even if the statute seems to be framed in relatively clear terms, the facts surrounding a regulatory issue (including basic research and information about a problem confronting the agency) remain subject to interpretation. Analytic techniques, as Gifford states, can be considered "decisional referents" which operate within a well-defined context of policy formation:

> Operationally, this means that the major policy decisions of an agency which has been legislatively instructed to bring about a new state of affairs will be oriented primarily to the future rather than to the past. And since the agency has been described only imprecisely, the agency will require information about the subjects and subject-matter which it regulates so that it will be able to employ its freedom intelligently. It needs information about the possible consequences of various changes in the legal and regulatory environment which it is capable of bringing about. It will require knowledge about, or access to, analytical techniques or professional disciplines concerned with the subject matter of its regulation. In short, it is the task of the agency concerned to formulate as guides for its everyday operations, decisional criteria and other decisional referents which will assist it in looking to the future. And these decisional referents, to be useful, must possess more content than the vaguely phrased goals or directives contained in the statutory grant of power to the agency. [Gifford, 1972:15]

Thus the agency policy process includes choice about "referents" — the analytical methods or other tools — which are to be employed as inputs into substantive policy decisions such as standards or rules which define an enforcement program. However, the choice of such referents (for example, the extent to which the decision process will involve an incrementalist strategy or an attempt at comprehensive rationality) also occurs through processes of social construction between policymakers and others within the agency. In this sense, the "bounded rationality" of policy decisions is a function of interpretations and symbols which arise through interaction, and as Gifford has further observed, this dynamic can have significant consequences:

> The referent concept is useful in demonstrating the manner in which the factors employed by individual officials blur into decisional factors employed by the sub-units, bureaus, or agencies in which those officials work. . . . A focus upon the referents actually employed focuses attention upon informal rule and non-rule referents which *arise from personal interaction among officials,* and which have often been the subject of inquiry by social scientists. These informal referents may "fill in" or "complete" open-ended formal rules, or, at times, may even effectively countermand them. [Gifford, 1972:47; emphasis added]

In our introductory chapter we drew attention to some of the central features of the law in action of agency policymaking. One involves the disjunction between external demands for more rational policy formation and what actually occurs because of the influences of bureaucratic factors. While the tendency toward more comprehensive rationality or incrementalism ("muddling through") is likely to depend, among other things, upon the nature of regulatory problems, it is the case that established organizational norms and operating procedures often dictate rule making, as Gifford notes. An agency will have difficulty responding to demands for comprehensive rationality because many regulatory issues simply do not lend themselves to this approach and because coalitions and units within the organization have conflicting goals. To the extent that internal bureaucratic conflicts become a major influence, policy formation will then fail to include reasonable bargaining with interest groups affected by the regulatory process. Policy rules become highly general, difficult to apply to individual cases, and "over inclusive" (Ehrlich and Posner, 1974; chapter 7 in this volume). This pattern in turn creates a further disjunction between agency policy and the implementation, or enforcement, stage. The uncertainties and undesirable consequences created by overinclusive rules must be resolved through flexibility, accommodation, and discretion in enforcement practice.

The design of substantive rules which are translated into effective programs of enforcement requires a significant degree of consensus on the part of agency professionals. Gifford, for example, notes that effective programs depend upon the capacity to discern regularities in the factual patterns of case and agency judgments about the importance of cases for broad goals. Agreement on these issues, however, can be adversely affected by internal agency politics. Similarly, as Diver observes, the capacity to avoid overinclusiveness and underinclusiveness in the design of rules depends upon some reasonable degree of agreement on the underlying policy objective. To the extent that necessary agreement is not forthcoming because of conflicting value orientations within the agency, inefficient rule making resulting in unreasonable regulatory enforcement may be the consequence.

As we noted in the introductory chapter to this volume, the social constructionist perspective draws attention to the way agency officials interpret demands for regulatory intervention and define organizational goals based upon a system of professional beliefs and ideologies. If rational policy formation is bounded by bureaucratic factors, the social constructionist perspective, with its focus on the interpretive process, provides valuable insights into how such factors unfold and impinge on policymaking activity.

The interpretive process defines the way in which decisions in specific cases are influenced by assumptions about the goals of regulation. These assumptions reflect basic values and ideologies and are seldom made explicit. This issue is particularly relevant in regulatory tasks which draw on experts whose function is to rule on risk and uncertainty. An example is the reliance of the Food and Drug Administration (FDA) on expert panels to screen new drugs. A case in point was the decision whether or not to license Panalba, a combination antibiotic that was recognized to be more effective than any of its ingredients sold separately (Breyer, 1982:142–43). The manufacturer of Panalba argued for licensure on the grounds that the drug effectively circumvented the tendency of doctors not to make detailed diagnoses which would result in the recommendation of a specific antibiotic. But the FDA advisory panel decided the drug was ineffective, and its reasoning illustrates the influence of a basic normative assumption: "The scientists believed that doctors *should* make precise diagnoses and use antibiotics more precisely designed to fit the disease. A different panel with more practicing physicians and fewer academics might have been swayed by the claim that what matters is what doctors *will* do, not what they *should* do" (Breyer, 1982:143).

Another example illustrates the significance of the interpretive process at the rule-making stage of regulatory policymaking. In implementing the consumer product warranty provisions of the Magnuson-Moss act, the Federal Trade Commission was called upon to issue a rule defining how much a defective product should be discounted for actual use in calculating a refund. This provision was designed to provide some equity for manufacturers, the argument being that consumers should pay the cost for use rather than receive the full purchase price (Denney, 1979). The development of this rule involved controversy and uncertainty, but a possible source of information for calculating the life of products could be the data of manufacturers themselves. One proposal by Federal Trade Commission professionals charged with the responsibility for policymaking was to require warrantors to supply the agency with estimates of product life. For our purposes, the interesting point about this decision process is that it illustrates the way in which information in the rule-making process can incorporate assumptions which, arguably, transcend the original objectives of the regulatory law. In this case, the decision to require information from manufacturers as the basis for rule making was intimately bound up with a view that this could have the important side effect of increasing market competition in consumer products (Lund, 1979:12). An objective of providing a measure of equity to manufacturers was thus transformed into another goal based upon a particular ideology of consumer rights and the marketplace. The point of this example is not to argue the correctness or morality of the view but rather to illustrate the way in which the interpretive process enters into policymaking decisions with seemingly clear-cut, focused objectives. In this case, the values of agency professionals affected key choices about the type of information which should be used in rule making—choices which conflicted with the original intent of lawmakers.

Discretion in Enforcement

In considering the basic tasks of policymaking, it is important to bear in mind the fundamental relationship between policymaking and implementation, that is to say, between agency policy and enforcement practice. Policymaking and implementation are reflexively connected: agency officials often develop policy on the basis of their interpretations of the realities of enforcement, and enforcement practice is constrained by perceptions of the requirements of regulatory goals. One prominent theme in studies of the regulatory process is the central part in the enterprise played by enforcement agents as they exercise discretion in specific cases (see, for example, Hawkins, 1984). In the day-to-day routine behavior of these agents the law is made reality, hence Lipsky's point that those who ostensibly only apply the formal law do in fact *make* policy. That agents are effectively in a position to create policy "derives from two interrelated facets of their roles: relatively high degrees of discretion and relative autonomy from organizational authority" (Lipsky, 1980:13). Thus policy is, in a fundamental sense, to be seen as defined by the "dispositions of implementors—how field level officials exercise discretion" (Van Meter and Van Horn, 1975), since for practical purposes agency policy is that which is defined and presented as such to the regulated by enforcement officials. Officials implement agency policy according to their own assumptions about the basic causes of regulatory offenses. Violators may be categorized as "bad," "incompetent," or "socially responsible" (see, for example, Kagan and Scholz, 1984). These designations, which stem from features such as the nature and context of the violations, the cooperativeness or otherwise of the regulated officials, their past history of encounters, and so on, all influence enforcement decisions at field level (see generally Hawkins, 1984). Thus it is quite possible that patterns of interaction in the actual process of enforcement compete and often conflict with interpretations of formal policy whose implementation may be preferred and intended by higher-level officials.

In general, the management of discretion is a form of relational "contract" (see Williamson, 1986) between regulatory policymakers and enforcement officials. A policy which defines this "contract" in a highly structured fashion may be dysfunctional for regulatory objectives in three ways: (1) it may fail to recognize that laws are generally overinclusive and require the delegation of discretion; (2) the overcontrol of enforcement officials may fail to account for the fact that the task of achieving compliance is based upon a socially constructed process of interaction; and (3) it may fail to recognize the limited ability of both regulatory agents and the regulated to cope with uncertainty and information distortion. In this sense, the goal of efficiency can be enhanced by recognition that rationality is bounded. As Williamson has recently stated: "Views to the contrary not withstanding, the set of issues on which economic reasoning can carefully be brought to bear is enlarged rather than reduced when bounds on rationality are admitted" (Williamson, 1986:46).

The idea of bounded rationality encompasses the set of institutional constraints on the problem-solving and information processing capacity of policymakers. From this perspective, policy developed and implemented at higher levels of the regulatory agency can affect the exercise of discretion in individual cases at the field level. When the regulatory task requires extensive inspection, for example, discretion is governed by explicit or implicit agency policy defining inspection priorities. It is necessary for agency policymakers to recognize this dynamic and attempt to formulate and implement procedures which reinforce the desired relationship between substantive regulatory goals and compliance.

The history of the Occupational Health and Safety Agency (OSHA) provides a valuable illustration of the impact of ill-conceived policies concerning enforcement priorities on the exercise of discretion by inspectors. When the agency, at one stage, gave priority in its management control system to numbers of inspections and violations cited, inspectors allocated their time to small businesses which could be inspected quickly and where violations, albeit trivial, could be found (Diver, 1981a:2). This policy also resulted in discretionary decisions heavily weighted in favor of nonserious violations: "Of the 380,000 violations discovered by OSHA in 1976 less than 13,000 were categorized as serious, willful or repeat violations" (Diver, 1981a:2). Similarly, in response to the political fallout of the 1975 "Kepone disaster" – a chemical accident which caused several deaths in a pesticide plant – OSHA shifted to an enforcement policy that covered all complaints. This constraint channeled inspection activity into certain types of business, to the neglect of others. However, a General Accounting Office study found in 1978 that 80 percent of the complaints addressed led to no violations of OSHA standards. The example illustrates the importance of an enforcement policy governing inspection procedures that links substantive goals – standards – with the nature and seriousness of complaints about violations of those standards.

The regulatory process is populated by bureaucracies intent on avoiding criticism, since after all they are government agencies whose policies reflect external political demands. To fail to recognize this dynamic is to assume that an optimal degree of discretion can be defined and structured. To the contrary, the management of discretion requires what might be described as a contingency framework, an effort to match delegation with the nature of substantive rules, and the capacity to recognize the reasons for deviations from accepted models of policy development. If an agency, for example, seeks to formulate policy through formal methods of decisionmaking such as cost/benefit analysis, it needs to understand how and why decisions in individual cases may deviate from such models. Similarly, if the agency attempts to respond to the demands of competing interests and values, it needs to understand why there may be resistance among enforcement officials to defining cases in terms of basic political tradeoffs.

Interest-group politics affect substantive rules in ways which influence the exercise of discretion. One example has been felicitously termed the "safety valve" phenomenon in regulatory decisionmaking (Diver, 1980:279). Discretion is necessary as a functional response to agency rule making which results in more or less absolute commands: "At the enforcement stage, the agency can adjust to the uncertainties and variations necessarily overlooked or smoothed over at the rule-making stage" (Diver, 1980:279). In this sense, policymaking and discretion are highly interdependent. If the management of field-level officials fails to recognize this interdependence, by emphasizing, for example, a rigid legalistic approach, the legitimacy of policy can be undermined. Moreover, the failure to allow discretion in the application of overinclusive rules may be an efficient approach to the enforcement of regulatory policy (see Ehrlich and Posner, 1974). The problem, however, with discretion which is efficient in applying overinclusive rules is that it can lead to uncertainty of treatment and violation of the equitable maxim that like cases should be treated alike.

One perspective on the relationship between external political demands and regulatory policymaking views the latter as essentially a function of competing interests: the role of policymakers is to reconcile conflicts and achieve workable compromise (see Reich, 1979). This view conflicts with an approach to discretion which emphasizes the authority of the office or the expertise of the officeholder (see Nonet, 1980). The frameworks of bounded rationality and social construction highlight the fallacy of adopting any one model as a governing principle. Certain policy issues require formal analysis, and one should not be averse to technical analyses of risk in these areas. The concepts of bounded rationality and social construction illustrate, however, the extent to which formal methods are limited by assumptions about problems and by the fact that decisions reflect the shared ideologies and values of decisionmakers as well as those of affected interest groups.

In addition to the well-known constraints of the external political environment, the exercise of discretion is a function of the type of decisionmaking task and the professional values of officials. As a consequence, it is highly problematic to control and change the amount of discretion in the regulatory process. While this difficulty must be accepted, it is useful to recognize certain principles which should guide efforts at reform. One is that efforts to constrain discretion should be based upon a careful analysis of the nature of the substantive rules which are to be enforced. Chapter 7 in this volume illustrates the point very well in the context of the problem of designing prosecutorial standards governing the transportation of hazardous materials. As this study notes, when the rules, or policy, to be implemented tend to be highly detailed or precise – in effect over-inclusive – it is rational to allow considerable discretion in citing and prosecuting violations. An effective approach emphasizes a management policy structure which strives to maximize interaction among prosecutors and inspectors (Gifford, 1972), systematic reflection on "hard" cases, and training programs which use knowledge from past experience. Additional strategies concentrate on improving the effectiveness of prior stages in the regulatory process – for example, procedures to screen out cases of questionable liability and the targeting of enforcement resources (see chapter 7). Such a perspective allows regulatory policymakers to "capitalize on discretion for improving the reliability and effectiveness of policies" (Elmore, 1979–80:610).

In general, research on the relationship between rule making and managerial strategies governing the delegation of discretion should recognize basic distinctions among types of regulatory problems. As Gifford notes, two basic dimensions of problems are the importance of a decision for agency goals and whether or not the pattern of facts in a case is such that it is possible to define standards for the exercise of discretion. Again, it is useful to draw on the perspectives of bounded rationality and social construction in seeking to understand these matters. The "importance" of a case is in part a function of definitions of organizational goals, which are difficult to formulate, particularly in areas of social regulation, such as health and safety, the environment, and consumer protection. The concept of importance is a socially defined construct, reflecting the complex interaction between the agency and its external political environment as well as the diverse values of agency professionals and careerists (see Wilson, 1980). A rational, let alone optimal, policy of discretion depends upon a consensus of views as to what constitutes an important case. Shared meanings of events evolve and come to be labeled as "important." On the other hand, the extent to which policymakers can discern patterns in the basic facts of cases is bounded by both information processing capacity and the uncertainty of many regulatory problems.

The importance of the process of interpreting regulatory events is implied in Diver's analysis of situations calling for greater or less precision in rules of substantive policy. Diver notes, for example, that the effectiveness of investing resources in the design of more precise rules can be a function of assumptions about the risk-taking propensities of the regulated. Similarly, a policy of allowing less precise rules and, consequently, more discretion to enforcement officials, is functional to the extent that officials believe violations result primarily from the incompetence of the regulated rather than from premeditated strategies (chapter 7). Both of these factors – assumptions about risk-taking propensity and about the motives of potential violators – are socially constructed in that they reflect the values of regulatory officials and the interdependence of these values and judgments about the attitudes and behavior of the regulated.

The ability to steer a course between the errors of undue leniency and an overly legalistic approach requires a clear understanding of the impact of a particular enforcement policy on compliance. Traditional command-and-control strategies of environmental control, for example, have resulted in inefficient enforcement and a failure to monitor continuous compliance. According to Ackerman and Stewart: "The present system does not put pressure on agency policy makers to make the large investments in monitoring and personnel that are required to make the tedious and unending work of credible enforcement a bureaucratic reality" (Ackerman and Stewart, 1985:1345). A policy governing discretion will be relatively ineffective if a lack of resources threatens the legitimacy and credibility of those who must exercise that discretion. The problem of linking policy with a clear assessment of enforcement realities also exists, however, with newer market incentives strategies. An important analysis of the impact of the "emissions trading" system for air pollution control – a market incentives approach aimed at the problem of inefficiency in the command-and-control model – has demonstrated that continuous monitoring for compliance remains a critical need (Tietenberg, 1985: 183; see also Drayton, 1980:8-7; and Russell, Harrington, and Vaughan, 1986:221). Thus an important degree of discretion exists that will have to be systematically addressed in regulatory management if the predicted compliance effectiveness of one policy relative to another is to be realized. In this sense, a rational policy – one that links enforcement with compliance – requires some understanding by regulatory policymakers of the norms adopted by lower-level field officials to define and interpret cases.

Conclusion

Recent studies of discretion in the enforcement of regulation suggest several conclusions concerning areas of potentially useful future research. First, it is necessary to conduct studies which can further our understanding of the contingency perspective. Such studies would analyze the relationship between enforcement in individual cases and the design of substantive rules (chapter 7 in this volume). Another dimension of research adopting a contingency view would emphasize the complex relationship between the nature of regulatory problems which Gifford (see chapter 8) has specified (importance to the agency and the routinization of facts in cases) and managerial policy aimed at promoting voluntary compliance. Second, research should probe more systematically the organizational and political context of particular styles of discretionary decisionmaking. Studies suggest the importance of broad classes of variables: the nature of the relationship and interaction between regulatory officials and the regulated; bureaucratic factors, including the way in which officials are rewarded and performance evaluated; and the nature of the substantive rules to be interpreted and enforced. Third, research should focus on ways in which policy executed at higher levels in agencies in response to political demands affects the exercise of discretion at the field level and, subsequently, compliance with regulatory goals.

The importance of understanding agency decisionmaking as a matter of process is underscored by evidence that regulatory bureaucracies are, and will remain, relatively impervious to executive and legislative attempts at control (Wilson, 1980:391). Thus an important first step in improving the making of regulatory policy is recognition on the part of those who seek major reforms in agency decisionmaking that considerable discretion is both necessary and inevitable (see Baldwin and Hawkins, 1984). It is useful, as Magat and Schroeder (1984:316), have recently observed, to "put aside earlier pretentions that discretion is merely residual or mechanical or that it can be controlled by neutral application of expert techniques of analysis and administration." One result has been the advent of persistent debate concerning the proper institutional role of the judiciary in the interpretation of regulatory decisions. A major implication for the improvement of regulatory policy is that the courts should consider alternative models for interpreting agency decisions. One possibility in this regard is the use of conceptual frameworks which reflect a basic understanding of the realities of policymaking in agencies. Diver, for example, has argued persuasively that incrementalism and comprehensive rationality may both be appropriate approaches, depending upon the nature of the regulatory task (Diver,

1981b). Problems involving a high degree of technological uncertainty and a low probability of catastrophic effects are amenable to an incrementalist approach. In contrast, the "synoptic," or comprehensive rationality, model should be attempted with regulatory issues that would lead to serious harms or situations in which value conflicts pose a need for formal procedures in the choice of alternative solutions. An understanding of the limitations of rational agency policymaking becomes all the more important, however, if rule design is to become increasingly responsive to demands for more comprehensive rationality. One significant result of this trend, it has been observed, may be greater judicial deference to the agency policymaking process:

> By about 1990 the judiciary will face a crisis of legitimacy vis-à-vis the agencies. The agency will represent the capacity of technical experts to produce substantively correct decisions on the basis of synoptic processes at a time when the strongest desire of the society will be to be technologically right. The courts will represent the democratic virtues of the lay mind, but a lay mind demonstrably incapable of even understanding, let alone making an independent judgment on, the technical matter put before it. The judges will withdraw to await the next know-nothing rebellion. [Shapiro, 1982:25]

To sum up, knowledge of the way in which agencies actually make policy will be of considerable value in efforts to confront the implications of this type of judicial deference. It will also be needed to help create institutional structures which can contribute to a sense of legitimacy in the process. But there is little doubt that, like the field of administrative law in general, study of the making of regulatory policy will remain, to borrow Richard Stewart's phrase, a matter of "dense complexity" (Stewart, 1976:1813).

At this stage of empirical research into the way in which discretion is used by field-level regulatory officials, we know little about either the antecedents or the consequences of particular styles of applying law and interpreting cases. Most research to date has concentrated on elaborating the norms associated with enforcement styles and the processes of bargaining with violators to obtain compliance. The focus of a number of these studies has been the detailed analysis of the interaction between regulatory agent and the regulated; analysis has concentrated on the subjective interpretation of events and the reflexive nature of attitudes and behavior which shapes this relationship as a case unfolds. Policy reform, however, should also reflect an understanding of the aggregate use of discretion – patterns of interpreting evidence and responding to violations – and the relationship between such patterns and legal impacts, including compliance and deterrence. Similarly, a focus on antecedents, or factors which influence the adoption of styles in the exercise of discretion, highlights the importance of the structural or material bases for decisionmaking (see Paris and Reynolds, 1983:190). The exercise of discretion in a single case is strongly affected by the way in which officials perceive and categorize cases and organize work around a caseload defined in time (see Emerson, 1983). Thus, in order to pursue meaningful policy change, it is important to understand both the "cognitive world" of the regulating official and the reality of caseload structures: resource availability and allocation, procedures for defining priority cases, role pressures arising from formal and informal reward systems, and external political demands.

References

Abel, Richard L. 1985. "Risk as an Arena of Struggle." *Michigan Law Review* 83:772–812.

Ackerman, Bruce A., and Richard Stewart. 1985. "Reforming Environmental Law." *Stanford Law Review* 37:1333–65.

Baldwin, G. R., and K. Hawkins. 1984. "Discretionary Justice: Davis Reconsidered." *Public Law* (Winter).

Bardach, Eugene, and Robert Kagan. 1982. *Going by the Book: The Problem of Regulatory Unreasonableness.* Philadelphia: Temple University Press.

Bernstein, Marver. 1955. *Regulating Business by Independent Commission.* Princeton, N.J.: Princeton University Press.

Breyer, Stephen. 1982. *Regulation and Its Reform.* Cambridge, Mass.: Harvard University Press.

DeLong, James V. 1979. "Informal Rulemaking and the Integration of Law and Policy." *Virginia Law Review* 65:157–356.

Denney, William Michael. 1979. "F.T.C. Rulemaking." Public Policy Analysis Case Study, Massachusetts Institute of Technology, Cambridge, Mass.

Diver, Colin. 1980. "A Theory of Regulatory Enforcement." *Public Policy* 28:257–99.

———. 1981a. "OSHA Case B." Public Policy Analysis Case Study, Harvard University, Cambridge, Mass.

————. 1981b. "A Policy-making Paradigm in Administrative Law." *Harvard Law Review* 95:393–434.

Drayton, William. 1980. "Economic Law Enforcement." *Harvard Environmental Law Review* 4:1–40.

Ehrlich, Issac, and Richard A. Posner. 1974. "An Economic Analysis of Legal Rulemaking." *Journal of Legal Studies* 3:257–86.

Elmore, Richard F. 1979–80. "Backward Mapping: Implementation Research and Policy Decisions." *Political Science Quarterly* 94:601–16.

Emerson, R. 1983. "Holistic Effects in Social Control Decision-Making." *Law and Society Review* 17:425–55.

Gifford, Daniel J. 1972. "Decisions, Decisional Referents, and Administrative Justice." *Law and Contemporary Problems* 37 (Winter): 1–48.

Hawkins, Keith. 1984. *Environment and Enforcement: Regulation and the Social Definition of Pollution.* Oxford: Oxford University Press.

Kagan, R. A., and John Scholz. 1984. "The Criminology of the Corporation." In *Enforcing Regulation,* ed. Keith Hawkins and John M. Thomas. Boston: Kluwer-Nijhoff.

Lipsky, Michael. 1980. *Street-level Bureaucracy.* New York: Russell Sage.

McKean, Roland N. 1980. "Enforcement Costs in Environmental and Safety Regulation." *Policy Analysis* 6:269–89.

Magat, Wesley, and Christopher H. Schroeder. 1984. "Administrative Process Reform in a Discretionary Age: The Role of Social Consequences." *Duke Law Journal* (April): 301–46.

Mashaw, Jerry L. 1979. "Regulation, Logic, and Ideology." *Regulation* 3 (November/December): 44.

————. 1985. "Prodelegation: Why Administrators Should Make Political Decisions." *Journal of Law, Economics, and Organization* 1:81–100.

Nonet, Phillipe. 1980. "The Legitimation of Purposive Decisions." *California Law Review* 68:263.

Paris, David C., and James Reynolds. 1983. *The Logic of Policy Inquiry.* New York: Longmans.

Reich, Robert B. 1979. "Warring Critiques of Regulation." *Regulation* 3 (January/February): 37–42.

Russell, Clifford S., Winston Harrington, and William J. Vaughan. 1986. *Enforcing Pollution Control Law.* Washington, D.C.: Resources for the Future, Inc.

Shapiro, Martin. 1982. "On Predicting the Future of Administrative Law." *Regulation* (May June): 18–25.

Stewart, Richard B. 1976. "The Reformation of American Administrative Law." *Harvard Law Review* 88:1669.

Tietenberg, Thomas H. 1985. *Emissions Trading: An Exercise in Reforming Pollution Policy.* Washington, D.C.: Resources for the Future, Inc.

Tuohy, Carolyn. 1985. "Procedural Rationality and Regulatory Decisionmaking: A Decision Framework Approach." *Law and Policy* 7:345–74.

Van Meter, Donald, and Carl Van Horn. 1975. "The Policy Implementation Process: A Conceptual Framework." *Administration and Society* 6:445–88.

Williamson, Oliver. 1981. "An Economist's View." In *The Scientific Basis of Health and Safety Regulation,* ed. Robert Crandall and Lester Lave. Washington, D.C.: Brookings Institution.

———. 1986. *The Economic Institutions of Capitalism.* New York: Free Press.

Wilson, James Q. 1971. "The Dead Hand of Regulation." *Public Interest* 25:51.

———. 1980. *The Politics of Regulation.* New York: Basic Books.

Notes on Contributors

Barry Boyer is Professor of Law and Director of the Baldy Center for Law and Social Policy at the State University of New York at Buffalo. His primary research and teaching interests are in the fields of administrative law and environmental regulation. He has also served as a consultant to the Administrative Conference of the United States and the U.S. Environmental Protection Agency.

Colin S. Diver is Dean and Professor of Law at the University of Pennsylvania Law School. He is the author of *Administrative Law: Cases and Materials,* with Ronald A. Cass, and numerous articles on government regulation.

Daniel J. Gifford is Professor of Law at the University of Minnesota Law School. He is the author of *Federal Antitrust Law Cases and Materials,* with Leo J. Raskind, and many articles on antitrust legislation and regulatory agencies, among other topics.

Keith Hawkins is Deputy Director of the Centre for Socio-Legal Studies at Oxford University. He is the author of *Environment and Enforcement: Regulation and the Social Definition of Pollution,* and a number of publications addressing legal decisionmaking, criminal justice processes, and law as a regulatory device.

Peter K. Manning is Professor of Sociology and Psychiatry at Michigan State University. He is author and editor of many books – most recently *Semiotics and Fieldwork* and *Symbolic Communication* – and has published widely in scientific journals. His general research interests are in occupations and organizations, medical sociology and criminology, and legal decisionmaking.

Errol Meidinger is Professor of Law and Jurisprudence at the State University of New York at Buffalo. He has published on research methodology, natural resources policy, and administrative regulation. His current research is on the social organization of environmental regulation and its relationship to the ideals of democracy.

281

Robert L. Rabin is A. Calder Mackay Professor of Law at Stanford Law School. His research and teaching interests are in the fields of torts, environmental law, and administrative law, and he has written extensively in each of these areas.

Paul Rock is Professor of Sociology at the London School of Economics, University of London. He is editor of *The British Journal of Sociology,* and his recent publications include *A View from the Shadows, Understanding Deviance,* with David Downes, and *A History of British Criminology,* an edited volume.

John M. Thomas is Associate Professor of Organization and Human Resources, School of Management, and Adjunct Associate Professor of Law at the State University of New York at Buffalo. He is co-editor with Keith Hawkins of *Enforcing Regulation* and articles on the legal process and government regulation.

Pitt Series in Policy and Institutional Studies

Bert A. Rockman, Editor